VEGANISM

Contemporary Food Studies: Economy, Culture and Politics

Series Editors: David Goodman and Michael K. Goodman
ISSN: 2058-1807

This interdisciplinary series represents a significant step toward unifying the study, teaching, and research of food studies across the social sciences. The series features authoritative appraisals of core themes, debates and emerging research, written by leading scholars in the field. Each title offers a jargon-free introduction to upper-level undergraduate and postgraduate students in the social sciences and humanities.

Emma-Jayne Abbots, *The Agency of Eating: Mediation, Food, and the Body*
Terry Marsden, *Agri-Food and Rural Development: Sustainable Place-Making*
Peter Jackson, *Anxious Appetites: Food and Consumer Culture*
Philip H. Howard, *Concentration and Power in the Food System: Who Controls What We Eat?*
Tania Lewis, *Digital Food: From Paddock to Platform*
Hugh Campbell, *Farming Inside Invisible Worlds*
Henry Buller & Emma Roe, *Food and Animal Welfare*
Kate Cairns and Josée Johnston, *Food and Femininity*
Claire Lamine, *Sustainable Agri-food Systems: Case Studies in Transitions Towards Sustainability from France and Brazil*

VEGANISM

Politics, Practice, and Theory

Eva Haifa Giraud

BLOOMSBURY ACADEMIC
LONDON • NEW YORK • OXFORD • NEW DELHI • SYDNEY

BLOOMSBURY ACADEMIC
Bloomsbury Publishing Plc
50 Bedford Square, London, WC1B 3DP, UK
1385 Broadway, New York, NY 10018, USA
29 Earlsfort Terrace, Dublin 2, Ireland

BLOOMSBURY, BLOOMSBURY ACADEMIC and the Diana logo are trademarks of
Bloomsbury Publishing Plc

First published in Great Britain 2021

Cover design: Terry Woodley
Cover photo by Ollie Millington/Getty Images

A catalogue record for this book is available from the British Library.

A catalog record for this book is available from the Library of Congress.

ISBN: HB: 978-1-3501-2492-9
PB: 978-1-3501-2491-2
ePDF: 978-1-3501-2493-6
eBook: 978-1-3501-2494-3

Series: Contemporary Food Studies: Economy, Culture and Politics

Typeset by Deanta Global Publishing Services, Chennai, India
Printed and bound in Great Britain

To find out more about our authors and books visit www.bloomsbury.com and
sign up for our newsletters

For my parents, Annie and Abdulrahman

CONTENTS

ACKNOWLEDGMENTS

First, thanks must go to Mike Goodman—for encouraging me to write this book in the first place and for being so supportive throughout the drafting and editing process. I really can't emphasize enough how appreciative I am. I also wouldn't have been able to write key parts of this book without the thoughtful and rich reflections offered by my interviewees. It was a privilege to talk to each and every one of you and the issues raised have not only been valuable in the context of this book—for thinking through what veganism is and means in the current moment—but also in reflecting on my own scholarship and practice: thank you.

I'm incredibly grateful to friends and colleagues who have offered feedback on specific chapters of the book: thanks to Josh Bowsher, Matthew Cole, and Alex Lockwood for comments. Thanks too, to the anonymous reviewers for their incisive, constructive, and supportive feedback on my first draft, and to the reviewers who offered instructive feedback on my initial proposal. All of the external comments have shaped the book in meaningful ways and I am very appreciative. In the very early stages of formulating ideas I also received helpful comments and suggestions at a workshopping session at Lund University and want to express enormous thanks to people who attended, including Iselin Gambert, Tobias Linné, María Ruiz Carreras, Helen Thompson (as well as anyone who attended but didn't write their names down afterwards!). Particular thanks to Tobias for inviting me and Iselin for being so generous with time when I was visiting. Finally, thank you to everyone who took time to help with some last-minute proof-reading, particularly Greg Hollin, Adam Searle and Jonathon Turnbull, I will be ever appreciative of your generosity with your time. More broadly, thank you everyone I know who has been involved—in some way—with vegan practice and who I've talked to about so many of the issues discussed in this book over the years, but particular thanks to Brent Reid. Any royalties from this book will go to Brinsley Animal Rescue: a place that I know is close to a lot of your hearts.

It's been a hard year for all the obvious reasons and I'd like to express thanks to my colleagues and all of the friends we've shared lockdown experiences with, who have made this year as manageable as it could be with everything from general collegiality to Zoom quizzes. There are a few people I'd like to single out in this regard. I am ever appreciative to Katie Higgins and Jack Decie for letting us sit in their garden (when we were allowed after initial lockdown easing!) and to Cat Gold and Jeff Whyte for the first outdoor drinks (again when it was possible!). Heartfelt thanks must also go to Clive Hollin and Felicity Schofield (and Toby), who put a roof over our heads for longer than originally anticipated in late 2019 (a time period that coincided with me writing a major chunk of the book!) and very special thanks to Greg, again, who I'm sure was getting sick of me mulling over things by the time I submitted my final draft (if not well before). Finally, despite all of the stress of this year, one real bright spot over the course of writing the book has been becoming an Auntie (on both sides!), so I wanted to give special mention to Hani May and Leo—it's been such a privilege.

Chapter 1

INTRODUCTION

MORE THAN A DIET

"What if plants feel pain too?," "what about mice killed in harvesting?," "do you refuse to use a computer or drive a car due to the animal products involved?," "what about all the human suffering?," "if a neighborhood cat died of NATURAL causes, would it be vegan to wear it as a hat?" Depending on context, these questions might stem from genuine curiosity, from a desire to puncture perceived moralism, or simply be a joke. Something all of these queries have in common, however, is that anyone who has been vegan for any length of time would have been asked at least one of them. Well, perhaps not the last question— although it certainly sticks in my mind even though it happened in 2003. What also sticks in my mind is that at the time—as a new vegan—I found these discussions engaging or sometimes even amusing and was happy to talk through various ethical debates. In contrast, a friend found everything less funny due to feeling worn down by years of bad faith "gotcha" moments, which were posed as questions but really designed to highlight perceived hypocrisies. As described in recent texts about vegan practice, these experiences are not unique and "gotcha" provocations are commonplace in everyday discussions about veganism (see Hamilton, 2019: 185; Ko, 2019: 7).

This opening range of questions—the varied motivations behind them, different possible responses they can elicit, and frequency with which such debates occur— evokes something significant about veganism itself. Everyone has some sort of relationship with nonhuman animals, be it related to consumption, recreation, or everyday interactions with environments.[1] The centrality of animals to society thus means that the questions posed by veganism, with its call to rethink and contest some of the most commonplace of these relationships, are not just relevant to the small (albeit rapidly growing) number of people who identify as vegan themselves.[2] Instead, veganism speaks to practices, values, and relationships with animals that have integral socioeconomic or cultural roles, even as these relationships vary significantly between, and indeed within, particular national contexts.

The vastness and complexity of the issues posed by vegan practice mean that even jokingly worded provocations cannot be resolved in a straightforward way. My aim in this book is, therefore, not to offer a simplistic riposte to questions about veganism that I feel I should have addressed more thoughtfully in the past. Nor does the book launch a defense of vegan practice against imagined, or anticipated, criticism. Rather than providing any neat resolution, what I aim to do here is to offer a sense of the theoretically, politically, and ethically complex issues that veganism poses, at an important juncture in its contemporary history. I argue throughout this book that, in order to grasp veganism's distinctiveness as a form of food culture, it is, paradoxically, necessary to understand it as *more than a diet*: not just due to veganism's concern with animal ethics beyond food, but because of the broader ethical implications of its criticism of many existing human-animal relations. At the same time, in order to grasp the tensions that surround vegan practice, it needs to be situated as something that is in constant negotiation with markets, specific social formations, institutions, and particular discourses about nonhuman animals, which attempt to reduce veganism to *just a diet*.

The overarching aim of the book is to offer a sense of how these struggles between "more than" and "just" are negotiated, in ways that open up (and sometime shut down) the more radical political and ethical potentials associated with veganism. I approach this task by turning to a range of informative contexts, including the formation of vegan identity, vegan activism and campaigning, popular commentaries that highlight affinities and tensions with other social justice issues, and the recent popularization of "plant-based" food. Engaging with a range of examples from popular culture, debates within existing vegan scholarship, and original interview materials with long-term vegans themselves, the book develops a picture of veganism as something that is more multifaceted and complex than is often recognized either in certain academic contexts or within mainstream media depictions. Together, the examples and debates I draw upon throughout the book underline the importance of preserving the sense of veganism as something that interrogates the relationships that people have with nonhuman animals in a manner that goes beyond diet, as well as the wider political ramifications of this interrogation, in order to retain a sense of the "more than."

One of the difficulties of conceptualizing veganism as more than a way of eating or fashionable diet, in the present forum, is that this book series is dedicated to contemporary *food* studies. Due to the book's necessary emphasis on food, therefore, there is a risk of falling back onto the sense that veganism is solely about eating. Yet what I illustrate across the book's eight chapters is something that perhaps sounds paradoxical: even when discussing food itself, the discussion always ends up moving decisively beyond it. Chapter 3's discussion of high-profile criticisms leveled at vegan food, due to environmental and labor politics that are masked by labeling these products "cruelty free" (see Harper, 2010a), for instance, is generative of wider debates about purity politics, lifestyle activism, and identity. Furthering this sense of complexity, Chapter 5's initial discussion of big-budget campaigns designed to promote vegan diets leads to wide-ranging discussions about animal subjectivity. Elsewhere in the book, such as Chapter 2's overview of vegan scholarship or Chapter 4's analysis of grassroots activism, I discuss a range of academic and political initiatives that have sought to articulate connections between veganism and other social justice movements. The final chapters pick up on these discussions, drawing out the limitations of certain iterations of contemporary vegan practice in ways that speak to broader concerns about the classed and racialized inequalities associated with alternative lifestyle politics and limitations of market-based popular veganisms. Before sketching out more in-depth overview of the book, however, it is important to set the stage for its overarching arguments by developing a clearer sense of what it means to describe veganism as more than a diet and how recent developments have begun to complicate this claim.

The Difficulty of Defining and Situating Veganism

Veganism is more difficult to define than it might seem. Recent years have seen a number of events that speak to shifting definitions of what veganism is and means. Depictions of elite vegan athletes in popular cultural texts such as *The Game Changers* (2018) and related celebrations of health-food veganism (Braun and Carruthers, 2020; Scott, 2020) offer a marked contrast from dominant media discourse even just ten years ago, with its focus on restriction and asceticism (Cole, 2008; Cole and Morgan, 2011). Though holding very different implications, the rise of "junk food veganism" and increased accessibility of vegan food in chain restaurants such as Subway and even McDonald's, or campaigns like Veganuary and Meat Free Mondays, also stand in stark contrast to earlier cultural understandings of veganism as something rigid, marginal, and extreme. These developments have seen a corresponding ascendancy of terms including "plant-based food" and "flexitarianism" that associate veganism with a food politics emphasizing flexibility and individual choice, which seems to herald a departure from its association with more radical forms of activism (cf Cherry, 2010). Recent shifts in vegan practice thus hold a complicated, and often uneasy, position in relation to its longer political histories. What makes things more complex still are a number of tensions that are generated by any attempt to pin down a normative definition of veganism against which these recent events can be contrasted.

A useful starting point for establishing a working definition of veganism, for example, could be the UK Vegan Society. The society themselves were founded in 1944 and played an important role in supporting individuals who wanted to eliminate the consumption of animal products. Perhaps best known for a founding member, Donald Watson, coining the term "vegan," the Vegan Society's early activities also included providing nutritional information for new vegans, publishing early recipe books, and supporting the emergence of vegan societies in other national contexts such as the American Vegan Society in 1960 (Batt, 1964).[3] Later, the society developed an international trademark to designate vegan products (a V evolving into a leaf and sunflower motif) which has become one of the most iconic signifiers of veganism.

The society's own, much-cited, definition of veganism is that it marks "a way of living which seeks to exclude, as far as is possible and practicable, all forms of exploitation of, and cruelty to, animals for food, clothing or any other purpose" (Vegan Society, 2020a). Yet even this apparently straightforward definition expands rather than resolves discussion of veganism's meanings: opening up a can of worms related to everything from the meaning of terms such as "exploitation" and "cruelty" to how the caveat "possible and practicable" should be understood. In addition, care must be taken not to treat *a* history of veganism as the *definitive* history of animal product elimination, as this framing excludes spiritual, religious, and ethical movements with different cultural or geographical origins (Harper, 2012). Indeed, while particular dietary and spiritual practices might be described as "vegan" today in the wake of the uptake of the Vegan Society's terminology, they have far longer histories than this institution itself and complicate any neat sense of veganism "beginning" with a particular organization (a point that was emphasized by the society themselves in their original definition of the term [Cole, 2014]). This is not to say there isn't considerable value in unpacking particular, influential, institutional definitions of veganism, more that it is important to resist using these histories in a manner that shuts down rather than opens up more complex discussions about vegan ethics.

Bearing these tensions in mind, the Vegan Society's definition remains useful, in part, due to what it *does* open up. Something that the society's early work underlines is how some of the most high-profile conceptions of contemporary veganism have understood and enacted it as more than a diet. Veganism, here, is not just about eating and encompasses any relationship with animals where they are used for the primary benefit of humans. Vegan practice, in other words, has historically not just focused on rejecting particular animal products but has also posed a series of more fundamental questions about the way particular humans relate to other beings. This definition of veganism not only unsettles classifications such as "livestock" or "food animals" (see Arcari, 2020) but also the principles underlying many other institutions and practices, from zoos and recreational hunting, to horse racing and uses of animals in laboratory research.

To put things more precisely: what makes this conception of vegan ethics significant is that in societies marked by "anthroparchy"—"a complex and relatively stable set of hierarchical relationships in which 'nature' is dominated through formations of social organization which privilege the human" (Cudworth, 2011: 67)—a vegan way of living has historically sought to unsettle the inevitability of these formations and the institutions that support them. This book is written from one such context whose social relations are informed by anthroparchy, the UK, though it touches on a number of theories, debates, and controversies that resonate with other national settings in which contemporary veganism has become popularized and commercialized.

Veganism's Complex Relationship with Human Inequalities

Even when focusing on the situated lineage of veganism that is evoked when beginning with the Vegan Society's definition, vegan practice throws up a multiplicity of ethical concerns that have wide-reaching implications beyond food. What becomes explicit when turning to vegan scholarship and debate in more depth, is that this form of veganism is also understood as acting as more than a diet in a second sense. While nonhuman animals have historically assumed a central role in vegan praxis, so too have attempts to draw connections between the treatment of nonhuman animals and social justice issues related to *human* suffering (Cole, 2014). As Corey Lee Wrenn puts it, from its emergence "the Vegan Society presented plant-based consumption as a solution to famine, war, environmental devastation, health, and especially Nonhuman Animal suffering" (Wrenn, 2019: 191). While, Wrenn (2020) argues, these linkages have waned over time in more formal, professionalized institutions, in its radical activist iterations there is a rich history of vegan activism that has (and continues to) identify, interrogate, and contest sites in which specific human and nonhuman animal oppressions overlap (a point discussed in further depth shortly; see also Cherry, 2006; White and Cudworth, 2014; White, 2015; White and Springer, 2018; Giraud, 2019: 69–97). These activist histories cut against more recent understandings of veganism as an individualistic, single-issue form of politics.

However, while it is useful to turn to longer histories in order to debunk stereotypes about veganism that portray it as something monolithic or single-issue, it is also important to resist constructing uncritically positive narratives. To situate my own perspective: I am vegan myself and my stance throughout this book is broadly sympathetic toward veganism or, more specifically, the hopeful potentials of grassroots vegan practice. Yet, as also traced throughout the book, vegan politics is heterogeneous, and sometimes overly generalizing and problematic claims are made both in vegan campaigning and some strands of scholarship. Productive existing directions in research and activism, which further more complex analyses, have carefully situated the entanglement of human and animal exploitation in broader critical analyses of capitalist social relations (e.g., Cudworth, 2011; Wadiwel, 2015). What entanglement means here is, in part, a practical point, referring to the sort of violent intersections between human inequalities and animal suffering that occur in sites such as slaughterhouse kill-floors. As detailed in visceral long-form journalism and ethnographic research about meat-processing plants, racialized class hierarchies tend to determine who gets the dirtiest, most socially undesirable work, and economic precarity—often intensified by workers' insecure immigration status—is frequently leveraged to undermine attempts to improve working conditions (LeDuff, 2003; Pachirat, 2011). Recently, for instance, much has been made of the role of meat processing as hotspots for Covid-19 in the United States (Specht, 2020), in a manner that has been replicated across Europe: with new virus outbreaks emerging within German meat factories as well as mink fur farms in the Netherlands and Denmark (Maron, 2020). These analyses illustrate how institutions that violently transform animals into capital (Shukin, 2009) are also reliant on the transformation of particular groups of people into expendable resources (cf Moore, 2017).

Awareness of the entanglement of human and nonhuman animal oppressions is not new. In activist settings there have been long histories of groups articulating the relationship between different forms of oppression: from overlaps between Victorian suffragist and anti-vivisection movements (Kean, 1998), to incisive anti-capitalist pamphlets that incorporate animals into Marxist analyses of social inequality (Dominick, 2010 [1997]). Initiatives such as Food Not Bombs, which emerged in the United States in 1980 but have since established charters globally, likewise, have a long history of highlighting the social injustices associated with food waste and food poverty by sharing vegetarian and vegan food in public space (Heynen, 2010; Giraud, 2015; Winter, 2015; Spataro, 2016; Giles, 2018). The (contentious) role of veganism in the new climate movements echoes these legacies of entanglement between animal ethics and other social justice issues, with veganism increasingly positioned as the one thing people can do to both reduce their climate footprint and rearticulate their relationship with other species.[4]

Yet literal, physical relationships between humans and animals are only part of the story. Existing vegan research, scholarship, and activism have a rich history of interrogating veganism's relationship with unequal food systems, including groundbreaking scholarship from Black feminism (Harper, 2010a, 2010b, 2012; Ko and Ko, 2017; Ko, 2019), critical disability studies (Taylor, 2017), queer theory (Dell'Aversano, 2010; jones, 2014; Stephens Griffin, 2017; Brueck and McNeill, 2020); Indigenous scholarship (Robinson, 2013, 2014, 2017; Womack, 2013; Belcourt, 2015); and ecofeminism (Adams, 2000 [1990]; Gaard, 2002; Gruen, 2015; Wright, 2015). This body of research has highlighted further material and discursive connections between the oppression of humans and nonhuman animals, with a prominent argument being that categories such as "animal" and "species" not only serve to portray animals as "lower beings" but are also routinely used to exclude particular people from rights and privileges that "the human" are normatively regarded as possessing. The emerging academic field of Vegan Studies, for instance, centers around the recognition that human and animal oppression are "enmeshed," as author of *The Vegan Studies Project* (2015), Laura Wright, puts it (see Wright, 2018, 2019). Aph Ko's *Racism as Zoological Witchcraft* (2019), moreover, offers insight into how this enmeshment is manifested in practice, via an incisive analysis of popular media texts that explicates the ways that white supremacism anchors itself in discourses of animality, arguing that "*Animal* is a signifier that is always convenient and changing, and any group the dominant class deems unworthy is immediately branded with this label" (2019: 37; italics in original).

The exclusionary constructions of "the human" detailed by Ko and Wright are argued to have their roots in Anglo-European philosophy that emerged during the Enlightenment (see Latour, 1993; Wolfe, 2003; Haraway, 2008; Braidotti, 2013), which were tightly bound to projects of colonial expansion (Kim, 2015; Jackson, 2020). The legacies of this brand of humanism, however, persist today. In contemporary Europe, for instance, discursive linkages between animality and particular groups of people remain routine in tabloid newspapers, as when imagery of cockroaches or the language of "vermin" are used in anti-immigration media discourse to legitimize xenophobic policy (a discourse that has led to high-profile condemnation by the United Nations (2015); also Berry, Garcia-Blanco and Moore, 2016).

Existing activism and scholarship, therefore, have pointed to variegated connections between human and animal oppression, to position veganism as something that is not solely about nonhuman animals and holds scope to connect to other social justice campaigns. Yet realizing these connections in practice is not necessarily straightforward. All too often, rather than opening up space to understand the complex relationships between oppressions, high-profile vegan campaigns have approached this sensitive task in a manner that perpetuates inequalities (for more on this point see Chapters 5 and 6). In North America, for instance, crude comparison-making between animal abuse and the violence faced by people of color and Indigenous communities, particularly in publicity stunts by large NGOs such as People for the Ethical Treatment of Animals (PETA), have been intensely damaging (Kim, 2011). In addition, calls by white, middle-class activists to prohibit particular practices (hunting, meat consumption) can be manifested as a universalizing imposition of norms that restages the logics of settler-colonialism (Robinson, 2017). A further problem, Ko (2019: 6) suggests, is that the focus in popular commentaries, everyday discussion of veganism, and even some instances of grassroots activism, tend to bring things back to the most well-known aspect of vegan practice: food.

The issue with narrowing the focus to food is that changing dietary, or even lifestyle, practices does not offer a route into "cruelty-free" living (to use Harper's turn of phrase, 2010a) unless other inequalities—and the institutions and systems that support them—are also disrupted. As the case of environmentally devastating monocrops illustrates, poorly paid migrant labor and inequality are not just problems associated with animal agriculture (Hetherington, 2020). In addition to plant-based food production being implicated in colonial legacies, intersectional vegan scholarship has pointed to similar tensions from the perspective of consumer politics: highlighting that who is able to "opt-out" of oppressive food systems can equally be bound up with inequalities (Harper, 2010a, 2012).

Some of these tensions are drawn out in Julia Feliz Brueck's edited essay collections, which offer a platform for critical voices who detail barriers to engaging in vegan and animal activist praxis due to the centralization of a white, middle-class vegan experience in both activism and popular culture (see Brueck, 2017, 2019; Brueck and McNeill, 2020). These high-profile depictions of veganism are not only dangerous because of who is portrayed as a "typical vegan" but also due to perpetuating "post-race" narratives about food (Harper, 2012), or the sense that racialized and classed inequalities do not shape access to food choices. Such narratives are thus problematic in neglecting the structural inequalities that affect all food systems, by displacing ethical responsibility onto the individual in an archetypal neoliberal discursive formation (see Littler, 2017). In sum, veganism holds potential to trouble the social positioning of animals and, in doing so, open questions about the relationships between human, animal, and environmental injustices in specific cultural contexts. However, vegan practice does not *intrinsically* avoid perpetuating other inequalities.

The critical engagements with veganism that I have outlined here, in the context of vegan scholarship, offer nuanced accounts of the tensions and barriers to engaging in vegan food practice. The problem, Ko argues, is that this nuance is often missed in wider media and popular conceptions of veganism. What is commonplace instead is that veganism is reduced to a way of eating, which means debates about vegan ethics are restricted to reflecting on the accessibility of particular dietary choices within existing food systems. Rather than opening up discussion about the problems with these systems themselves, moreover, criticisms related to food inequities are often deployed in ways that foreclose discussions about structural change or the "multidimensional" relationships between animal oppression and other inequalities (Ko, 2019: 10). For this reason, Ko argues, it is important to resist attempts to reduce veganism to a way of eating or lifestyle, and instead conceive of vegan practice as something that—like other social movements—is "not about items or consumption, but powerful conversations for change" (2019: 8). Instigating the sorts of conversations that Ko is calling for, however, is precisely where the problem lies in the present moment. Creating connections between veganism and a wider interrogation of structural inequalities is precisely what has been rendered difficult in recent years, if not by the popularization of vegan practice itself, at least by certain facets of this popularization.

Shifts in Vegan Practice: From "Activist Veganism" to "Plant-based Capitalism"?

As hinted at earlier, during the second decade of the twenty-first century, and from 2015 in particular, vegan food culture has moved to the mainstream, especially in the Global North and urban, industrialized South. Large fast-food chains who were originally the target of protest by animal activists now sell vegan burgers, while hipster cafés offer dishes—from BBQ jackfruit and mock duck bao, to dosa to tempeh satay skewers—from food cultures with far longer plant-based histories. In many national contexts, these developments have resulted in veganism shifting from holding a DIY countercultural status to becoming something unaffordable and coded as only accessible to the middle classes (Polish, 2016), with vegan cafés and restaurants often associated with gentrification (Hamilton, 2019: 174–5). Against this backdrop, there has been growing concern from scholars and activists about whether some of the more radical dimensions of veganism that characterized its origins and practice until recently are being lost. The popularization of plant-based foods has again shifted the focus firmly back to veganism as a diet, as opposed to a holistic understanding of vegan practice that questions human-animal relations more broadly and their connection with other forms of oppression.

Richard White's valuable essay "Looking Backward, Moving Forward" (2018), for instance, sounds a note of caution about veganism shifting from a more radical, grassroots movement to the mainstream. Though this change carries all sorts of democratizing potentials, he suggests, it also holds the danger of veganism being co-opted and turned into just another dietary choice on a menu or fashionable lifestyle. While there might be potential in broadening veganism's appeal, White points out that the assumption that more widespread engagement with a vegan diet equates to profound societal change has not thus far materialized in practice— with animal product consumption continuing to rise. Moreover, the framing of plant-based eating as "cruelty free" is dubious; echoing Harper's (2010a) critique of the same label, White points to harrowing accounts of abuse faced by agricultural workers in the fruit and vegetable sectors across several European countries. As White asks: "if veganism is not having a positive impact on human or nonhuman animals, and indeed is contributing to greater levels of suffering and exploration, then what, or indeed for whom, is twenty-first century veganism of the greatest value and use for?" (White, 2018).

An informative example of these tensions can be found in Nathan Clay et al.'s (2020) discussion of the emergence of new markets oriented around plant milks (or mylks, made of produce such as nuts, oats, or hemp). The rise of these products could potentially be a "disruptive practice" (as Gambert, 2019, puts it) that de-naturalizes certain relationships with nonhuman animals, with the growth of plant-based markets also hinting at scope for more dramatic transitions in food systems. Indeed, the threat that these products are perceived to pose to animal agriculture—in part—accounts for the y in mylk. This alternative spelling originally arose in response to legal challenges by US-based dairy corporations who aimed to prohibit uses of the term "milk" for non-animal-based products, with similar battles over non-dairy milks and meat alternatives raging in Europe (Gambert, 2019: 801–3). Some of the most widely available mylks, however, are produced by large dairy corporations who effectively try to have their (non-vegan) cake and eat it, by capitalizing on the growing ethical disquiet surrounding cows' milk though emphasizing perceptions of plant milks being healthier and more environmentally friendly alternatives, while continuing to be implicated in dairy production. Other, independent brands, such as Oatly, *do* present their mylks as marking a radical break with existing forms of consumption (and indeed with other, dairy company-owned mylk brands), but even these products resist association with activist-vegan politics: avoiding "disgust at animal death and the 'extremism' of vegan activism" (Clay et al., 2020: 956).[5] Mylks, in other words, carefully negotiate their branding, in order to circumvent any "disagreeable opinions of those who stand to lose out from this reorganization of the dairy system" as well as "unpalatable ruminations over whose economic interests [mylk] serves, and the social relations involved in producing almonds, soy and oats" (Clay et al., 2020: 956). While promising—and in some instances even promoting themselves as offering—disruption to food systems, therefore, these products often just serve to facilitate business as normal.

It might be tempting, in light of these issues, to give up on notions of the radical ethical potentials of veganism, or—at least—give up on any sense that a vegan *diet* responds to oppressions that are entangled. What I illustrate in this book, however, is that although it is important to be reflexive about the limitations of vegan (and indeed any) political praxis that operates in the messy space between collective and individual change, there is still something important in veganism that should not be dismissed. Recognizing that there is no such thing as ethical consumption under capitalism is not the same thing as opting-out of difficult questions about how to rework the practices and institutions that reduce nonhuman life to resources on such a staggering scale and it remains valuable to explore scope for veganism to serve as a form of "counter conduct" that resists these processes (Wadiwel, 2015).[6]

White's own response to negotiating tensions related to a vegan diet is to make a differentiation—though one he acknowledges is imperfect—between "lifestyle" and "activist" veganism, urging that before uncritically embracing "lifestyle veganism" as a democratizing force, it is important to "look backwards" and derive lessons from the more complex forms of vegan ethics enacted by earlier grassroots social movements. This distinction is informative due to illustrating the stakes of the rise of popular veganisms, or, to use the label I put forward in Chapter 7, plant-based capitalism. The risk of veganism's popularization is that plant-based capitalism has the potential to reduce a movement that has a long history of being "more than a diet" into "just" a diet. This process of commodification not only marks a disconnection from broader questions about human-animal relationships also but severs connections between veganism and other social justice issues: reducing the issue to eating animals rather than anthroparchy writ-large.

Yet while it is useful to recognize differences between "activist" and "lifestyle veganism" or long-standing iterations of vegan praxis and plant-based capitalism, it is important not to romanticize vegan activism. Even aside from the racially and culturally problematic large-scale vegan campaigns discussed previously, grassroots vegan praxis has itself sometimes veered toward single-issue politics or elitism (see Chapters 4 and 6, this book). The activist/lifestyle distinction remains useful as a loose heuristic, however, as *because* of these ongoing issues, the sorts of tensions that have boiled over in the recent commodification of plant-based foods have already been subject to a long history of debate and discussion in the context of vegan activism and scholarship. It is, of course, vital to engage with new research and perspectives—including those that are critical of veganism— but much can be learned from revisiting earlier debates rather than attempting to initiate conversations about vegan ethics and politics from scratch.

Perhaps most productively, existing vegan scholarship and activism offer resources for navigating debates that can sometimes prove stultifying. As hinted at in the opening questions, one of the biggest sources of tension associated with veganism is the sense of moral judgment that it is seen to carry. No matter if stereotypes of the "preachy" or "angry" vegan are accurate or not (and as described in Chapter 3 these tropes are complex; see also Stephens Griffin, 2017), the ethical implications of vegan politics and practice can still infer moralism. To grasp these implications, it is helpful to again revisit the Vegan Society description of veganism as a "way of living which seeks to exclude, as far as is possible and practicable, all forms of exploitation of, and cruelty to, animals for food, clothing or any other purpose." What is significant about this definition is that it reframes ways of relating to animals, which are commonplace within particular cultural contexts, as being exploitative. Reframing normative cultural practices as ethically questionable means that people, say, who might see themselves as animal lovers but eat meat (a position that is not treated as incompatible in national contexts such as the UK, for instance), are implicated in animal cruelty. What makes this reframing discomforting for many people is that it does not just cut against the ideological grain (as Joy, 2011, argues), but can generate frictions in light of other inequalities that are bound up with food systems and that might make veganism difficult to realize (see Chapter 3).

What is perhaps underemphasized in critical narratives about veganism, however, is the activist-vegan tradition pointed at by White, which positions vegan praxis in structural rather than liberal-individualist terms. Indeed, an emphasis on structures, institutions, and systems is present even in the Vegan Society's early definition of veganism, as with the phrase "possible and practicable" itself. Sociologist Matthew Cole (2014) draws out the meaning of this phrase, describing how the Vegan Society's early work embedded the recognition that it is impossible to be entirely vegan in an agricultural system where everything—including fertilizers and manure—is entangled with animal agriculture. Indeed, recognition of the impure basis of any sort of political action was central to these early debates, with activists repeatedly arguing that the exploitation of nonhuman life "dirties us all": vegans included (in Cole, 2014: 214). As Cole describes, early initiatives by the society were attempts to support individuals in attaining what was feasible within the constraints of this system, as well as maximizing this feasibility through pioneering infrastructures (such as alternative farming methods) that were needed for more wholescale, systemic change. These efforts continue today in initiatives such as the development of veganic agriculture or the work of thousands of small-scale food cooperatives across the globe that are trying to find less harmful ways of distributing food.[7] What is notable, therefore, is that veganism has historically not been seen as something promising moral solace or purity, but instead been positioned as an ongoing process that is in constant negotiation with systemic constraints.

More recently, relational understandings of veganism have been developed into sustained political frameworks, as with Sunaura Taylor's (2017) conception of a "social model of veganism" that draws inspiration from the social model of disability to see veganism as a valuable heuristic to aspire toward while recognizing the constraints that might make this difficult in practice. While I delve into these arguments in more depth in the rest of the book, what is important about Taylor's approach is that it again firmly shifts away from narratives of veganism as an individual choice and firmly articulates it as something enabled and constrained by existing socio-technical infrastructures.

In light of the shaky premise of some of the dominant critiques of veganism, which have focused on accusations of moral inconsistency and purism that can perhaps be complicated by pointing to definitions and activist practice that show it has never seen itself as pure, it could be easy for vegan activism and scholarship to sweep aside criticisms. Yet, work such as Taylor's does not lead to this conclusion either. Contemporary veganism *does* carry tensions that need to be grappled with; just because some iterations of activist veganism recognize structural problems does not mean that this recognition is universal (Dominick, 2010 [1997]).

It is important, therefore, to distinguish between vegan histories that see it as "more than a diet" and recent iterations of plant-based capitalism that submerge the more radical potentials of veganism, as this distinction clears space for critical questions about variegated material, discursive, and infrastructural connections between human and animal oppression. At the same time, it is important not to exempt even these earlier grassroots forms of veganism from critique, and recognize that vegan practice has a history of being criticized even by those sympathetic to its aims. As activist pamphlet *Beasts of Burden* states:

> While it addresses a single issue, animal liberation does pose fundamental questions about the relationship of humans to the world. This can be a starting point for a fundamental questioning of the way we live our lives; on the other hand animal rights ideology can become a limit which prevents a wider critique of society. We need to go beyond this ideology without abandoning what is subversive in what it represents. (Anon, 2004)

Though the histories of animal activism and veganism are not synonymous (see Chapter 4) this quote is one I have repeatedly come back to in previous works (e.g., Giraud, 2013a, 2019: 69), because it captures something important about vegan practice. As touched on at the start of this chapter, veganism holds potential to trouble something fundamental about the way humans relate to other beings. With the rise of plant-based capitalism, however, long-standing problems associated with vegan practice could be intensified: especially if veganism becomes something neatly satisfied through existing food systems in ways that delimit scope for more fundamental critique of the way that particular humans relate to non-human animals. One of the aspirations of this book is to chart, and draw hope from, some of the existing ways veganism has—and continues to have—potential to act as more than a diet, while also examining some informative contexts in which these potentials are being limited, which have become intensified in the contemporary moment.

Chapter Overviews

The book approaches the complex relationship between "more than" and "just" in vegan praxis by offering a sense of existing scholarship, activism, and ethical debates, before turning in a more sustained way to veganism's (complex) relationship with other social and environmental injustices in the contemporary moment. In light of the rapidly emerging and expanding body of work about veganism, the book does not offer an exhaustive overview but focuses on the issues and debates that speak most clearly to concerns set out in this initial chapter regarding what it means—in material and conceptual terms—to be a lifestyle movement that wrestles with the need for both democratization and more radical change, even as these needs sometimes pull in opposite directions.

Chapter 2 offers a sketch of some productive strands of existing vegan scholarship and scholarship about veganism, fields which are not synonymous due to the marked distinction that currently exists between research that holds normative commitments to veganism and research that treats vegan practice and identity as an interesting object of study. It begins with recent calls for Vegan Studies to be seen as a field in its own right, which—to use Wright's terminology (2015: 11–14)—is distinct from the "three prongs" of existing animal studies research: critical animal studies (CAS), posthumanism and human-animal studies. After tracing some of the ecofeminist lineages of this emergent field, as currently conceived, I highlight both overlaps and informative sites of tension with the other prongs of animal studies. The purpose of tracing these, often messy, academic relationships, however, is not simply to offer a mapping of the field of Vegan Studies, but point to productive future directions. To give a sense of what some of these directions might look like, I close by arguing for the importance of engaging with research and critical perspectives that do not fit neatly into Vegan Studies as it currently stands. In particular, I draw upon work in more-than-human geographies, media studies, and the sociology of consumption, as well as bodies of research that might exist outside of animal studies entirely but are useful for understanding the fraught political terrain that contemporary vegan practice is operating within.

The third chapter builds on the complex picture of veganism developed by existing vegan scholarship, to rethink some of the debates that I have touched on throughout this introductory chapter: the perception that vegan practice is a form of individualistic purity politics (see Shotwell, 2016). Starting from the premise that veganism has historically not been enacted as something "pure" (Cole, 2014), the chapter shows how popular discourses that perpetuate purity stereotypes can sometimes (inadvertently) segue with more reactionary narratives that criticize *any* ethical stance that tries to question existing social norms. The chapter then moves onto recent sociological research, which traces how a sense of necessary inconsistency and impurity is manifested in contemporary expressions of veganism.

The fourth chapter's aims are crystallized by its title, "Learning from Vegan Activism," in focusing on what can be learned from turning to some of the existing ways that ethical complexity has been recognized—and engaged with—in activist practice. The first half of the chapter focuses on visibility politics, or the long-standing argument that highlighting how animals are treated in certain agricultural contexts can mobilize support for veganism. I then move onto activism that foregrounds the limitations of assuming that visibility leads to change, including the Save Movement (who hold vigils outside slaughterhouses), Animal Rebellion (an offshoot of climate change movement Extinction Rebellion), and anti-McDonald's protest (that first emerged in the 1980s but persists today). Rather than seeing "visibility" as enough in itself, these movements instead illustrate the need for a more fundamental contestation of both categories such as "livestock" that render animals unworthy of mourning and wider narratives that support these categories by portraying human and animal needs as lying in opposition to one another. Yet, even as these instances of activism illustrate the need to disrupt existing categorizations and create alternative social relationships between humans and animals, they also illustrate the practical difficulties associated with this task. The chapter closes by probing these difficulties in more depth, turning to initiatives that do not just seek to unsettle the way things are but actively prefigure alternatives: food-sharing activism and protest camp infrastructures that try to realize egalitarian vegan politics in the present. Though these forms of activism are—inevitably—imperfect, they offer scope for new forms of responsibility and accountability toward the worlds that they attempt to bring into being, which, I suggest, offer helpful inspiration moving forward.

The fifth chapter, "Animal Subjectivity and Anthropomorphism," picks up on questions about how to change the social status—and position—of animals, by bringing animals themselves more firmly into the frame. Throughout the chapter I examine the ambivalent role of anthropomorphism (cf Parkinson, 2019), or the act of highlighting affinities between humans and animals to mobilize support for vegan ethics, in the context of three examples: PETA's attempts to question the consumption of animals by mapping "livestock" attributes onto human bodies; Animal Equality's attempts to reverse this tactic by mapping human emotion and experience onto animals in slaughterhouses; and—in stark contrast—the unsettling of classifications that distinguish between pets and food animals (Joy, 2011) that can be found in the home of Esther the Wonder Pig and the sanctuary movement more widely. On one level, comparing these examples offers a means of critically interrogating campaign tactics that have sought to treat animals as subjects rather than objects (elaborating on issues raised in Chapter 4). However, in the process, the chapter also interrogates different frameworks that have arisen in academic contexts—but are increasingly gaining purchase in campaign settings—for centralizing animal subjectivity. The chapter ultimately argues that for all of the value of finding new ways to identify with animals, which are emerging in scholarship and activism, classifications such as "livestock" or "pet" are not altered just by changing perceptions, but the institutions and social formations that sustain species' difference. It is these questions of structural change that have become increasingly difficult to address in light of the developments discussed in the closing chapters.

The book's final two substantive chapters shift the focus to some of the most pressing concerns within the book, exploring how veganism's push to be more than a diet has become still messier with veganism's move to the mainstream. While the other chapters are predominantly documentary analysis, engaging with existing scholarship and examples from popular culture, in the final chapters this approach is complemented by my own interview materials.

The penultimate chapter draws on concerns raised by my interviewees in order to approach an increasingly high-profile set of arguments for a more intersectional form of veganism, which recognizes and seeks to dismantle the connections between human and animal oppression within specific (capitalist) social relations (Harper, 2018). Mirroring what Patricia Hill Collins (2015) describes as the wider "definitional dilemmas" of intersectionality, the concept of intersectional veganism holds a slightly different range of meanings in the context of vegan activism and scholarship, with some commentators arguing that the term is not especially helpful (e.g., Ko, 2019). The chapter traces how these debates have manifested themselves in relation to two different forms of erasure that have arisen in contemporary vegan cultures. First, the problems associated with the cultural phenomena of "white veganism"; what Harper (2012) frames as a "post-race" mode of ethical consumption that relegates classed and racialized inequalities to the past and suggests no barriers to ethical lifestyle choices exist. The chapter then, second, examines how an interrelated form of erasure can emerge in criticisms of veganism, which treat white veganism as though it is representative of all veganism: in the process cutting away vegan experiences, practices, and identities that are already excluded from middle-class "Westernized" iterations of vegan praxis. The chapter outlines how these two forms of erasure manifest in especially problematic ways in narratives of veganism as a global phenomenon, arguing that these tensions both illustrate the need to centralize existing research from fields that have interrogated inequalities in vegan praxis and create space for more situated narratives about veganism's expression in specific national contexts. At present, however, these approaches are often obscured within both pro- and anti-vegan narratives in popular culture.

While Chapter 6 foregrounds important criticisms of ethical lifestyle politics that operate within a post-race landscape, the final chapter asks if this neglect of structural inequalities has been intensified by the rise of plant-based capitalism. The chapter draws insights from research that has critically analyzed the cultural phenomenon of postfeminism, a "sensibility" that Rosalind Gill (2007, 2017) argues characterizes depictions of feminism in popular culture wherein there has been a shift away from narratives of collective or structural change toward individual empowerment (often expressed through consumption choices). I argue that the recent popularization of contemporary veganism shares structural similarities with postfeminism's depoliticization of feminism as a collective mode of politics. More specifically, recent developments in vegan politics have emphasized individual choice, while neglecting the structures that constrain who is able to make particular lifestyle decisions. To tease out the characteristics of plant-based capitalism, or post-veganism, I draw, in particular, on fifteen of my interviews that have discussed how these developments are manifested in the UK: focusing on this specific bounded context in recognition of the varied and uneven uptake of veganism even across settings that seem similar (such as North America and Northern Europe, see Aavick, 2019a, 2019b). Yet, although some of the key developments outlined in the chapter might be articulated from a situated perspective, they have broader significance in terms of illustrating the tensions that can rise when a movement such as veganism shifts to the mainstream. The chapter, in other words, makes the promise and pitfalls of veganism's popularization and commercialization explicit; while popularization holds democratizing potentials, it also runs the risk of turning something that (to reiterate the core concern of the book) began as "more than a diet" into just a diet.

Approaching Veganism: A Final Note on Methods

Before closing this introductory chapter, I wish to make a brief note about the book's overall disciplinary and methodological orientation. Due to the broad implications of veganism—in terms of its interrogation of wider entanglements between humans, animals, and environments—there have been calls to develop an interdisciplinary approach to vegan studies.[8] As Wright (2015) points out in her important body of work, veganism is bound up with an expansive array of concerns, including animal ethics, cultural understandings of the body, political institutions, globalized economies of production and consumption, popular media depictions, and even issues related to health and psychology. In this book, therefore, it would be tempting to draw together an interdisciplinary set of tools that are capable of mapping onto these issues. Rather than taking this path, however, I focus here on a more specific tool kit offered by a particular tradition of media and cultural studies.

As Chapter 2 explores, both existing vegan scholarship and scholarship about veganism are themselves complex to define, drawing—as they do—on a heterogeneous variety of theoretical influences and hailing from a range of disciplinary contexts. The relationship between vegan research and other (equally complex) interdisciplinary fields such as animal studies, which have distinctive histories and commitments of their own, makes things even more unwieldy. On a practical level, bringing still further disciplinary perspectives to the table could make things unmanageable. Pragmatics aside, one of the ethical and epistemological commitments of the approach I have taken to writing this book is that, to borrow Donna Haraway's turn of phrase, "nothing comes without its world" (Haraway, 1997: 37; see also Puig de la Bellcasa, 2012). No piece of knowledge, framework, or disciplinary tool can be fully extracted from the sociopolitical context, norms, and assumptions that govern its context of production. Uprooting any given piece of knowledge from its constitutive world is dangerous, because it can render the underlying assumptions and context of a particular disciplinary insight difficult to detect.

As research focused on common tensions in interdisciplinary research has elucidated, overly "ebullient" (Fitzgerald and Callard, 2015) borrowing from other disciplines can run the risk of things being taken out of context and misrepresented or fail to recognize when knowledge from different disciplinary contexts carry assumptions that clash with one another. Issues can arise, for instance, when drawing together fields such as neuroscience, psychology, and cultural studies to gain insight into human relationships with animals, due to these fields conventionally holding very different understandings of the relationship between individuals and society. To do justice to a synthesis of different disciplines, therefore, it is important to first recognize and then carefully negotiate any such tensions. Giving a full sense of the worlds that come with the different disciplinary insights that could be brought to bear on veganism, however, is beyond the scope of this book. To echo a point that Cary Wolfe makes in the context of similar debates about animal studies (2010: 115), it is sometimes more productive to produce work that is explicitly from a specific disciplinary perspective in order to offer an anchor-point for conversation with other fields.

To this end, while this book aims to contribute to an interdisciplinary conversation, it is informed by a specific tradition of cultural studies that is associated with the Contemporary Centre for Cultural Studies, Birmingham, UK. There is no scope here to go into depth about the rise (and sad decline) of this form of cultural studies as a formal, institutionalized discipline (see Webster, 2004), but, to briefly give a sense of its core commitments, what was (and remains) important about this body of work is that it takes popular culture seriously as an object of study. From punk subcultures (Hebdige, 2005 [1979]) to mediated nationalism (Gilroy, 1991), and youth magazines (McRobbie, 1990), or, to draw on more recent work engaging with the legacies of CCCS that has gone well beyond a UK focus, queer identity (Bao, 2020), popular feminisms (Banet-Weiser, 2018), and transnational meat cultures (Chatterjee and Subramaniam, 2021), cultural studies seeks to identify the shared meanings or collectively recognized "codes" associated with everyday practices in specific cultural contexts (Fiske, 2010). More specifically, cultural studies has been especially concerned with how these codes are bound up in struggles over dominant meanings between the producers and consumers of popular cultural texts or products. Central to the field is an understanding that battles over meaning take place on an uneven terrain; as Stuart Hall (1980, 2010) argues, publics always interpret, or decode, cultural meaning in a landscape that is already inscribed with dominant values and ideologies. Resistant or nonnormative cultural readings and practices are thus difficult to realize as they cut against the grain of established meanings.

The book is informed by this tradition of cultural studies in three ways. First, in methodological terms it recognizes the conceptual value of texts that are not straightforwardly "academic": drawing inspiration from sources including activist pamphlets, marketing literature, and recipe books, alongside conventional academic sources. Due to the rapidly evolving affordances of veganism, some of the most informative reflections about vegan practice do not appear in peer-reviewed articles and books but online: notably in blogs and social media sites. Indeed, traffic between the "academic" and "nonacademic" in these contexts is difficult to disentangle, with prominent academics often choosing to publish short, but valuable, reflective essays as blog-posts. Some of the most significant recent books about veganism, moreover, are both informed by academic research and have in turn fed into vegan scholarship, but themselves focus on making complex theoretical debates accessible to wider audiences. Though I work to situate the sources I engage with carefully and do not wish to entirely flatten important distinctions related to, for instance, the intended audience of particular publications, I nonetheless argue that popular texts that are sometimes sidelined in academia are not just valuable subject matter for analysis but can offer powerful conceptual insights and provocations.

The second way the book is informed by cultural studies is in resisting the assumption that problematic texts, products, or examples from media culture can be used to make assumptions about how people actually enact, think, or feel about a particular set of political values. While anthropomorphic imagery used on the social media accounts of animal sanctuaries or angry debates on vegan forums might give a particular impression of veganism and need to be taken seriously (and critically), it is important not to draw overly general conclusions from these texts alone. It is here that the final chapters' engagement with interview data is especially informative.

Although the main methodological approach I take throughout this book is textual analysis, as I began to write the initial chapters, I realized that the issues I was engaging with were evolving so rapidly that something additional was needed. Every day a new controversy about vegan practice was emerging online, a new vegan campaign was grabbing the media spotlight (often for the wrong reasons), or a new plant-based product-line was emerging. What was absent in many of the discussions emanating from these developments (as others have also pointed out, see Hamilton, 2016, 2019) were the perspectives of vegans themselves. It is for this reason that the final chapters of the book include original data from a series of interviews I undertook as part of a larger project, in order to gain insight into what long-term vegans themselves felt about contemporary veganism. The rich qualitative data gathered from these interviews not only adds another complex layer to this book's conceptualization of vegan practice as more than a way of eating but also offers insight into some of the dominant characteristics of the recent phenomenon of "plant-based capitalism" more specifically. As described in the chapter overviews, interviewees also often troubled assumptions about vegan ethics, particularly the notion that this ethics results in overly simplistic, universalizing modes of political practice.

The interviews themselves focused on three broad themes that were designed to explore the perceptions of long-term vegans about veganism's increasing popularity:

- What do long-term vegans feel about veganism's recent popularization?
- What political opportunities and challenges do long-term vegans think are posed by veganism's popularization?
- What do long-term vegans think needs to be done to negotiate these challenges (e.g., to make veganism more inclusive/accessible, or challenge its characterization as apolitical lifestyle politics).

These themes were approached through a series of subquestions, which asked people about issues related to the biggest changes associated with veganism, what connections people felt veganism had (or didn't have) with other social justice campaigns in the wake of these changes, and if they had any thoughts about the dangers and potentials about veganism's growing popularity.

After initial interviews, I made two adjustments to the framing of the project. Though the research was originally designed to engage with both academics engaged with veganism and activists, in practice these distinctions broke down: with long-term activists often keen to reflect on academic frameworks (especially ecofeminism) and academics choosing to speak from their perspective as activists. In addition, the transnational nature of vegan scholarship meant that veganism was not evenly popularized: with participants from the United States, in particular, describing very different experiences to the United Kingdom. For this reason, the chapter where I engage most substantively with interview materials (Chapter 7) is based on insights from the fifteen interviews I have undertaken with long-term vegans based in the UK, although other materials are touched on in Chapter 6 in relation to wider debates about intersectional veganisms. "Long-term vegan" is, of course, a relative term and I use this label here in reference to individuals who have practiced veganism for ten years plus, as this marks a period prior to the popularization I have discussed in this book. In line with this definition, I have labeled any quotations from interviewees with a designated pseudonym along with the length of time they have practiced veganism (as specified during the interview itself).

The final way the book is informed by a cultural studies tradition is its conceptual orientation, which focuses on identifying the struggles over meaning that are emerging in relation to contemporary vegan practice and teasing out the political and ethical stakes of these struggles. Echoing other recent work that has adopted an emphasis on struggles associated with the popular (e.g., Littler, 2017; Banet-Weiser, 2018), throughout the book I pay close attention to the discourses and practices that constitute the battleground that contemporary vegan practice is negotiating. While recognizing that contestations over meaning are always messy and uneven, and offer few easy answers, by focusing on contestation this book interrogates the political and ethical stakes of veganism's popularization. While the book is primarily situated in relation to contemporary *food* politics, therefore, in order to reflect the broader concerns of the series it is situated in, the struggles I engage with go beyond a focus on diet: echoing the aspirations of vegan politics, practice, and theory itself.

Chapter 2

VEGAN DEBATES

TRACING VEGAN SCHOLARSHIP

The aim of this chapter is to trace some of the key issues and debates that have animated research about veganism across the humanities and social sciences. What makes this task difficult is that various (sub-) disciplines have constructed slightly different narratives both about veganism itself and about its emergence as an area of academic inquiry. In the overview of existing research that I provide here, therefore, I am not aiming to create one homogenous story about vegan scholarship, nor provide an exhaustive overview of a singular academic field. Instead, I offer a snapshot of conceptual and empirical approaches to engaging with veganism, which have emerged across a range of academic contexts, and are valuable for grappling with the politics of its popularization.

I begin by turning to recent attempts to formalize vegan studies as a distinct area of academic study, or, put differently, the shift from vegan studies to Vegan Studies. I then move onto work in critical animal studies (CAS), the field where initial references to vegan studies as an area of research began to emerge. The next section of the chapter turns to engagements with veganism in so-called mainstream or posthumanist animal studies, grouping this heterogeneous body of work into two categories: theoretical work influenced by science and technology studies (STS) and literary animal studies.[1] Finally, I engage with research about veganism that has tended to be categorized under the label human-animal studies, as well as work from geography, social movement studies, and the sociology of consumption. Though the material I engage with throughout this chapter is wide-ranging, what it shares is the sense that even though food is an important area of concern for vegan scholarship, the ethical implications of veganism go well beyond diet.

From vegan studies to Vegan Studies

As noted earlier, a degree of dissonance and heterogeneity exists across academic work that has engaged with veganism; that said, a number of texts do recur as touchstones. In the first decade of the twenty-first century, for instance, a series of journal special editions emerged, which sought to carve out a place for animal studies within particular conceptual and disciplinary contexts, with veganism emerging as a central theme. These editions included an issue of the *Journal for Critical Animal Studies* (Yarbrough and Thomas, 2010) that focused on the work of women of color and contained influential work about veganism by A. Breeze Harper (with Harper's *Sistah Vegan* coming out in the same year). An edition of *Feminism & Psychology* (Potts, 2010) emerged at a similar time, which included a dialogue between Donna Haraway and Annie Potts that addressed tensions between critical and "posthumanist" animal studies (subfields explained in more depth subsequently). Two years later saw the publication of an issue of *Hypatia* (Gruen and Weil, 2012), which explored the relationship between feminism and animals, and veganism was again a prominent theme.

Perhaps the most decisive academic engagement with veganism, however, has been Laura Wright's call for a Vegan Studies that moves away from being seen as a subfield of animal studies, to instead be treated as a field in its own right. This argument is articulated most prominently in Wright's 2015 book *The Vegan Studies Project: Food, Animals, and Gender in the Age of Terror*, but has also been developed through a series of other publications, including a 2018 special section of the journal *ISLE* (Interdisciplinary Studies in Literature and Environment) and edited collection *Through a Vegan Studies Lens: Textual Ethics and Lived Activism* (2019), alongside two forthcoming handbooks. As touched on previously, Wright is not alone in focusing on veganism; other lineages of thought exist and have engaged with vegan politics using different conceptual tools (for overviews of alternative trajectories, see Hamilton, 2016; Gillespie, 2017). While research that both overlaps with and departs from Wright's work is discussed further in the rest of this chapter, it is nonetheless useful to begin by mapping out her arguments due to *The Vegan Studies Project* being the first monograph-length attempt to situate Vegan Studies as an academic field in its own right.

One of Wright's primary concerns is how particular bodies are constructed as normative and others as nonnormative within US culture, indeed the original title for *The Vegan Studies Project* was *The Vegan Body Project*. This focus on the body was complicated, however, by realizing the range of different issues and concerns that were entangled with veganism and so, instead, Wright oriented the book around examining "the mainstream discourse surrounding and connecting animal rights to (or omitting animal rights from) veganism, with specific attention to the construction and depiction of the U.S. vegan body as a contested site manifested in contemporary works of literature, popular cultural representations and news media" (2015: 19). The body, then, was transformed from the book's primary focus to a lens through which to approach broader issues related to food politics and animal ethics, and through which to make sense of a cultural landscape that is often hostile to nonnormative ways of eating (unless there is potential to commodify them).

In *The Vegan Studies Project* itself, correspondingly, Wright engages with a broad range of topics. The book discusses the potential for popular cultural texts (from post-apocalyptic novels to television series focused on vampires) to unsettle norms surrounding animal product consumption, examines associations created by the media between veganism and disordered eating, and explores tensions surrounding celebrity veganism. What underpins all of these examples is the sense, again, that veganism is more than an object of study. Or, at least, veganism is such a *complex* object of study, that examining it encompasses a broad range of themes—ranging from ethics to health, and contemporary politics to questions of media representation—which can only be fully analyzed using an interdisciplinary approach.

In the wake of *The Vegan Studies Project* and as calls for a Vegan Studies have taken firmer shape across Wright's subsequent body of work, several prominent characteristics have emerged. First, Wright repeatedly emphasizes that veganism is both an *identity* and a *practice* (2015: 2). In light of this recognition, the field, second, has tended to focus on the construction and contestation of vegan identity and practices in contemporary culture (while Wright's focus is on the United States, others who have taken up her work have engaged with a wider range of national contexts, e.g., Castricano and Simonsen, 2016). A third key aspect of this formulation of Vegan Studies, and one Wright consistently reasserts, is its grounding in ecofeminism. Her approach builds directly on foundations laid by ecofeminists—particularly the work of Carol J. Adams and Greta Gaard—who have emphasized intersections between the oppression of women and animals, and argued for veganism as a conceptual and ethical means of contesting these oppressions.[2] Indeed in one of Wright's succinct formulations of the aims of Vegan Studies, she explicitly draws on an ecofeminist framing to argue that "at this point in history, the task of the vegan theorist is to disaggregate enmeshed oppressions in order to understand more fully the mechanisms that support them" (2018: 28). For Wright, in other words, a vegan perspective is the starting point for rethinking not only human-animal relations but a whole host of other classed, racialized, and gender inequalities that are entangled with these relationships.

Ecofeminism and "Enmeshed Oppressions"

The concept of enmeshed oppressions that Wright evokes is drawn from the ecofeminist argument that vegetarianism and veganism can serve as feminist practices that unsettle the mutually supportive relationship between patriarchy and speciesism (e.g., Gaard, 2002, 2011; Kheel, 2004; Sturgeon, 2009). This understanding of veganism is predicated on the argument that the oppression of nature and women is interlinked. The treatment of the natural world as a series of resources that can be used for human benefit is, for ecofeminist thinkers, a key component of patriarchy. Once it is possible to view the world as something that humans have dominion over, they argue, it also becomes possible to legitimize the oppression and objectification of particular groups of humans, namely those who have historically been treated as somehow "closest" to nature (including women and people of color, as well as animals). As Marti Kheel puts it:

> Ecofeminists argue that Western patriarchal society operates by means of a series of gendered dualisms. The male half of the dualism is associated with "culture," "good," the "rational," and the "spiritual," while the female half is associated with "nature," "evil," the "nonrational," and the "profane." (2004: 328)

As Kheel points out, while strands of feminism have tried to combat oppression by contesting the association between women and nature (which is seen as supporting essentialist conceptions of gender), ecofeminism takes the opposite approach. From an ecofeminist perspective it is the devaluation of nature that needs to be challenged, because as long as this dualism exists it can be drawn upon to portray particular groups of people as less-than-human. In this formulation, the enmeshed oppressions of women, nature, and animals are also seen to be entangled with the stigmatization of qualities such as care and emotion, while rationality is valorized. To combat these dichotomies, one of the central projects of ecofeminism has been to reclaim care as the foundation for developing less anthropocentric forms of ethics (see also Tronto, 1993; Donovan and Adams, 2007; Puig de la Bellacasa, 2011, 2017; Gruen, 2020). By extension, ecofeminism has criticized conventional animal rights and liberations frameworks that are grounded in rationalist approaches to ethics—such as the work of Tom Regan and Peter Singer—for focusing on one aspect of enmeshed oppression while perpetuating other dualisms that sustain the Othering of "nature" by sidelining care ethics (Seager, 2003).

Ecofeminism thus holds significance for vegan ethics and politics in two specific ways. First, by highlighting how oppressions are enmeshed, ecofeminism argues that contesting the exploitative treatment of the more-than-human world, and animals in particular, is important to a feminist project. On the other hand, second, these arguments create space for veganism to be rearticulated as an (eco) feminist act due to unsettling some of the routine, everyday practices (such as meat consumption) that enact animals as something "Other" and allow dualistic thinking to be naturalized as "the way things are." It is this latter point that has been stressed by perhaps the key figure in ecofeminism who has informed Vegan Studies: scholar-activist Carol J. Adams, whose book *The Sexual Politics of Meat: A Feminist Vegetarian Critical Theory* (2000, originally published 1990) was a foundational text arguing there is a connection between the oppression of women and animals.

Both women and animals, Adams argues, are objectified in contemporary culture via a mechanism that she terms the "absent referent" (2000: 51). Grounded in a critique of pornography, Adams asserts that while women's bodies are often placed front and center, their agency and any sense of subjectivity is erased. A similar mechanism, she suggests, occurs when decontextualized parts of animals are consumed in a more literal sense, as all traces of the sentient animal are erased while its body parts are rendered edible (often taking on shapes—sausages, burgers—and even names—pork, beef—that obscure the origins of these products). Adams's project speaks directly to what she describes as the central aim of ecofeminism, namely, to address "the various ways that sexism, heteronormativity, racism, colonialism, and ablism are informed by and support speciesism and how analyzing the way these forces intersect can produce less violent, more just practices" (Adams and Gruen, 2014: 1).

This connection between ecofeminism and vegan politics, however, has not gone uncontested. Within ecofeminism itself some have voiced concern about veganism becoming a totalizing moral imperative (Plumwood, 2003) or been wary about perceived affinities being drawn between women and animals (George, 1994, 2000). Carrie Hamilton (2016) goes further still, arguing that it has become difficult to ask constructively critical questions about ecofeminism itself, due to the prominence of narratives that argue ecofeminism has been overshadowed by posthumanist theory in mainstream academic contexts (e.g., Fraiman, 2012). While Hamilton does not deny the problem of erasure, she points to a set of problems that can be inadvertently generated by erasure-narratives themselves. In academic debates about veganism, Hamilton argues, scholars' desire to recompense for the historical erasure of ecofeminism—by instead centralizing this body of scholarship—can make it difficult to engage in constructive discussion about any inadvertent over-simplifications and exclusions found within particular ecofeminist texts themselves (2016: 121).

A number of thinkers have, nonetheless, posed sympathetic, but critical, questions about the prominence of ecofeminism as a framework for thinking about veganism due to the primacy it gives to patriarchy over other oppressive structures such as racism (e.g., Deckha, 2012). Erika Cudworth suggests, for example, that "there is often a tendency in this literature to conflation—the use of an all-encompassing theory of gender relations to explain intersected oppressions" (2014: 26). Indigenous scholars writing from a North American context have also pointed to the danger of treating the "absent referent" as a universal mechanism that accounts for the way that animals are "Othered" (for an overview, see Gillespie, 2017). In an article that underlines the need to develop more situated approaches to analyzing animal product consumption, for instance, Margaret Robinson points out that "the detachment Adams describes is not foundational to the Mi'kmaq oral tradition" (2013: 191), describing instead how "In our stories, the othering of animal life that makes meat-eating psychologically comfortable is replaced by a model of creation in which animals are portrayed as our siblings" (191). Robinson, however, does not use these important differences as a reason to entirely dismiss Adams, but as a starting point to explore where ecofeminist theory needs to be—carefully and critically—adapted in order to extend beyond the contexts in which it originated. While thinkers such as Robinson do not reject ecofeminism, therefore, and often embrace some of its key ethical arguments, they also highlight the need to avoid using ecofeminist work to make broad, univeralizing arguments about how humans relate to nonhuman animals (such as the notion that acts of distancing and separation always underpin killing). Debates about universalism are revisited in more depth later on in this chapter, but before doing so it is necessary to flesh out a few final characteristics of Vegan Studies itself.

Vegan Studies and Animal Studies

In focusing on veganism's relationship to enmeshed oppressions, Wright argues that

> A vegan studies approach examines texts (broadly speaking) via an intersectional lens of veganism as a practice, an identity category, and theoretical perspective

in order to complicate our understandings of, our relationships with, and our access to food, animals, the environment, and other humans. (2019: xv)

Informing this sense of Vegan Studies as an *approach* is the ethical commitment of its scholarship; like CAS (discussed shortly), the field has been populated by those committed to veganism as a means of contesting the oppression of humans and nonhuman animals. Rather than perceiving this normative commitment to veganism as a "distorting lens" (to use Sara Ahmed's turn of phrase; 2017: 157), those working within the field have framed Vegan Studies as a form of situated knowledge akin to feminist scholarship, which recognizes the importance of being upfront about ethical commitments rather than presuming neutrality in relation to an issue where no position is truly "neutral."

Many of the attributes of Vegan Studies thus overlap with other fields that have engaged with veganism. In the field's ethical commitments there are affinities with CAS, while Vegan Studies' theoretically informed attempts to unsettle ethical divides between humans and animals resonate with work in the posthumanities. To distinguish Vegan Studies from other areas, therefore, Wright does not just work to describe what Vegan Studies *is* but defines it *against* what she terms the "three prongs" of Animal Studies more broadly (2015: 11–14, 2019: vii): human-animal studies, CAS, and posthumanism. She argues that Vegan Studies is distinguished both by its focused subject matter and the diverse range of issues bound up with veganism (many of which exceed the scope of animal studies). For this reason, Wright claims Vegan Studies is simultaneously more focused than other strands of animal studies while going beyond their direct concern with animals themselves. It should be noted, however, that the separate status of Vegan Studies is not a "done deal" and boundaries between this body of work and other branches of animal studies are often articulated in slightly different ways, especially by those who produce vegan scholarship but have long-standing associations with existing fields. While the emergence of Vegan Studies is an important development, therefore, it is equally important to have a sense of some of the other academic bodies of work and theoretical lineages that have played a significant role in the study of veganism.

Critical Animal Studies and Veganism

An area that overlaps significantly with Vegan Studies is CAS, a field set up in explicit opposition not only to particular human-animal relations it deems to be exploitative, such as animal agriculture and experimentation, but also against a "mainstream" animal studies that was perceived to take an apolitical stance toward (and even be complicit in) normalizing these relations (e.g., Best et al., 2007; Best, 2009). Though these early CAS texts detail several aims, at heart the field aspired to develop research that contributed in concrete ways to contesting animal exploitation. Echoing ecofeminist arguments, to achieve this end it was recognized that human oppression (rooted in capitalism and imperialism) also had to be contested. As a practice veganism was actively advocated in several of the early CAS texts that instigated the formation of the field, which situated it as a "crucial and necessary step" for attaining "total liberation" (Best, 2007: 44).

Early work in CAS was highly polemical and more activist in tone than academic, with its aggressively critical stance toward academia leading to it being regularly dismissed as a single-issue approach in wider commentaries about the state of animal studies (e.g., Lorimer, 2013). Yet even in these strident early CAS mission statements, a more nuanced account of vegan praxis was articulated than might be expected. Steve Best, for instance, displayed wariness of veganism being co-opted by capitalism, at the same time as criticizing overly dogmatic approaches to animal advocacy that leave activism vulnerable to becoming another "Western, white, middle class movement" (2009: 43). Indeed, he argued that "Until this insularity is recognised and effectively addressed, it will continue to seriously compromise any achievements of the 'vegan revolution'" (2009: 43). Yet although recognition of tensions surrounding veganism was present in these early texts, it was not until slightly later that attempts to fully *address* these tensions began to emerge.

CAS, Critical Race Studies, and Vegan Food Politics

Though CAS was always *intended* to be bound up with anti-capitalist, feminist, and de-colonial politics, the field began to realize this aim in a more concrete sense in 2010 with the publication of the aforementioned special edition of the *Journal for Critical Animal Studies* "Women of Color in Critical Animal Studies." The edition itself was designed to redress the way that "the voices and perspectives of women of color were eerily absent from critical animal studies and vegan studies in general" (Yarbrough and Thomas, 2010: 3). Central to the edition were two essays by A. Breeze Harper and Maneesha Deckha, which interrogated intersections between racism and animal oppression. Harper's article, for instance, drew on critical race studies and feminist geographies to elucidate how the use of labels such as "cruelty free," in reference to products containing ingredients such as sugar or cocoa, erases the way these products are imbricated in colonial legacies and contemporary geopolitical inequalities. "Who," Harper asked, "are the non-white racialized populations who are harvesting chocolate, under conditions that help certain USA vegans practice modern ethics through vegan chocolate food consumption?" (2010a: 14). Both the article itself and Harper's edited collection *Sistah Vegan* (2010b) aimed to counter the erasure of racial politics from vegan praxis (2010a: 19) while Deckha's (2010; see also, 2008a, 2012) research likewise brought together animal and critical race studies, in a move that has emerged as increasingly vital to both critical and mainstream animal studies (e.g., Brueck, 2017; Ko and Ko, 2017; Boisseron, 2018; Ko, 2019; Jackson, 2020).

Partially in response to Harper and Deckha's interventions, in more recent CAS scholarship an ecofeminist focus on enmeshed oppressions has frequently been drawn together with a commitment to intersectionality as derived from Black feminism (Pendergrast, 2018; Nocella and George, 2019). Recently, however, caution has been raised about uses of the term "intersectionality," due to the concept being applied in overly broad ways that depart from (and sometimes even obscure) its roots. Despite coining the term, for instance, Kimberlé Crenshaw (2017) has voiced concern about intersectionality's popularity, due the risk of the concept being treated as "a grand theory of everything" rather than centering on the experiences of African-American women. Aph Ko (2019) echoes Crenshaw's concerns in the context of animal studies for slightly different reasons, questioning whether intersectionality's expansion beyond its original legislative focus is well suited to the specificities of the dialogue that needs to unfold between critical race studies and vegan ethics.

These debates illustrate how care needs to be taken when using the term "intersectional veganism" in a CAS or Vegan Studies context, and the importance of avoiding an entire conflation of intersectionality with the sorts of enmeshed oppressions discussed in ecofeminism (despite potential affinities between these two bodies of feminist thought). Because these issues are so important from a political and ethical perspective, rather than delving into them further here I dedicate a whole chapter to discussions related to intersectional veganism later in the book (see Chapter 6).

Growing Engagements with CAS in Academia

As with debates surrounding intersectionality there is no scope to discuss the history of CAS in more depth here, but, in the context of veganism, it is useful to note that since the emergence of the Institute for Critical Animal Studies in the United States in the mid-2000s (Best et al., 2007), Institutes have emerged in other international contexts and the concerns of CAS have increasingly been engaged with in more "mainstream" academic contexts (Taylor and Twine, 2014).

Taylor and Twine's edited collection *The Rise of Critical Animal Studies: From the Margins to the Centre* (2014), for instance, centralizes veganism in its introduction, arguing that "In subverting the taken-for-granted devaluation of the 'animal', veganism is a key practice [for CAS], yet is only an ethico-political beginning to addressing the interconnected oppression of people and animals" (2014: 12). The book also contains a substantive section on veganism, which includes chapters on the history of the Vegan Society (Cole, 2014) and examination of vegan activism that incorporates illegal actions (Glasser, 2014). Even outside this section of the book, veganism plays a central role in other chapters on themes that range from methodological issues in CAS in the context of research about vegan identity (Stephens Griffin, 2014) to auto-ethnographic analysis of anxieties faced by vegans themselves (Salih, 2014).

The eclecticism in aim and scope of research within *The Rise of Critical Animal Studies* reflects the way that work engaging with vegan themes from a CAS tradition has risen to prominence and again there are important overlaps with Vegan Studies. One of the other key texts that has positioned itself as elaborating on Wright's arguments—*Critical Perspectives on Veganism* (Castricano and Simonsen, 2016)—for instance, explicitly approaches the subject from a CAS lens with the aim of contributing to a practical sense of how total liberation can be attained, incorporating research from disciplines (including geography, philosophy, and cultural studies) to explore challenges facing veganism in a range of global contexts. Other work related to CAS commitments that explores vegan themes has emerged in contexts including media studies (Almiron, Cole and Freeman, 2016, 2018; Linné, 2016; Parkinson, 2019), film (Pick, 2012, 2018), sociology (Cudworth, 2011, 2014; Cole and Stewart, 2016; Wrenn, 2016, 2020), criminology (Flynn and Hall, 2017), and law (Gambert, 2019), as well as philosophy and critical/political theory (Kymlicka and Donaldson, 2011; Wadiwel, 2015), among other fields.

CAS and Vegan Studies

As CAS research about veganism suggests, the field shares important conceptual affinities with Vegan Studies: both have centralized vegan politics, highlighted intersecting oppressions, and possessed similar normative ethical goals of contesting these oppressions through advocating vegan practice. As well as this conceptual traffic, scholars identifying with CAS have published in some of the Vegan Studies contexts described earlier; Wright's *Through a Vegan Studies Lens* and *ISLE* special edition, for example, contain pieces by scholars who have published other work under a CAS banner.

The productive traffic that has been generated by the fairly porous boundaries between academic fields is not just true of CAS and Vegan Studies, moreover, but between other bodies of work in animal studies that have been concerned with veganism. To gain a clearer sense of these overlaps, the next section of this chapter moves onto another of the "prongs" of animal studies (to use Wright's framing), so-called posthumanist animal studies. This field, however, is not just useful for mapping the contours of scholarship about veganism, but is also valuable in highlighting fraught debates about veganism that have consolidated tensions between scholarship committed to vegan ethics and work that remains critical of it.

A "Posthumanist" Vegan Studies?

Due to its title, Cary Wolfe's *What is Posthumanism?* seems to promise an introductory overview of this body of theory and, while this is definitely not the case, the opening chapter still contains a helpful definition of "posthumanism" as marking "a historical moment in which the decentring of the human by its imbrication in technical, medical, informatics, and economic networks is increasingly impossible to ignore, a historical development that points to the necessity of new theoretical paradigms" (2010: xv–xvi). Although here Wolfe focuses on technologies, elsewhere in his work animals have taken center stage as beings who humans hold interdependent relationships with. Wolfe's arguments thus resonate with ecofeminism in underlining that humans are not individual, autonomous beings, because every aspect of human existence is reliant on nonhumans. While these interdependencies have always existed, Wolfe argues that recent cultural and technological developments have made such entanglements more explicit. For Wolfe, posthumanism is thus an attempt to meet the challenge of recognizing that "the human" is not an autonomous being, separate from the material, nonhuman world. Feminist strands of posthumanism have highlighted the political stakes of this recognition, arguing that human exceptionalism is not only inaccurate but also dangerous. Theorists such as Donna Haraway (2008, 2016), Rosi Braidotti (2013, 2016), and Stacy Alaimo (2016), for instance, have argued that contemporary environmental crises such as climate change and mass extinction require new ways of thinking, which do not privilege the human (or to be precise certain humans). The new conceptual frameworks developed by these thinkers focus instead on finding new ways of sharing a precarious world with all of the beings who inhabit it.

It is perhaps notable that although animals play a central role in posthumanism, the focus in this brand of theory is more expansive and often concerned with human entanglements with nonhumans in general (from microbes and minerals, to technologies and elements; see Giraud et al., 2018). In their attempts to extend ethics beyond the human, aspects of posthumanism have, nonetheless, proven so influential for rethinking human-animal relationships that insights from this body of theory deserve consideration. Although there are overlaps, broadly speaking two strands of conceptual work inform posthumanist animal studies. First, work in STS, which argues that the social cannot be understood by focusing on humans alone and, second, contemporary philosophy and literary theory, which has drawn more directly on continental philosophy to understand the mechanisms of anthropocentrism.

Before delving into the value of these, respective, bodies of theory, however, it is important to add a caveat. There are a few issues with using the label "posthumanism" as a means of grouping together theoretically focused work in animal studies that is concerned with unsettling "the human." While some theorists in animal studies and the environmental humanities do explicitly frame themselves as posthumanist (Alaimo, 2016; Braidotti, 2013; Cudworth, 2011; Cudworth and Hobden, 2013; McCormack, 2016; Wolfe, 2010, 2012), a large body of theoretical work that has challenged anthropocentrism does not, strictly speaking, fall into this category. For instance, work inspired by theorists who are more commonly associated with post-structuralism, (new-) materialisms, or queer theory (notably Jacques Derrida, Gilles Deleuze, Karen Barad, and Judith Butler), are often grouped with more explicitly posthumanist theorists. Prominent thinkers such as Donna Haraway, moreover—who is regularly cited as a key influence on posthumanism (Wolfe, 2012: xiii)—are sometimes keen to avoid this label (Haraway, 2008: 19). These complications are quite aside from the use of alternative labels, such as more-than-human (Whatmore, 2006), or nonhuman (Latour, 1992) that have slightly different resonances to posthumanism but still share concern with unsettling the human. I continue to use the term "posthumanism" here for the sake of brevity, so from here on in I will bracket aside problems with terminology to one side in order to examine the *content* of this body of work.

Expanding Agency Beyond the Human in Science and Technology Studies

A shift of focus beyond "the human" has been pioneered by two intertwined branches of STS in particular: those associated with actor-network theory or ANT (such as Bruno Latour, Michel Callon, John Law, and Annemarie Mol) and feminist science studies (such as the work of Donna Haraway, Karen Barad, Vinciane Despret, Isabelle Stengers, Maria Puig de la Bellacasa, and Joanna Latimer). Central to these bodies of work is a redistribution of agency, so that the capacity to shape social action is not just seen as a property of humans. From scallops (Callon, 1984) to mushrooms (Tsing, 2015), dogs (Haraway, 2003, 2008), sheep (Despret, 2006; Despret and Meuret, 2016), and horses (Latimer, 2013), to microbes (Paxson, 2008), slugs (Ginn, 2014), and alien undersea life (Barad, 2007; Helmreich, 2009), this body of work has not only sought to *include* nonhumans in understandings of the social but also emphasized their *agency* in profoundly shaping and even constituting human life.

Michel Callon's (1984) work on scallops, for example, argues that the shellfish exert agency due to where and how they live, which shapes the actions of fishermen, scientists, and technological infrastructures. More recently, geographer Franklin Ginn (2014) has engaged with work from an STS lineage to illustrate how slug agency transforms people's negotiation of their own gardens, often shaping what plants are grown and how gardens are arranged. Perhaps the most prominent figure in this field, however, is Donna Haraway, whose work has proven influential in asking what ethical questions are opened up in the wake of recognizing the liveliness and agency of nonhumans. To pose these questions, Haraway often turns to specific examples, or "figurations" (2008: 4; for elaboration, see Giraud et al., 2018), which crystallize particular social and cultural issues and, in doing so, elucidate the ethical dilemmas posed by these issues.

While Haraway's most famous instance of a figuration is her cyborg, from the early 2000s she has explored how ethical insight can be found in everyday relations with domestic companions: from grand evolutionary narratives about the coevolution of humans and dogs to everyday care relations in the home with pets, Haraway has traced how what it means to be human is profoundly shaped by relations with other animals. Both the *Companion Species Manifesto* (2003) and *When Species Meet* (2008) offer intimate, and deliberately provocative, accounts of her own relationship with her dog Cayenne, whose "red merle Australian Shepherd's quick and lithe tongue has swabbed the tissues of [her] tonsils" and given rise to all manner of microbial exchange (2008: 16). In addition, these texts examine the geopolitical networks associated with animal agriculture and economic relationships forged by the global pet industry. Domestic encounters between humans and animals thus offer rich grounds for Haraway to pose the central ethical question that informs all of her work: "what counts as nature, for whom, and at what cost?" in any situation (1997: 104). In other words: Whose values, and even lives, are naturalized in a particular setting and what is devalued, and can the relationships that create this distribution of value be organized in less oppressive ways?

Haraway's commitment to exploring whether new forms of ethical responsibility can be opened up once the human has been decentered might seem like a promising opening for vegan ethics, due to challenging the notion that humans act in the world while nonhuman animals are passive recipients of this action. In her introduction to Vegan Studies in *ISLE*, for instance, Wright draws inspiration from Haraway to argue that "we are bodily enmeshed with nonhuman others in ways that should require us to consider the embodied nature of our relationships to them" (2018: 731). Yet while the recognition that animals have agency too might offer less anthropocentric ways of thinking about the world, in Haraway's own work—and the vast body of research inspired by her—this recognition has not always supported calls to transform material relations with nonhuman animals (or certainly not along the lines called for by CAS or ecofeminism).

Haraway herself has been directly critical of animal rights, liberation, and advocacy movements, arguing that "we do not get very far with the categories generally used by animal rights discourses, in which animals end up as permanent dependents ('lesser humans'), utterly natural ('nonhuman'), or exactly the same ('humans in fur suits')" (2008: 67). For Haraway these discourses undercut their own aims in attempting to extend ethics beyond the human while shoring up human privilege in the process (as humans are often depicted as those holding the privileged agency to speak for nonhumans, see also Haraway, 2011). As an alternative (building on allied scholars Vinciane Despret and Isabelle Stengers), Haraway emphasizes situated, bodily engagements with animals. It is through everyday interactions, observations, and care-work, Haraway argues, that humans learn to be affected by animals and begin to understand their bodily cues, thus creating space for animals to "speak back" and impose their obligations upon humans. These arguments are complex (and I unpack them in more depth in Chapter 5), but they are also important to touch on here because this emphasis on situated, bodily ethics has generated some of the most significant friction between Haraway—and the vast array of research informed by her work—and vegan perspectives.

What puts Haraway slightly at odds with Vegan Studies is that her work has drawn inspiration from sites that, from a CAS perspective, are seen as perpetuating exploitation and human exceptionalism, such as animal laboratories (Weisberg, 2009; Giraud and Hollin, 2016), animal product consumption (Adams, 2006; Wadiwel, 2015), and the domestication of "pets" (Collard, 2014). While acknowledging the often-instrumental relationships that take place in these sites, Haraway argues that interpreting these relations as wholly oppressive is dangerous because it perpetuates the myth of human mastery over the nonhuman world. Seeing these sites as oppressive, she argues, fails to acknowledge the roles of animals as actors and erases their agency.

As described in further depth within the next chapter, more specific criticisms of veganism also punctuate *When Species Meet* and even though these references are often brief, they have huge resonance; first, Haraway's arguments have underpinned a burgeoning body of work within animal studies that has been suspicious of dogmatism, labeled veganism as dogmatic, and dismissed it on this basis. Second, and more hopefully, as Tom Tyler (2018) notes, Haraway's framing of veganism has resulted in a number of counter-arguments that challenge such criticisms of veganism (leading Haraway to modulate her arguments slightly, see Haraway, 2017). I engage with these counter-arguments further in the next chapter, but, for now, it is important to note that one of the central responses to Haraway's critique of veganism has been to offer alternative conceptions of vegan practice, which reverse narratives about what veganism is or does. This body of work has suggested it is not *vegan ethics* that shuts down ways of being, but *society itself* that excludes less anthropocentric ways of acting in the world. It is this re-working of veganism to position it as a disruptive conceptual approach, that highlights and troubles existing anthropocentric norms, which is a central concern of the second body of theory that I turn to now.

Veganism as Theory

The idea that veganism can serve as something that *disrupts* rather than *imposes* norms has been pursued in a second body of work that is sometimes labeled "posthumanist": this time hailing from a literary studies tradition that draws extensively upon continental philosophy. Broadly speaking, theorists in this area argue that "modern," post-enlightenment systems of thought have conventionally carved existence up between human subjects (who are rational, capable of reflecting on the conditions of their own existence, and have autonomous agency to act in and on the world) and nonhumans (who lack these qualities).

Unlike STS branches of posthumanism, the literary variety has more ready affinities with Vegan Studies due to slight differences in the conceptual traditions it draws upon. Jacques Derrida's (2008) writing, for example, has proven especially influential due to his explicit discussion of the role of animals. These insights have then been built upon by thinkers such as Matthew Calarco, whose work has proven valuable in more fully articulating the significance of Derrida to Animal Studies. Calarco describes how, for Derrida, "the meaning of subjectivity is constituted through a network of exclusionary relations that goes well beyond a generic human-animal distinction" (Calarco, 2008: 131). Derrida uses the term "carnophallogocentrism" to describe this network of exclusions. This concept refers to Derrida's analysis of how what it means to be human has often been defined against "the animal." This exclusion of animality, moreover, is tied together with other forms of exclusion, wherein particular groups of people are also excluded from the rights and privileges afforded to liberal human subjects, on the basis of being portrayed as "lacking in one or another of the basic traits of subjectivity" (Calarco, 2008: 131), or, to put things differently, on the basis of being portrayed as somehow closer to animality.

Paralleling ecofeminism, it is thus argued that in order to contest the Othering and oppression of specific groups of humans it is not enough to challenge their association with animals (as this allows the concept of "animality" to survive as a stigmatizing label that must constantly be battled). Instead, the concept of the animal must itself be deconstructed in order to offer a more sustained contestation of the violent exclusions that render both animals and certain humans as legitimately "exploitable" for the benefit of others.

Derrida's arguments perhaps offer a more hopeful engagement with vegan practice than STS strands of posthumanism, but tensions still exist. As Calarco points out, unlike vegetarian ecofeminism, Derrida's work is not designed to lend itself to a vegan ethics as his deconstructive approach works to unpick rather than support the development of ethical frameworks (see also Calarco, 2014). Cary Wolfe makes a more forceful point in this regard, echoing Haraway in characterizing perspectives that *do* maintain a decisive ethical stance (such as animal liberationism) as a form of "humanist posthumanism" (2010: 121), that seeks to extend ethical consideration beyond the human, but undercuts its own aims in doing so by relying upon humanist frameworks of rights (which, he argues, tend to value animals seen as somehow closest to the human).

As Vegan Studies has begun to emerge in a more formal sense, these tensions between deconstructive or posthumanist approaches and vegan ethics are increasingly being addressed head-on. Emilia Quinn and Benjamin Westwood's *Thinking Veganism in Literature and Culture: Towards a Vegan Theory* (2018), for instance, is an important touchstone for exploring the conceptual significance of veganism, which contains interventions by both emerging and established scholars in animal studies, who reflect on the conceptually disruptive potential of veganism in different disciplinary contexts: ranging from philosophy to literature to film studies. Though broadly aligning with Vegan Studies as Wright conceives it (indeed she contributes the first chapter of the book), the text seeks to open up new theoretical trajectories and also marks a (partial) departure from CAS-informed work on veganism (e.g., Castricano and Simonsen, 2016). For Quinn and Westwood, veganism as a lens of academic enquiry is not just a means of analyzing depictions of veganism, nor is it solely a means of implementing, supporting, or promoting veganism. Instead, they argue, veganism also offers a distinct way of *thinking*.

Quinn and Westwood's opening chapter situates veganism in the context of queer theory, asking how vegan thought can trouble, or queer, preexisting norms surrounding what it means to be human. Veganism, they argue, offers a means through which to denaturalize "a world that has normalized and industrialized the exploitation of nonhuman life" (2018: 2). This re-framing of veganism as a way of disrupting existing norms can be neatly elucidated when turning to one of the most evocative chapters in *Thinking Veganism*: Robert McKay's essay "A Vegan Form of Life." Within the chapter McKay hints at the provocation offered by veganism as a subject-position, by stating "I am vegan, not human" (2018: 250). The backdrop to these arguments is a personal encounter with a family member, who regularly invited McKay for meals. While the relative did take pains to provide vegan food (though it was "almost always ratatouille"), every time they served his meal they proclaimed "Here we go Robert, your lesbian food" (McKay, 2018: 250).

McKay offers a deliberate over-reading of this moment, suggesting its significance goes beyond a mere articulation of hegemonic masculinity where gender, sexuality, and dietary preferences are Othered in mutually reinforcing ways. Instead, McKay questions the specific work that is accomplished by Othering veganism, reading it as an attempt to distance his relative's (human) identity from a lifestyle practice seen to threaten his sense of humanity itself: "it is the normality—read centrality—of my host's very humanity that is endangered by what is (to him) an unimaginable identification with nonhumans, inherent in veganism" (McKay, 2018: 251). Two particular conceptual tools aid in McKay's over-reading. First, Derrida's aforementioned carnophallogocentrism, which understands human subjectivity as predicated on the exclusion of the nonhuman. Drawing also on Foucault and Butler, McKay points out, however, that the symbolic positioning of the animal is always entangled with specific practices that constantly *enact* these exclusions. Jokes about McKay's diet (and corresponding normalization of animal product consumption) are one such exclusion and, he argues, mark the separation of the nonhuman from the human. For McKay, then, the cultural denigration of veganism is not just about criticizing a particular way of eating, but undermines ethical affinities with other species. McKay's arguments thus reframe veganism so it shifts from being a normative diet that is associated with liberal humanist conceptions of "animal rights," to instead being a provocation that unsettles anthropocentric norms in ways that perhaps even exceed posthumanism. McKay's chapter crystallizes the central contention of *Thinking Veganism*: that vegan practice and identity is not something that denies or cuts away existing entanglements between humans and animals (as is often claimed). Instead, veganism is a way of thinking that highlights the preexisting exclusions created by everyday relations with animals, in order to create space to imagine what alternative relationships might look like.

A broader critical engagement with posthumanism has also come to the fore in postcolonial scholarship, which holds implications for both animal studies more broadly and Vegan Studies specifically. These criticisms, in part, resonate with ecofeminism's concern with the limited canon of texts that are typically associated with posthumanism (cf Adams and Calarco, 2016). While ecofeminism has pointed to gendered exclusions within posthumanist animal studies, Zakiyyah Iman Jackson (2013) is critical of posthumanism's tendency to treat thinkers such as Foucault or Latour as forefathers of its attempts to decenter the human, as opposed to postcolonial theorists such as Sylvia Wynter or Aimé Césaire. Jackson does not simply highlight these exclusions, moreover, but shows how redressing such omissions can push posthumanism in new directions.

One of the problems with posthumanism is that it often treats the human/animal, or human/nonhuman, dichotomy as foundational, the primary exclusion from which others follow. This assumption is evident even in Wolfe's early recognition

that traditionally marginalized peoples would be skeptical about calls by academic intellectuals to surrender the humanist model of subjectivity, with all its privileges, at just the historical moment when they are poised to "graduate" into it. But the larger point I stress here is that as long as this humanist and speciesist structure of subjectivization remains intact, and as long as it is institutionally taken for granted that it is alright to systematically exploit and kill nonhuman animals simply because of their species, then the humanist discourse of species will always be available for use by some humans against other humans as well. (Wolfe, 2003: 8)

Here Wolfe overcomes potential criticisms that could be leveled at posthumanism, by suggesting that dismantling the idea of "species"—and the violence that this concept legitimizes—lies at the root of challenging other inequalities. What Jackson's work has emphasized, however, is that species is not necessarily the primary form of exclusion, as, historically, this concept emerged alongside colonial constructions of race (Jackson, 2016, 2020; see also Kim, 2015). Discourses of species and race, in other words, coevolved at a particular moment and needs to be unpicked *together*.

In making these arguments Jackson highlights the need to avoid seeing "humans" in general as privileged above the nonhuman world, and to focus critique instead upon a geographically and historically specific understanding of "the human" (see also Sundberg, 2014; Todd, 2016; TallBear, 2017). What is thus underlined by Jackson's arguments is that, without reflecting carefully upon the racialized dynamics of how the concept of "the human" operates, it is easy to make broad-brush statements that depict "humans" in general as always privileged above "animals," in a manner that neglects the way that the deaths of racialized people are also frequently treated as "mundane, normal, and expected" (Ko, S. 2017: 86). The need to develop context-specific frameworks, so as not to generalize about what veganism means or how it is enacted, therefore, deserves further attention; something that is gradually being addressed by the final body of work Wright sees as overlapping with but distinct from Vegan Studies: human-animal studies.

Human-Animal Studies . . . and Beyond

Wright describes human-animal studies or HAS, a term used by numerous scholars concerned with the role of animals in culture and society (DeMello, 2012), as a third "prong" of animal studies. Although I do discuss research that uses the HAS label here, I also wish to go beyond material falling under this rubric. Like some of the other strands of animal and Vegan Studies discussed in this chapter, pinning down a definition of HAS is hard. The label tends to be used within specific fields—especially sociological contexts and organizational studies (e.g., Wilkie, 2015; Hamilton and Taylor, 2017)—in reference to research that is concerned with animals, but many thinkers within these fields *also* identify explicitly with CAS. The reason why I have grouped the scholarship in this section of the chapter together, then, is more of a difference in orientation. While the research I outlined earlier, in relation to the other "prongs" of animal studies, was seeking to define the boundaries of CAS as a subfield of animal studies or delineate posthumanist animal studies as a novel body of theory, the work described in this section has gone in the opposite direction: pushing for established academic disciplines (such as sociology and geography) to take animals seriously as the focus of scholarship. This distinction, however, is just a loose heuristic and some thinkers could have equally been discussed in previous sections of this chapter.

Regardless of how this work is categorized within animal studies, what begins to emerge when touching on sociologically-focused research is that, when it comes to examining veganism, some important scholarship does not fall under the remit of animal studies at all (or at least only tangentially). In this section, therefore, I also incorporate work that is valuable for the study of veganism but does not neatly sit within either of the other "prongs" of animal studies, notably research in geography, sociology, and social movement studies. While some of this work defines itself as HAS, other research belongs to subfields, such as the sociology of consumption, or interdisciplinary research areas such as food studies.

Vegan Sociology

As touched on previously, Cudworth has raised some (sympathetic) criticisms of ecofeminism, questioning the priority it has historically given to gender over other oppressions (related to race or political economy, for instance). One of the most valuable points she raises is that ecofeminist work tends to have a broader theoretical orientation, which makes arguments about cultural attitudes to animals in general rather than discussing the specific institutional contexts in which human-animal relations are materialized. Though Cudworth is not blaming ecofeminism for this omission, recognizing it instead as a difference in aim and focus, her arguments nonetheless point to a gap in existing knowledge that the social sciences need to fill. It is time, she argues, for "sociology to step up to the task of outlining the social institutions in which the discourse of species is embedded and to provide an analysis in terms of social relations" (Cudworth, 2014: 27). As a discipline, however, sociology has been slow in introducing questions about animals: let alone veganism.

Despite calls for sociology to engage with animals coming to prominence in the early 2000s—most notably in David Nibert's *Animal Rights/Human Rights* (2002)—numerous sociologists have noted the challenge of having their work taken seriously within the discipline (Peggs, 2013; Carter and Charles, 2018). Though ethnographic work about veganism has been developed in allied and sub-fields such as social movement studies, notably Elizabeth Cherry's sustained body of work (2006, 2010, 2015; see also Giraud, 2015; Lockwood, 2018), the sense that concern with animals is something "fringe," "radical," or "activist" has traditionally meant vegan subject matter has been underexplored in the context of mainstream sociology (for key exceptions, see Cole, 2008; Greenebaum, 2012a, 2012b; Wrenn, 2016, 2020). Even in work about animals there has been a sense that they are primarily worthy of study due to their entanglements with humans, with dominant notions of "the social" oriented around human communities, though due to the influence of actor-network theory, posthumanism, and new materialism this is gradually shifting (see Wilkie, 2015; Fox and Alldred, 2016; Hamilton and Taylor, 2017).

Recently, however, changes have begun to emerge, in part due to the popularization of veganism and its positioning as a response to climate crisis by key institutions such as the IPCC (Intergovernmental Panel on Climate Change) and UN (United Nations). These developments have allowed work focused on veganism to be framed as a "mainstream" political concern and appear in key sociology journals (e.g., Twine, 2017), as well as giving rise to international conferences dedicated to Vegan Sociology.[3] What is often shared by sociological work focused on veganism is an emphasis on vegan ethics, with several of the key figures in the field hailing from a CAS tradition. Matthew Cole and Kate Stewart's research (Stewart and Cole, 2009; Cole and Stewart, 2016), for instance, has explored how speciesism is reinforced via childhood engagement with media, toys, and visual culture in general, in ways that naturalize meat consumption (with the aim of questioning this naturalization). Nathan Stephens Griffin (2017) has turned to the embodied experiences of vegans themselves and the way that their identity is negotiated in everyday environments that often make veganism difficult to realize (see Chapter 3 for a more in-depth discussion of these arguments).

Collectively, therefore, sociologically-oriented research has begun to build up a complex picture of veganism, which explores how both vegans themselves and vegan activist groups work to negotiate tensions between vegan lifestyle politics and the need for structural change (themes discussed further in Chapter 4). What is particularly important about this work is that it has begun to offer theoretically informed but empirically grounded responses to claims about what veganism is and means, which complicate and even contest overly reductive framings of veganism as single-issue dogmatism.

Vegan Geographies

While sociology has tended to focus on human-animal relations, other disciplines—notably geography—have long histories of engaging with animals in their own right, offering fertile foundations for vegan scholarship to flourish. Julie Urbanik (2012) identifies three major "waves" of animal geographies. The third "wave," emerging from the early 1990s, generated valuable work exploring the geographies of animal agriculture. Chris Philo's research, for instance, outlined how, from the mid-nineteenth century onwards, animals classified as "livestock" were removed from public space (see Chapter 4). A number of contemporary texts in animal geography build on these arguments, framing vegan politics as a means of combatting the invisibility of animals that has been created by particular spatial arrangements (Oliver, 2020a).

Similar to other strands of animal studies, posthumanism and post-structuralism have gained increasing purchase within geography with the focus on *animals* often shifting to *nonhumans* in general. Haraway has been a central figure in these shifts and, as such, several of the tensions outlined earlier in relation to her work and veganism have persisted in geography. Like animal studies writ-large, one of the responses to the uptake of posthumanism in geography has been calls for *critical* animal geographies. While not quite as antagonistic as early work in CAS, this research has adopted a more critical approach than other work in animal and more-than-human geographies, interrogating examples—such as dairy farming (Gillespie, 2018) or the global wildlife trade (Collard, 2014)—that trouble some of the positive framings of human-animal entanglements that have been prominent in posthumanist contexts.

The eponymous edited collection *Critical Animal Geographies* itself (Gillespie and Collard, 2015) perhaps best speaks to this commitment to engage critically with the existing treatment of nonhuman animals in particular cultural contexts and includes chapters focused on vegan ethics specifically (e.g., White, 2015 and my own contribution, Giraud, 2015). The long-standing intersections between radical geographies and social movement studies mean that it is perhaps unsurprising that work on veganism as a social movement has also gathered further momentum in geographical contexts and these insights look set to be further developed in forthcoming edited collection *Vegan Geographies* (Hodge et al., 2021). Aspects of animal and vegan geographies, moreover, not only go beyond HAS but point to valuable areas of research that are useful for the future study of veganism but exceed the bounds of animal studies.

Future Trajectories

This chapter has provided an overview of some of the key debates within Vegan Studies itself as well as charting the role of veganism within overlapping strands of animal studies. As hinted at in the final section of this chapter, and as Wright argues, however, research about veganism also goes beyond these fields. What I suggest, in addition, is that aspects of vegan studies also go beyond Vegan Studies, as currently formulated: with some references to vegan studies preceding the capitalized field's formulation (notably work in CAS), while other research offers slightly different conceptual and empirical genealogies. To trace these dynamics, I conclude this chapter by turning to research which offers productive trajectories that complement but also depart from work currently falling under the rubric of Vegan Studies.

As argued in the introductory chapter, veganism is more than a diet and strives to unsettle oppressive relationships between humans and nonhuman animals—and the ways that these relations are bound up with the oppression of particular groups of humans—in contexts that go beyond food. This chapter has offered an examination of a range of academic texts, which have extended a sense of what "more than a diet" means in practice. The scholarship discussed here positions veganism as a form of political praxis or way of thinking about the world, which has the capacity to articulate connections between the oppression of animals, humans, and wider environmental degradation. Yet, ironically, while veganism is more than just a way of eating, some particularly expansive work about veganism can be found in academic work that does focus on food. The interdisciplinary field of food studies—which has a strong geographical emphasis but also draws on other social scientific work, such as the sociology of consumption, and cultural theory that loosely falls within the bracket of posthumanism—is increasingly discussing veganism. Vegan politics, for instance, is a key theme in Mike Goodman's work on ethical foodscapes (2010), while some of the recent key work in sociology (mentioned earlier) engages with theories of consumption. Other aforementioned work in feminist geographies (e.g., Harper, 2012) suggests a need to consider factors such as markets, food production systems, and racialized socioeconomic inequalities that might make it difficult to produce and consume food in particular ways.

Some valuable research that lies at the intersection of the sociology of consumption, more-than-human geography, and STS, for instance, is concerned with the ethical significance of meat substitutes, particularly in vitro meats developed through technoscientific innovation (e.g., Stephens, 2013, Stephens et al., 2018; Sexton, 2016). This work has addressed fundamental questions about what in vitro meat is and how it is being developed that highlights practical issues for veganism, such as the fact that this foodstuff is still currently reliant on animal slaughter as well as its imbrication in the market logics of Silicon Valley. In addition, research about meat substitutes poses *conceptual* challenges; as Alexandra Sexton argues, even meat products made entirely from plant-based foods can serve as absent referents: this time not masking the animal that lies behind them (as with Adams's analysis) but the networks of commerce and industrial agriculture that are bound up with their production. The production of particular meat substitutes, Sexton illustrates, entails a complex process where certain aspects of the development of these foods are highlighted and made to "matter" to consumers (such as their visceral affinity with "real" meat while being distanced from "real" animals) in a manner that "draws attention away from the ingredients and political economies" that perhaps fit less neatly with constructions of these products as ethical alternatives (Sexton, 2016: 75).

Research about meat substitutes offers a snapshot of work that is important for the study of veganism, but does not necessarily exhibit the same overt form of critique that has thus far characterized Vegan Studies. Work in this area is nonetheless important in meeting future ethical challenges that are arising with veganism's popularization and commercialization.

Throughout the rest of this book, therefore, while I engage with research that identifies with Vegan Studies, I also draw on work that offers useful tools for thinking through the dynamics of contemporary veganism, but that comes from slightly different disciplinary or conceptual traditions. In particular I draw on work in allied fields that are valuable for the study of veganism, but stray even beyond animal studies' focus, fields which pose questions about markets, consumption, and the politics of anthropocentrism more broadly. These topics might emanate from discussions of food, but ultimately go well beyond it. As argued in the introduction, veganism is more than a diet. Perhaps befitting of something that is "more than" how it is often conceived, therefore, the approaches to studying veganism that I engage with throughout this book often exceed Vegan Studies, or at least how this field has emerged thus far: although they still hold potential to feed back into this vibrant, complex, and emerging research area.

Chapter 3

VEGAN IDENTITIES

PURITY AND IMPERFECTION

"Can vegans stomach the unpalatable truth about quinoa?" This question, posed in the title of Joanna Blythman's (2013) article for UK newspaper *The Guardian*, is useful in evoking some of the central issues raised in this chapter and indeed in relation to veganism more broadly. The piece was shared 167,511 times on various social media platforms and gained traction to the extent that large NGOs such as PETA were prompted to write counter-responses (e.g., Bekhechi, 2013). The reason why this article is informative, however, is less due to its circulation and more the way it speaks to wider discourses about veganism that center on the alleged moral inconsistency of vegans themselves. As the title of Blythman's piece infers, the article's central argument is that just because individuals eat plant-based foods this does not mean their lifestyles are free from implication in violence and inequality. Blythman details a number of examples that illustrate problems with cereal and vegetable production, which range from quinoa itself (which has now become so popular that local Bolivian people can no longer afford what was a cheap stable) to water depletion in Peru from asparagus farming. More damning still is the piece's critique of soy bean agriculture:

> Soya, a foodstuff beloved of the vegan lobby as an alternative to dairy products, is another problematic import, one that drives environmental destruction . . . Embarrassingly, for those who portray it as a progressive alternative to planet-destroying meat, soya production is now one of the two main causes of deforestation in South America, along with cattle ranching, where vast expanses of forest and grassland have been felled to make way for huge plantations. (Blythman, 2013)

The whole article is thus framed as another "gotcha" moment for vegans, here projected as self-satisfied, self-righteous individuals, who fail to grasp the complexities of food systems and whose food choices are not nearly as ethical as they think.

What I argue in this chapter, however, is that arguments centering on the moral inconsistency of a vegan diet can themselves be overly simplistic and are sometimes in danger of enacting the same self-righteousness that they accuse the so-called vegan lobby of possessing. Indeed, what is notable about Blythman's piece in particular is the stubbornness with which it clung to this trope of the hypocritical vegan, even after the newspaper was forced to add disclaimers once the article's arguments were found to be inaccurate. For instance, a footnote was added after some of the core claims were debunked by members of the public: "while soya is found in a variety of health products, the majority of production—97% according to the UN report of 2006—is used for animal feed." Although this point fundamentally troubles the article's central argument, its inclusion as a footnote leaves the central thrust of the opinion piece intact. Other, similarly troubling, points raised in the comments were not addressed at all, such as the suggestion that the comparatively low percentage of vegans in the UK would have far less of an impact on quinoa than its broader fashionable status as a health food.

This chapter takes the construction of the self-righteous vegan consumer as a starting point, in order to grasp not just how this construction operates as a media trope but to understand its broader social function. On one level, this depiction of veganism could be debunked by turning to the vegan histories outlined in the introductory chapter: where high-profile institutions such as the Vegan Society founded themselves on the recognition that purity was impossible within existing food systems (Cole, 2014). But while it might be tempting to simply dismiss purity stereotypes as inaccurate, my aim in this chapter is to instead take them seriously as things that pose important questions for vegan politics and identity. Even though these stereotypes are often reductive, they can nonetheless raise important issues. As Alexis Shotwell argues: "food and energy systems are always systems. If we hold ethics to the level of the individual we restrict ethical choice to those who are most privileged by and within the system" (Shotwell, 2016: 125). Shotwell's point is made as part of a larger critique of individualistic lifestyle politics, but it is notable that she uses a vegan diet to illustrate these dangers and, in doing so, her work speaks to the types of negative portrayals of veganism that have become prominent in certain academic contexts as well as within popular culture.

This chapter begins by situating its discussion of veganism in relation to wider debates about lifestyle movements and moralism. I initially take a lead from the arguments articulated by Shotwell and engage with the concept of purity politics in more depth in order to understand how this concept speaks to both academic and broader cultural criticisms leveled at veganism. The second half of the chapter then offers a counterpoint to commonplace criticisms of veganism, turning first to depictions of vegan identity in popular culture that speak to these arguments before drawing on research derived from (sub-)cultural studies, social movement studies, and sociological perspectives, which offer a far messier and more complex picture of vegan practice. Although this research sometimes describes instances of veganism that mesh with more individualistic forms of lifestyle politics, or food being used as an exclusionary identity marker, it also foregrounds the danger of categorizing *all* vegan politics in this manner. I conclude by drawing hope from research that has shown how, in certain contexts, veganism does not function as something normative that promises purity, but works to unsettle existing norms surrounding not just food but human-animal relations more broadly.

Critiques of Vegan Identity and Practice

Shotwell's concern is that veganism has become a form of "purity politics" that bestows those who engage in a vegan diet with an individual ethical identity rather than enabling radical political change. These criticisms of veganism (or at least veganism as a food practice) are articulated in a nuanced way within Shotwell's *Against Purity*, but her arguments also resonate with more strident criticisms that have been made by a number of other influential cultural theorists. In addition, notions of purity politics are a recurring theme in popular media representations of veganism. Together, then, the academic and cultural significance of purity politics means that turning to this concept in more depth offers a route through some of the fractious academic and political debates that have gathered force over the past twenty years in relation to questions of vegan identity.

Debates about veganism as an ethical identity relate to a much broader set of criticisms that have been leveled at so-called lifestyle movements (Haenfler, Johnson and Jones, 2012). This label refers to people who share individual ethical lifestyle choices, but are not necessarily part of more organized social movements. Unlike environmental, anarchist, or animal rights groups, for instance, who might work strategically to achieve specific aims, members of lifestyle movements might never act collectively—or even meet—and are often only linked together in the abstract sense of engaging in the same practices. Although critics have begun to craft more hopeful, or at least more ambivalent, understandings of the relationship between lifestyle movements and social change (e.g., Littler, 2009; Carolan, 2011; Goodman, Maye and Holloway, 2010; Halkier, 2019), this form of politics has traditionally been seen as problematic for two reasons.

First, lifestyle movements are not associated with coordinated, collective action in the same way as other social movements, but consist of individuals choosing to live in a particular manner (whether this is by adopting a diet or engaging in acts of ethical consumerism). Lifestyle movements are often seen as consisting of "self-centered, largely individualistic projects of personal expression and affirmation, thus marking movements as serious contenders for social change and lifestyles as trivial in comparison" (Haenfler, Johnson and Jones, 2012: 1–2). Ethical lifestylism is thus often criticized, due to the presumption that those who participate in a particular form of consumption (and not others) are afforded moral solace by perceiving their behavior as "correct."

Criticisms leveled at lifestyle politics could certainly be extended to aspects of a vegan diet. If people feel that purchasing the right products or eating the right foods is ethically correct, this could be de-politicizing due to masking the need for more sustained structural change (see Huddart Kennedy, Parkins and Johnston, 2018). For instance, just because it is possible to purchase a vegan sausage roll in UK bakery chain, Greggs, a vegan burger in Finnish McDonald's, or a vegan

Burrito bowl in US branches of Chipotle does not mean that the systems that lie behind these food choices have somehow become less harmful. Problematic agricultural relations, employment practices, and environmental damage can still be caused by large-scale food systems, even if a small part of these systems has started to cater to vegan customers. Indeed, as scholars engaged in critical analysis of food systems have long argued, companies frequently target ethical consumers in order to capture new markets and create new revenue streams, a tactic that ultimately serves to sustain the problematic structures these forms of consumption are ostensibly contesting (Guthman, 2003, 2004). The dangers of ethical lifestyle politics only look set to intensify in the wake of new technological innovations such as in vitro meat that is grown artificially, which might attenuate one problematic aspect of food systems—cruelty to animals (though even this is not straightforward)—while leaving other problems intact, such as the scarcity and inequalities fostered by many globalized food systems (Sexton, Garnett and Lorimer, 2019).

   In the context of food, ethical lifestyle movements have also been seen as problematic for a second reason: they neglect the complexity of food systems (Probyn, 2000, 2016). An emphasis on complexity has played a significant role in criticisms of veganism. A vegetarian or vegan eschewal of animal products is often seen to draw an arbitrary ethical line that fails to recognize that eating is far too complicated to be navigated via simplistic ethical rules (Keith, 2009). To summarize some of the key criticisms that have been leveled at veganism: the promotion of vegan politics is often depicted as neglecting the complexity of both food *production* and food *consumption*. As touched on in Chapter 1, in terms of production, vegan politics is seen to mask the way that all food production—including plant-based products—can involve some form of killing: from mice killed during harvesting, to insects dying from certain forms of pesticide use (Haraway, 2008: 80; Shotwell, 2016: 120). These forms of inadvertent violence are aside from harm to particular human populations who live in regions that grow food that is shipped to wealthier nations (often creating a substantial carbon footprint in the process) (Harper, 2010a). Food consumption also carries a complex politics and the moralism associated with alternative food networks has been accused of neglecting class and racial inequality, as factors which can make it difficult to adopt particular ways of eating (Slocum, 2007; Guthman, 2008). It is worth questioning, however, whether veganism fits with narratives of purity politics as closely as is often assumed.

Veganism as "Purity Politics"?

In the introduction of *Against Purity*, Shotwell neatly encapsulates her concern with forms of politics that consist of an "ethos . . . that we can access or recover a time or state before or without pollution, without impurity." She continues that "A piece of this ethos is perhaps also the sense that we can buy a product that brings this natural state of purity back, though particularly in certain left scenes, ideological purity seems to behave as a one-step facial cleanser" (Shotwell, 2016: 3). What Shotwell is critical of, in other words, are actions or beliefs that people engage in as individuals in order to exempt themselves from systemic violence or broader social and environmental problems.

For Shotwell, whatever we do as individuals we are still implicated in structures that perpetuate systemic problems and inequalities. A stereotypical North American or Western European lifestyle, for instance, has a carbon footprint that is difficult to erase no matter how many choices an individual might make to reduce it (by transferring to renewable energy suppliers, taking public transport, or cutting down on animal products, for example). Likewise, these lifestyles are often entangled with longer histories of colonialism or dependent on contemporary labor and geopolitical inequalities that, again, cannot be altered through individual actions. Although Shotwell points to a number of different examples of products, values, and political practices that appear to promise purity—and hide the persistence of systemic issues in the process—one of her most significant chapters focuses on the politics of eating. Eating, and veganism in particular, has an important role in the book; in an interview to promote *Against Purity*, for instance, Shotwell explains:

> I started thinking about eating and purity because I eat vegan. I've had some of the most annoying conversations I can remember with fellow vegans . . . . As soon as you start really looking, you see you can't be cut off from the incredible suffering that's produced simply from the fact that we [have bodies]. All of my vegan friends who think that they're not actually participating in cycles of death and suffering, they're just wrong. (Shotwell, 2017)

Shotwell's frustration here is born not just because of her assertion that no form of politics is pure, but that any ethical practice that acts as though it *does* offer some form of purity denies the messiness and complexity of the world (in a similar manner to Blythman's quinoa-munching vegan). As well as being illusory, purity— and the moralism that it is associated with—is dangerous as it can lend support to hierarchies between those who adhere to morally "pure" practices and those who do not. There hierarchies are especially pernicious because not everyone is able to make particular choices, in light of financial restrictions and limitations of access to particular foods; as Shotwell neatly puts it: "No one wants only the rich to have the capacity to have ethics, since they frequently manifest little or no such behavior" (2016: 125). These arguments resonate with a number of criticisms of veganism, as sketched out previously, which have associated veganism with moralism and inadvertent elitism.

Though criticisms of purity politics are themselves vitally important, in the rest of this chapter I aim to trouble some of the ways in which veganism has been labeled as such. By providing an overview of key theoretical debates and empirical social science research, I illustrate that—although it is valuable to engage with questions of elitism and hierarchy—the characterization of veganism as a lifestyle movement in which self-righteous middle-class individuals try to impose norms on others is not quite as neat as is often suggested. These arguments, however, come with the caveat that it is nonetheless important not to dismiss criticisms of vegan politics, in light of the way that certain high-profile campaigns and examples *do* seem to place ethical responsibility upon the individual and treat vegan consumerism as an end in itself (problems that are engaged with in Chapters 6 and 7 in more depth).

To briefly illustrate why veganism is sometimes accused of being an individualistic lifestyle movement, it is informative to turn to the influential documentary *Cowspiracy* (dir. Anderson and Kuhn, 2014). The feature-length film takes its name from the concern—by Director Kip Anderson—that the role of animal agriculture in causing climate change has been masked. In Anderson and Kuhn's documentary, a lack of focus on animal agriculture is not portrayed as being solely due to a cover-up on the part of corporations and governmental institutions with vested interests in the livestock industry. Charities are also framed as culpable for their role in promoting other—more palatable—forms of lifestyle change, rather than tackling the more controversial issue of reducing animal product consumption.

The film, moreover, does not present veganism as a single-issue politics that relates to climate change but instead foregrounds intersections between environmental concerns and animal ethics. For instance, initially Anderson explores other alternatives to reducing his carbon footprint, such as small-scale, sustainable livestock farming, an approach that is ultimately seen as untenable due to the discomfort with the act of killing that he experiences when witnessing the slaughter of a duck on a smallholding. As Alex Lockwood argues, the message of this scene is clear: "if [Anderson] cannot bear witness himself to the slaughter of animals for consumption, even at this presumably less environmentally damaging backyard farm, then he cannot contribute to any form of animal agricultural practices" (2016a: 743). These moments in the film, in other words, help to illustrate how individual ethics can emerge in response to intersecting problems: here climate change and animal agriculture.

Taking a lead from these arguments, *Cowspiracy* has been seen as a powerful film that engages people with the politics of meat consumption in ways that foreground the messiness and complexity of lifestyle movements (Giraud, 2019: 69–97). I pointed out that other aspects of the documentary, however, undermine this more situated exploration of how felt ethical responsibility is dealt with in specific contexts. Vegan activist Danny Chilvers (2016), for instance, voices concern that

> *Cowspiracy* . . . seems to assume that the only people worth targeting with its message are white, Northern and middle-class. One of the most problematic lines in the film is when a commentator says "it's not possible to be a meat-eating environmentalist." This statement is presumably meant to prick the consciences of well-off US eco-activists but it sweeps the struggles of millions of poorer Southern and Indigenous peoples under the carpet. Most of the people fighting for a safer global environment aren't middle-class Northern folks with carbon-heavy lifestyles. They are the people engaged in frontline battles against fossil fuels, local pollution, and—yes—livestock megafarm projects around the world, and they are leading the way in the defence of our shared climate.

These arguments help to elucidate the paradox of purity politics in geopolitical terms. For Shotwell one of the key issues with this form of politics is that those living in the Global North and wealthy industrialized South not only have lifestyles that contribute disproportionately to ecological problems but then engage in individualistic forms of politics that offer solace for those who are most responsible for these systems. In contrast, those who already face racial, class, and other forms of discrimination are not only disproportionately affected by ecological problems but also find it far more difficult (if not structurally impossible) to engage with an ethical lifestyle politics that is often inaccessible and expensive.

Shotwell's critique of purity politics has been talked of in positive terms in general (e.g., Glabau, 2017) and offers a nuanced way of thinking about the tensions associated with lifestyle movements. Vegan herself, it is also important to note that Shotwell does not outright condemn veganism in general but *particular* strands of vegan practice that she argues are implicated in purity politics. Indeed, Shotwell is critical of scholars, such as Lierre Keith (2009), who see veganism as somehow worth singling out as especially problematic, arguing that despite Keith underlining "the need to understand eating as a system, and as a system within which we are never free from death" she still "devotes her energies toward convincing vegans and vegetarians to change their individual eating practices on the way to destroying agriculture" (Shotwell, 2016: 118). Shotwell argues that this treatment of veganism misses the point and reproduces the very contradictions that veganism itself has been accused of, focusing attention on individual practices instead of systems. Rather than veganism being intrinsically problematic, for Shotwell the issue is when an ethos of purity (and its associated moralism) becomes associated with particular forms of vegan identity politics.

Other thinkers, while sharing Shotwell's general concern with lifestyle movements that provide overly simplistic response to complex problems, *do* single out veganism as exemplary in this regard. Elspeth Probyn states, for instance, that "increasingly the choice to proclaim oneself vegan often seems to act as an opting out of the structural complexities of food provisioning, production, and consumption" (Probyn, 2016: 3). There is a subtle shift between Shotwell's work and more strident criticisms, therefore, from veganism being treated as an instance of purity politics, which can assume problematic characteristics in certain contexts, to being portrayed as *especially* simplistic and reductive. These critical arguments, moreover, do not exist in a vacuum and build on lineages from other thinkers, such as Donna Haraway (2008; see Chapter 2), who have argued that no ethical or political decision is ever "innocent" as each course of action will have some sort of consequence: "Try as we might to distance ourselves, there is no way of living that is not also a way of someone, not something, dying differentially" (2008: 80). Again, in Haraway's work, veganism is singled-out as an example of this form of distancing, which will inevitably fail because

eating means also killing, directly or indirectly, and killing well is an obligation akin to eating well. This applies to a vegan as much as to a human carnivore [. . .] There is no rational or natural dividing line that will settle the life-and-death relations between human and nonhuman animals; such lines are alibis if they are imagined to settle the matter "technically." (Haraway, 2008: 296)

Haraway makes these arguments in relation to an everyday example: conflict that surrounded a faculty social event where a colleague served roasted meat from a hog he had hunted. The solution to heated debates surrounding the event (a compromise where ready-prepared deli meats were served at future events, rather than hunted animals) was likely to have left everyone unsatisfied, but the way Haraway frames the problem is significant. She suggests that "If one knows hunting is theologically right or wrong, or that animal rights positions are dogmatically correct or incorrect, then there is no cosmopolitical engagement" (2008: 299). Two aspects of Haraway's argument are significant here: first, she infers that the most problematic aspect of such debates is dogmatism itself and, second, she suggests that commitment to a decisive political or ethical stance is necessarily dogmatic. While commitment to hunting is framed as potentially dogmatic too, Haraway's positioning of veganism as something that undermines reflection about the ethical complexities of eating is especially biting because it is a refrain that recurs throughout *When Species Meet*.

Similar debates have emerged within ecofeminism between those who advocate a vegetarian or vegan politics (e.g., Gaard, 2011; Adams and Gruen, 2014) and those who condemn it (George, 1994, 2000). Val Plumwood, notably, distinguishes between what she describes as "ontological veganism"—"a theory that advocates universal abstention from all use of animals as the only real alternative to mastery and the leading means of defending animals against its wrongs"—and "ecological animalism" (2003: 1). For Plumwood the politics offered by ecological animalism situates humans as *part* of nature in order to challenge the notion that humans have *mastery* of nature. In contrast, she argues that veganism is ethnocentric due to "universalising a privileged 'consumer' perspective" and in doing so inadvertently reinforcing distinctions between humans and the "natural world" by "extend[ing] human status and privilege to a bigger class of 'semi-humans' who, like humans themselves, are conceived as above the non-conscious sphere and 'outside nature', beyond ecology and beyond use, especially use in the food chain" (2003: 2). Following Plumwood, the construction and contestation of such characterizations of veganism has been a recurring debate within ecofeminism (for overviews, see: Gaard, 2002; Giraud, 2013b; Hamilton, 2019).

While all of these theorists raise important issues that need to be engaged with, it is also necessary to critically reflect on whether this repeated portrayal of veganism as (to use Haraway's phrasing) an ethical "alibi"—that hides humans' ongoing implication in violence—is accurate or adequate in capturing the messiness of vegan politics or indeed of lifestyle movements in general.

Discourses of Veganism as "Purity Politics" in Popular Culture

The criticisms of lifestyle movements described previously hinge on the notion that no position is truly innocent or pure. Particular identities and practices that seem to offer purity are at best illusory and—at worst—mask ongoing violence and inequality. As crystallized by the arguments outlined here, veganism has been routinely used as an illustration of this problematic form of politics. Criticisms of vegan ethics, however, are not restricted to theoretical work and also circulate within popular culture.

Criticisms of plant-based foods are epitomized by a famous example from the early 2000s, from George Ouzounian's satirical website "Best Page in the Universe." Ouzounian (better known as internet persona Maddox) launched his site in 1997 and it rapidly rose to prominence. The site itself consisted of a series of articles skewering various targets. Even though Maddox did not make his political affiliation explicit—attacking targets on the left and right of the political spectrum—the particular vitriol the site reserved for so-called social justice warriors, along with its implied misogyny, have resulted in it being seen as a precursor in tone to contemporary alt-right online media (Kusz, 2017). Vegetarianism was one of Maddox's many targets; one of his most popular articles was entitled "Guiltless Grill? Is there Another Kind?" (Ouzounian, ND). The article itself detailed Maddox's annoyance at opening a restaurant menu to find a section of vegetarian dishes entitled "guiltless grill." The opening sentences set the tone, with Maddox describing how he "thought to myself 'boy, I sure am glad that I'm not a meat-hating fascist' and I skipped on to the steak section (because I'll be damned if I'm going to pay $15 for an alfalfa sandwich, slice of cucumber and a scoop of cold cottage cheese)." The "guiltless grill" label continued to irk him, however, and he continues:

> What pisses me off so much about this phrase is the sheer narrow-mindedness of these stuck up vegetarian assholes. You think you're saving the world by eating a tofu-burger and sticking to a diet of grains and berries? Well here's something that not many vegetarians know (or care to acknowledge): every year **millions** of animals are killed by wheat and soy bean combines during harvesting season (source). Oh yeah, go on and on for hours about how all of us meat eaters are going to hell for having a steak, but conveniently ignore the fact that each year millions of mice, rabbits, snakes, skunks, possums, squirrels, gophers and rats are ruthlessly murdered as a direct result of YOUR dieting habits.

A series of images—all with the deliberately crude aesthetic subsequently associated with sites such as 4Chan—were used to bring home this point, including a banner "~~meat~~ wheat is murder." In addition, the piece began with a cartoon (seemingly created in Microsoft Paint) that depicts one rabbit being crushed violently by a combine harvester while another rabbit watches on. Two speech bubbles (with text in comic sans, again in adherence to the overall aesthetic) radiate from the second rabbit, who states: "Hey look on the bright side: at least you're being murdered unintentionally" and "try not to make so much noise as your skull is crushed, we wouldn't want some self-righteous vegetarian to realize that 'guiltless grills' aren't so guiltless."[1] Though Maddox was discussing vegetarianism, in recent years—as anti-social justice warrior rhetoric has been taken up by the alt-right—veganism has emerged as the sustained target of critique (Gambert and Linné, 2018a; Stǎnescu, 2018).

What is significant is the resemblance these popular cultural arguments bear to theoretical critiques of veganism, which is again framed as offering an illusory sense of "purity" from the problems associated with industrial agriculture. Unlike theoretical texts, however, rather than using this critique in order to push for more complex and messier ways of thinking about food systems, Maddox is part of broader popular discourse that mocks those who engage in any sort of ethical action at all. As touched on earlier, this mocking of moralism foreshadows contemporary alt-right rhetoric, notably recent uses of epithets such as "soy boy" to denigrate not only those who explicitly identify as vegan but also so-called "beta men" who show commitment to gender and racial equality (with the inference being that over-consumption of soy has resulted in "emasculation"; see Gambert and Linné, 2018b). Although this weaponized usage of veganism might be novel, therefore, it speaks to a longer tradition of poking fun at vegan and vegetarian ethics in the context of popular culture.

Laura Wright, for instance, illustrates that anti-social justice warrior internet discourses are not unique, tracing a similar logic across other humorous popular cultural representations of veganism. Wright elucidates this point with reference to an episode of animated television series *The Simpsons* entitled "Lisa the Treehugger." In the episode Lisa's engagements with environmental politics are plagued by one-upmanship by fellow activist Jesse Grass, who—on hearing of Lisa's vegetarianism— infamously declares he is "a level five vegan" who "won't eat anything that casts a shadow" (cited in Wright, 2015: 5). Through satirizing the excessive moralism of veganism, what is being articulated here—as Wright succinctly puts it—is a logic of "infinite ethical regression: the only way to be 'genuine' or 'good enough' in such a formulation is not to do anything, because as soon as one does *something*, one is held to a standard (to which others do not hold themselves) that immediately assumes that one is not doing *enough*" (Wright, 2015: 21).

Without wishing to outright condemn a classic episode of *The Simpsons*, it is nonetheless informative to situate such imagery as part of the broader critique of lifestyle movements that exists within popular culture. This type of representation has historically stigmatized nonnormative diets (and other forms of personal ethical decision-making). Indeed, in their analysis of depictions of veganism within the UK media, Matthew Cole and Karen Morgan (2011) identify a specific discourse of "vegaphobia" wherein "Vegans are variously stereotyped as ascetics, faddists, sentimentalists, or in some cases, hostile extremists" (2011: 134). Dominant themes in these representations included "Ridiculing veganism," "characterizing veganism as asceticism," "describing veganism as difficult or impossible to sustain," "describing veganism as a fad," "characterizing vegans as oversensitive," and "characterizing vegans as hostile" (2011: 139). Collectively, Cole and Morgan argue, these themes constructed a discourse that resulted in the "marginalization of vegans themselves, evidenced through the ubiquity of the imagined omnivorous reader and the lack of articles addressing the beliefs, experiences or opinions of vegans" (2011: 149).

As explored in Chapter 7, the nature of these discourses has shifted slightly in the wake of veganism's rising popularity.[2] It is nonetheless important to recognize how representations of veganism that exist across both the news and popular media have traditionally worked to consecrate the status quo by making any attempts to question it seem moralistic and hypocritical (as with Blythman's piece on quinoa) as well as ineffective and doomed to failure. What is also significant, and perhaps disconcerting, about such representations is their resemblance with theoretical work that has made similar accusations about the hypocritic moralism of veganism.

Whether sympathetic or outright critical, these portrayals of veganism all hinge on an assumption: that vegans or vegetarians *themselves* believe that eating a particular way offers some form of ethical purity. In the case of Maddox, however, this belief is based not on encounters with those who eat plant-based foods, but due to the branding of a restaurant. Academic criticisms are grounded in more than this form of speculation, but often still present themselves as talking about veganism or vegans in general when actually drawing on evidence from vegan campaigns, which have often themselves been subject to sustained criticism from within the vegan community (see Chapters 4 and 5).

As Cole and Morgan (2011) point out, moreover, one of the notable dimensions of these recurring characterizations of veganism is that the voices of vegans themselves are absent. Even as veganism is repeatedly used to illustrate the problems of purity politics, or held up as a simplistic response to a world that is messy, entangled, and complex, very little empirical work about what vegan politics means to those who engage with it is ever cited to support this point. Currently there is scant evidence as to whether vegans in general *do* understand their identity as offering any form of moral solace (cf Hamilton, 2016). The evidence that is provided tends to be anecdotal, from reflections about negative encounters online to stories about irritating vegan friends and colleagues: a point C. Lou Hamilton underlines in her sympathetic critique of Probyn's monograph about fish consumption, *Eating the Ocean*:

> The word "complexity" is repeated time and time again . . . mantra-like. Probyn makes a convincing case that fish and other sea creatures are caught up in human life in complex ways, and that solutions to food sustainability will have to take account of this complexity. Yet the equally repeated claim that most food politics are too "simplistic" is backed up by fewer empirical examples, relying instead on sweeping generalisations about vegans and white, middle-class urbanites obsessed with local, organic produce. (Hamilton, 2019: 68)

Though made in relation to Probyn's specific text, Hamilton's concerns have far wider resonance in light of the cultural discourse of vegan hypocrisy traced in this chapter; in her words: "How did we get to the point where taking into account animals—their lives, feelings, intelligence and relationships to us—can be labelled 'simplistic'?" (2019: 69). While purity politics is deeply problematic, therefore, and I do not wish to dismiss the argument that certain forms of veganism might fall into this category, or to sweep aside negative personal experiences (many of which I've shared!), the extent to which a number of prominent critiques of veganism make universalizing claims while using fairly anecdotal evidence to support these claims remains concerning.[3]

In the rest of this chapter, I work to complicate the assumption that vegan politics is by necessity a form of purity politics, or, more generally, an instance of lifestyle politics that is inherently apolitical. In order to develop this argument, I turn to an emerging body of sociological research that has troubled some of the criticisms that have been leveled at veganism in theoretical and popular cultural contexts.

Veganism: Normative or Contesting Norms?

Critical depictions of veganism often hinge on the assumption that it acts as a normative identity marker, which delineates between which forms of eating are ethical and which are seen as unethical. What this portrayal of veganism misses is that vegan practice is not just about imposing norms, but *unsettling* them. What I mean by this can be elucidated by briefly turning to popular mock-documentary *Carnage* (2017), directed by comedian and writer Simon Amstell, which uses vegan politics to elucidate how particular (omnivorous) ways of eating are routinely treated as a neutral default. The mockumentary is set in a future where veganism itself is a norm, its subject matter ostensibly being on how this normalization unfolded historically (see also Hamilton, 2019: 155–9). A key turning point in veganism's journey to becoming mainstream is when fictional activist Troye King Jones is interviewed on a high-profile news program and responds to the interviewer's accusation that veganism is an extreme form of moralism by stating: "We are not 'vegans' THEY are 'carnists'" (Amstell, 2017). Here the consumption of meat shifts from being neutral (and naturalized) to simply normative, opening space to ask questions about the ethical implications of these norms. The process of veganism becoming normative, in this context, is thus impossible to separate from the act of unsettling existing norms regarding which forms of consumption are seen as socially acceptable.

The shift from practices being seen as "natural" to merely normative has long been seen as important within sociological theory. In Pierre Bourdieu's (2008: 164) terms, norms that govern social conduct (or "doxa") are at their most powerful when they exist beneath the radar and are not even acknowledged as existing, but just treated as "the way things are." As soon as alternative (or in Bourdieu's framing "heterodox") ways of doing things emerge, however, existing social norms lose some of their power, as they are no longer beyond question but are seen as merely the "orthodox" (i.e., normal or mainstream) way of doing things. While socially orthodox norms and practices are still dominant—and often vehemently defended—they are never as powerful as when these norms function imperceptibly.

The capacity of vegan politics to serve as a heterodox practice that de-naturalizes existing norms (rather than just as something that imposes its own moralistic values) has already been argued for within cultural theory (see Giraud, 2013a, 2013b, 2019 for overviews). Indeed, the term "carnism" was originally used in critical animal studies (Joy, 2011) and played a central role in informing Vegan Studies as a field by establishing meat consumption as orthodox, rather than doxic and beyond ethical question. However, although these conceptual arguments remain valuable, many of the stereotypes about veganism make empirical claims about what vegans think and feel; thus to complicate these assumptions it is necessary to engage with the understandings and beliefs of vegans themselves.

In the final section of this chapter, therefore, I turn to existing sociological research that highlights, first, how normalizing pressures play a significant role in shaping vegan practice and, second, how sustaining veganism is often contingent on resisting these norms. Both of these arguments are illustrated by Nathan Stephens Griffin's book *Understanding Veganism: Biography and Identity* (2017), which is a valuable text in being one of the few publications that addresses the complex ways that veganism is navigated in practice. What the book underlines is that the status of veganism as a nonnormative diet has significant implications for how vegan identity itself is realized. Through interviews with a number of vegans, Stephens Griffin shows that vegan identity is always articulated in relation to mainstream food cultures that work to undermine it in a range of ways. In line with a growing number of other texts within vegan studies, his analysis draws explicitly on a Foucauldian theoretical tradition in order to examine the different social relations that produce and regulate vegan subjectivity (e.g., Acari, 2020; Cole, 2008; Potts and Parry, 2010; Stanescu, 2013; Dean, 2014; Pedersen and Stanescu, 2014). In particular, he draws upon the notion of "normalization," a "process by which all conduct is judged, and rewarded or punished accordingly" (2017: 20). In line with this framework, the vegans Stephens Griffin interviews constantly have to struggle to realize their identity in the face of social relations that work to impose more normative (i.e., omnivorous or "carnist") ways of eating.

On an everyday level, a number of interviewees described how pressures from friends, families, and even fellow activists informed how veganism could be enacted. On a more extreme level, a preexisting medical condition on the part of one interviewee limited how they were able to realize veganism, due to institutional arrangements and medicines that made it difficult to remain vegan. Vegans who had encounters with the criminal justice system because of involvement with other forms of animal rights activism were also often encouraged to conform to non-vegan diets in prison, or even forcibly given medication that was not vegan. What is underlined by revealing these, sometimes aggressive, processes of normalization is that, as Stephens Griffin concludes,

> far from being a politically benign "diet" or "lifestyle" choice, vegans routinely become the subject of normalising processes. These function to make it harder to be vegan, creating conflict in areas of daily experience that are otherwise unproblematized. (2017: 121)

The experiences described by Stephens Griffin's interviewees also illustrate how processes of normalization often intersect with other social inequalities; in the case of two interviewees, for instance, veganism fed into exoticizing discourses that were already working to marginalize them on the basis of religion and ethnicity. Another interviewee in a high-powered job deliberately hid their veganism for fear it would accentuate preexisting gender discrimination. In light of these varied forms of normalizing pressures, what Stephens Griffin concludes is that "Whilst 'veganism' remains rigid at its core, the process through which vegan identity is deployed and achieved is fluid and contextual" (Stephens Griffin, 2017: 123). In the contexts described by this research, veganism is not something that imposes norms in ways that neglect or reinforce existing social inequalities. Indeed, sometimes the opposite is the case, with veganism marking individuals as nonnormative in ways that can contribute to other more profound forms of exclusion.

Similar arguments about normalizing pressures have been made in auto-ethnographic research by critical animal and disability studies scholar Sunaura Taylor, who—likewise—describes how her veganism often plays a role in making her feel Othered along with her disability, arthorogryposis multiplex congenita (2017: 119). Toward the end of her book, *Beasts of Burden* (2017), Taylor describes being asked to speak at an event that was physically inaccessible (recalling how she and her partner were forced to wait downstairs while others attended an arts event upstairs). Her alienation was then compounded after the food she was served—a "special dish . . . that consisted mainly of roasted vegetables" made her feel like her lifestyle choices would be seen as similarly "isolating and different" (2017: 150). Like Stephens Griffin, Taylor is careful not to conflate everyday stigmatization due to veganism with other structural oppressions, while still foregrounding the persistent ways that normalizing pressures impact upon vegan identity.

What is significant about this emerging body of research focused on everyday vegan experience is that it works to unsettle simplistic accounts of veganism as a norm that individuals in positions of privilege try to impose on others (due to believing their diet offers some form of ethical solace). Indeed, the heterodox status of veganism—coupled with the moralistic stereotypes attached to it— means that in practice people often display keen awareness of the need to avoid being seen as "po-faced" or "preachy" (e.g., Stephens Griffin, 2017: 43, 73). These findings resonate with work that has likened the social dynamics of veganism to Sara Ahmed's concept of the "feminist killjoy" (Twine, 2014), a comparison made in the wake of a large research project about vegans' experiences wherein "thirty-three of forty [of the project's] participants (82.5%)" had experienced negative reactions on becoming vegan, ranging from dismissiveness to outright hostility (Twine, 2017: 629).

Ahmed's (2017) concept refers to the way that feminists are often perceived as disrupting others' happiness through their political beliefs. She offers an everyday example of the sorts of instance where the feminist killjoy is perceived by her friends and family as, quite literally, killing joy, by describing a dinner table scene where the feminist disrupts the atmosphere by failing to ignore casual misogyny. Though this seeming inability to "take a joke" and apparent readiness to take offence, the feminist herself is projected as the problem rather than the oppressive social relations she is objecting to. In contrast to Ahmed's feminist killjoy, the vegan killjoy, moreover, does not even have to verbally or affectively signify any objections. As this sociological research about veganism describes, happiness is sometimes disrupted just through others knowing a vegan is present, due to the inference of moral judgement (which often results in the vegan themselves being subject to hostile questioning).

The picture painted by existing social scientific research, therefore, complicates theoretical narratives in two important ways. First, sociological work with vegans helps to trouble the notion of veganism as purity politics by elucidating how this label is something vegans are acutely aware of and try to resist. Second, this research illustrates how assumptions about purism are often something that are applied to vegans rather than being integral to people's self-identity. Sometimes the presence of a vegan in itself creates discomfort about food practices that are routinely coded as culturally normative and ethically unproblematic: regardless of how vegans themselves act.

Navigating New Norms

Awareness of the normalizing pressures facing veganism has not just existed in academic contexts. Vegans themselves have also shown recognition of the social pressures that make their lifestyle subject to scrutiny, which online vegan culture has long sought to find ways of negotiating. Commonly shared memes in online vegan communities, for instance, include a vegan "bingo card" that lists routine "gotcha" questions that are asked to check for moral consistency—and catch vegans out in their hypocrisy—all of which point to normalizing pressures. The so-called defensive omnivore bingo card originally emerged on vegan online forum the Post Punk Kitchen after being designed by user Brian VanderVeen. The card contained squares such as "asks you where you get your protein," "expresses concern for plant suffering," "brings up PETA," "asks you why you care more about animals than human beings," "asks what would happen to the cows if we didn't eat them," and "wonders how we would grow enough food if we all turned vegetarian overnight" (along with many others). Of course, the tone of the bingo card is likely to, in turn, feed into the trope of the self-righteous vegan, with these options effectively acting as a series of "reverse gotcha" moments to anticipate criticisms.[4] This approach runs the risk of treating all commonplace queries about veganism as stemming from bad faith even if they arise from genuine concern or curiosity. What a more generous reading of the card points to, however, is the importance of vegan community in negotiating and ameliorating normalizing pressures. This argument has been borne out by the sociological research, discussed in the previous section, that suggests veganism can only be sustained through finding ways to resist the various normalizing processes that try to undermine it.

A growing body of work has pointed to the expansion of vegan food cultures that depart from stereotypes in order to portray vegan food as more "joyful" and "appealing," not just for potential vegans themselves but friends and relatives (Véron, 2016b; Scott, 2020): processes that are important for sustaining vegan practice. Commonplace practices that support normalization, Twine (2017) suggests, include the development of new products (including meat or cheese alternatives), vegan-led online depictions of veganism—such as Instagram communities #whatveganseat and #whatfatvegans eat—that disrupt perceptions of it as restrictive, and online cooking communities where people experiment with unusual ingredients like aquafaba. Aquafaba is a relatively recent discovery and consists of the "leftover" water from cans of beans, which has been found to have similar properties to egg whites and can be whipped up to create things that were formerly thought of as impossible to veganize (such as meringues and macarons). Since its emergence the ingredient has received high levels of publicity: even being central to one of the challenges on hit television series the *Great British Bake Off* (which itself had a vegan week for the first time in 2018). In addition to indicating veganism's increasing normalization, however, these shifts also elucidate a degree of ambivalence associated with such processes. The Facebook group "Vegan Meringue—Hits and Misses," for instance, has recently undergone a transformation to simply "Aquafaba." What this change in name points toward is the danger that along with normalization can come a degree of depoliticization, where things formerly marked as nonnormative become re-packaged in order to depart from their "killjoy" associations.

Yet it would be overly simplistic to read processes of normalization as straightforwardly depoliticizing veganism. The rise of meat, dairy, and egg substitutes, for instance, has routinely been identified as a food trend, something that large supermarket chains have themselves pointed to as a growing market to exploit. Yet, as I explore in more depth in Chapter 7, vegans are often cognizant of these tensions and try to negotiate them. Awareness of the tensions surrounding meat, dairy, and egg substitutes is also evident in other, more explicit, attempts to articulate the messiness and non-innocence of all food choices by artists and activists. For example, in 2014 a series of research and creative events were held at Lund University, exploring the "animal turn" that had emerged across the social sciences and humanities. Two years later, one of these events went viral after being reported on a popular blog under the title "These Vegans Cooking and Eating E.T. The Extra Terrestrial Will Ruin BBQ for You" (Kurp, 2016).

The barbecue in question was organized by a collective of artists from creative design studio Unsworn Industries—Helga Steppan, Nicklas Marelius, Livia Sunesson, Erik Sandelin, Magnus Torstensson, Sveta Suvorina, and Julia Zajac—along with artist Terje Östling. The group made a giant E. T. from seitan (a popular meat alternative made out of vital wheat gluten), which was barbecued on a spit and served to attendees. The attendees were then interviewed in order for the artists to explore, as Sandelin puts it, "issues such as the social function of mock meat, the legal and moral status of extraterrestrials, fictional atrocities and victimless crimes, and mock meats as potential surrogates for some of the complicated pleasures of meat eating" (Sandelin and Unsworn Industries, 2014: 49). What was important about this creative experiment was that it explicitly drew attention to the conditions and food systems that underpin *any* eating practice rather than just serving as a critique of animal product consumption.

Those consuming E. T. voiced discomfort at consuming the—alarmingly lifelike or at least true-to-fiction—body of the friendly alien, but negotiated this with comments such as "mock meat never was someone" and "no one is hurt" (2014: 53). Sandelin, however, doesn't let such sentiments offer any form of ethical closure, instead using the consumption of E. T. as a means to trouble such justifications. He points out that being meat free doesn't equate to being "guilt free" as "Industrial monocultures, such as wheat, are also part of the ongoing living and dying of humans and nonhumans." Sandelin draws, in particular, on the work of Anna Tsing (2011) to "unravel the historical transfer of affection from multi-species landscapes to focusing on one or two particular crops," a process that links "grain cultivation and the emergence of social hierarchies—as well as the rise of the state" (Sandelin and Unsworn Industries, 2014: 53). Rather than shutting down reflection on the politics of eating, therefore, this particular creative experiment with a meat substitute foregrounded the complexities of food systems. Though online discussion surrounding reports of the barbecue focused on its obvious critique of meat, the experiment was fundamentally designed to foreground the non-innocence of all forms of eating: in an act far removed from purity politics.

Conclusion: Holding Systems in View?

In her sympathetic critique of veganism or, to be more precise, strands of vegan politics that segue with purity politics, Shotwell argues that food ethics, instead, needs to be oriented around "holding in view" the systems that constitute food choices. In this chapter I have provided an overview of both theoretical and popular cultural discourses about veganism that focus on its alleged sense of purity and related moral inconsistency, before contrasting these narratives with other research from fields such as sociology and media studies. The picture provided by more sociologically-focused research, and its exploration of how vegans understand and negotiate their own identity, is that—rather than masking structural problems in food systems—veganism can serve to highlight important aspects of these systems. In other words, rather than eschewing structural complexity as certain commentators have suggested, veganism can instead serve as an "opting in," a starting point for peeling back the layers involved in food ethics.[5]

What I have also sought to convey in this chapter is that issues surrounding ethical food practice are never straightforward and need to be contextualized in relation to broader debates about lifestyle movements. As Haenfler, Johnson and Jones (2012) argue, lifestyle movements are often dismissed as problematic, liberal endeavors that place the responsibility on individuals rather than structural change. Issues discussed in this chapter suggest that a more complicated framing is needed in order to understand the political potentials (as well as attain a more in-depth grasp of the downfalls) of this form of politics. One of Haenfler et al.'s key points is that those who are part of lifestyle movements are engaging in forms of prefigurative politics that can—on occasion—translate into more sustained forms of activism if the opportunity arises, because often "manifestly political social movements overlap; indeed, they are often inextricably linked, as movement organizations regularly promote both lifestyle and collective action, and adherents of LMs occasionally engage in electoral and contentious politics" (Haenfler, Johnson and Jones, 2012: 12). More recent sociological work about veganism discussed in this chapter bears out this line of argument, elucidating how normalization might *start* as a form of individual resistance but is necessarily *sustained* by collective practice: an argument that helps to elucidate how lifestyle movements can serve as a vector for social change in more meaningful ways. Even research on the most maligned aspect of lifestyle movements—ethical consumerism—speaks to the messiness of food politics, illustrating how more collective modes of political action can emerge from (apparently) inauspicious beginnings (Littler, 2009; Evans, Welch and Swaffield, 2017; Carrigan, 2017). Debates about veganism, therefore, need to be situated within a changing landscape, where ethical consumerism itself is gaining more politicized meanings, though (as discussed in more depth in Chapter 7) consumerism also has clear limitations when it comes to social change.

Yet even while—to reiterate Hamilton—it is important not only to see both food systems and food politics as complex phenomena, for all of this complexity it is still necessary to recognize that veganism is not intrinsically anti-normative. Veganism's own norms might be heterodox at present and do important work in rendering preexisting norms perceptible, but they are still *normative*. As the sociological research I have discussed in this chapter argues, veganism is often only sustained by varied normalization processes that make it practically and emotionally possible to live a vegan life in cultural settings where dominant norms seek to undermine it. The normalization of alternative ways of eating, in other words, is vital in resisting normalizing pressures that exist more widely in particular societies. The sticking point to this argument is that although normalization processes are vital in supporting veganism, they are also where tensions are likely to emerge in the future due to the way that supporting and sustaining norms is (at least in the present moment) entangled with commercial processes, emerging markets, and cultural (or subcultural) value. If veganism moves more fully from resisting existing norms, to becoming socially normative in itself, therefore, further questions need to be asked about its capacity to be reduced to a less politicized— more exclusionary—mode of ethical lifestylism. These questions are taken up throughout the rest of the book but, before examining how they are negotiated in the context of vegan activism in the next chapter, it is necessary to reflect on one final concern.

Many of the discussions outlined in this chapter center on veganism as a way of eating. Debates about whether veganism is or isn't a lifestyle movement, or indeed its limitations if it is categorized in this manner, tend to hinge on the inevitable inconsistencies that are generated when making ethical choices in complex food systems. Yet, to echo the previous chapters, what vegan scholarship shows is that even when food is a starting point, discussions soon shift to more expansive reflections about socioeconomic relations or media discourses. It should also be noted that much of the vegan scholarship touched on in this chapter does explicitly go beyond food: such as Stephens Griffin's discussion of medicine, while elsewhere in Hamilton's work she describes the politics of clothing, particularly leather (2020: 132–54). Perhaps more fundamentally, to reiterate Aph Ko's (2019) arguments as discussed in Chapter 1, a focus on food is itself often the problem, because this sets the terms of debate in ways that limit more complex conceptions of veganism. It is thus important not to use tensions that might surround veganism as a diet in order to dismiss the more expansive questioning of human-animal relations that could be offered by vegan ethics. The next chapter builds on these arguments to examine some of the existing ways that vegan activism has wrestled with the problem of how to articulate veganism as something that pushes for wider structural change, rather than something that operates at the level of individual dietary politics.

Chapter 4

LEARNING FROM VEGAN ACTIVISM

The previous chapter concluded with a question: Is it possible for veganism to serve as a starting point for "holding in view" (Shotwell, 2016: 125) the complexity of food systems? More specifically, can vegan practice go beyond debates about how to eat ethically within existing systems to engage with questions about how to reorganize these systems? These questions necessarily draw together environmental politics and concern with human inequalities, as well as the complex social and cultural implications of rethinking human relationships with other beings, across a range of institutional contexts. In other words, even when starting with a narrow focus on dietary veganism, discussions soon become more expansive.

As outlined previously, the relationship between veganism and systemic problems has become the focus of heated debate between those sympathetic toward and those critical of veganism. A number of cultural theorists have bristled at the assumption that veganism is key to minimizing harm in any universalizing sense: instead depicting vegan practice as an overly simplistic, individualistic, and moralistic form of politics that has a narrow focus on food. Again, the adage "there is no ethical consumption under capitalism" perhaps best encapsulates this line of argument. From animals slaughtered in harvesting, to people exploited in the manufacturing of products, and inequalities that shape who is able to make consumption choices, *no* way of eating, or indeed living can offer moral solace: veganism included.

Yet, as I traced throughout Chapter 3, other scholarship (both theoretical and empirical) has offered a series of counter-arguments. Though it is critically important to recognize that there is no truly ethical form of consumption, all too often this point can work to shut down rather than open up more challenging questions about how to redress harms affecting both humans and nonhuman animals. Instead, the unethical nature of all consumption can sometimes be leveraged rhetorically as a "gotcha" moment that results in doing nothing at all for fear of hypocrisy (Wright, 2015: 21; Ko, 2019: 7). As outlined in the previous chapter, it is in order to move beyond this impasse that a number of thinkers who are more sympathetic to vegan praxis have offered alternative narratives. While recognizing problems and pitfalls associated with certain aspects of veganism, this body of research has offered two lines of argument that complicate commonplace criticisms: First, it has unsettled the sense that veganism is seen by vegans themselves as offering any form of solace or purity from structural problems. Second, and relatedly, this scholarship has begun to show that rather than *shutting down* engagement with the complex relationships between humans and nonhuman animals, in practice veganism has often provided an *entry point* to complexity.

This chapter offers a more in-depth appraisal of the extent to which veganism can serve as an opening to broader concerns about human-animal relations, by turning to vegan activism. Throughout the chapter I focus on a range of activist movements, some of which offer a narrow focus on changing eating patterns while others advocate a vegan ethics that is "more than a diet." The more hopeful of these initiatives construct multilayered narratives that highlight connections between human and animal oppression, or develop practices—and sometimes even alternative infrastructures—that offer a response to enmeshed oppressions. At the same time, the chapter does not seek to uncritically valorize vegan (or indeed any form of) ethico-political practice, but emphasize its heterogeneity and recognize the messy, complex nature not just of the terrain that activists are working within, but of activism itself. By focusing on how movements navigate complexity in practice, the chapter aims to move beyond the types of debates outlined previously, about whether veganism is or isn't a form of purity politics or is oriented toward individual or collective action. Instead, I ask what can be learned from contexts where veganism is *already* being enacted as something that is more than an individual dietary choice: as well as instances where these potentials have failed to materialize.

Initially I focus on activism that has highlighted animal suffering in order to raise awareness and instigate change, before turning to alternative approaches that have attempted to expose the structures and classifications that normalize the transformation of animals into resources. I then explore grassroots activism that has not just criticized existing structural oppressions but attempted to create alternative infrastructures. Before focusing on specific movements, however, it is important to provide some wider context about the histories and political landscapes associated with vegan activism.

Contextualizing Vegan Activism

Over the past two decades, research about a range of different forms of vegan activism has emerged: from analyses of awareness campaigns launched by large NGOs such as PETA (see Chapter 5), to veganism as a form of lifestyle activism (Haenfler, 2004; Wrenn, 2011; Greenebaum, 2012a; Véron, 2016; Dickstein et al., 2020), and vegan political praxis within social movements (Munro, 2005; Giraud, 2015, 2019; Lockwood, 2016a, 2018, 2019a, 2021). In practice, however, veganism often operates in the hinterland between organized social movements and everyday cultural activism that takes place outside spaces coded as activist (Stephens Griffin, 2017: 7).

This *both and* positioning of veganism could be seen as key to its potential to act as "more than a diet," by hinting at pathways through which individual resistance can feed into collective praxis that troubles human relationships with other beings in a more holistic sense. As discussed in the previous chapter, although critics of veganism have framed it as normative, those engaged in sustained sociological research about vegan politics have pointed out its counter-hegemonic position in relation to existing, normative ways of eating. Echoing work that has seen vegetarianism as a form of resistance to dietary norms (e.g., Kwan and Roth, 2011), veganism is also often framed as a form of everyday activism that challenges the ideological naturalization of meat consumption or "carnism" (Joy, 2011). Vegan practice has also been seen as a marker of resistance to other capitalist and patriarchal norms, due to values that have become associated with meat, such as wealth, masculinity, and colonial social formations (Adams, 2000; Harper, 2010b; Potts and Parry, 2010; Robinson, 2013; Dean, 2014). As discussed in further depth in Chapters 6 and 7, however, veganism does not *intrinsically* mark resistance to other forms of oppression (see Harper, 2010a, 2012; Brueck, 2017; Ko and Ko, 2017). Indeed, even more politicized forms of vegan activism that do try to draw connections are heterogeneous in aims and scope and sometimes unsuccessful.

"Vegan activism" can evoke a range of meanings in activist contexts. For instance, veganism can be an identity marker for animal activists, or even part of their protest repertoires, serving as a form of prefigurative political practice that reflects the worlds activists seek to bring into being (Cherry, 2006, 2010, 2015). This is not to say that veganism and animal activism are necessarily synonymous. High-profile Victorian anti-vivisectionist groups, for instance, existed in the UK over fifty years before the founding of the Vegan Society (Kean, 1998). At the same time, the contours of contemporary veganism have nonetheless been informed by these broader animal activist histories. For instance, the abolitionist/welfarist distinction (see Wrenn, 2016) between vegan practice (and its prefiguration of a world that seeks to eliminate animal exploitation) and welfarist groups (that focus on improving the conditions of animals within existing spaces and institutions) have roots in these Victorian activist histories. This distinction stretches back to the end of the nineteenth century when the first contemporary animal activist movement—the Victoria Street Society that was founded in opposition to uses of animals in laboratory research—split into two groups broadly along welfarist/ abolitionist lines: The National Anti-Vivisection Society (NAVS) and the British Union for the Abolition of Vivisection (BUAV) in 1897 (French, 1975).

These complex relationships between vegan and animal activism are themselves only part of a larger story. Veganism's relationship to activism is not limited to animal rights and liberation movements and can also serve as part of the identity of other activist groups, notably those engaged in environmental politics. But here the story becomes more complicated still, as it is often in environmentalist contexts that vegan practice has been subject to particular scrutiny. In certain contexts veganism has been accused of an exclusionary means of demarcating insiders and outsiders from radical grassroots groups (e.g., Saunders, 2008), but in other contexts veganism has itself been marginalized from mainstream environmentalism: something only starting to change in recent years with the rise of the new climate movements.

As conveyed by the previous thumbnail sketch, vegan activism is not easy to pin down (to say the least), and this is just when focusing on a few constitutive threads of activist history in one national context. While recognizing complexity is important, the aim of this chapter is not to offer a genealogy of the roots of vegan activism, nor to provide a typology of high-profile instances of activism that exist today (Wrenn, 2016, 2020, to get a sense of these relationships, and Stallwood, 2014 for an activist perspective). Instead, I engage with a series of particularly informative activist tactics that speak to the aforementioned question of how vegan activism can hold systemic problems in view.

Holding Animals in View

One of the reasons why veganism helps to lay bare the challenge of holding systems in view is because the tactic of revealing what is ordinarily perceived to be hidden by particular socioeconomic or cultural structures has been a central tenet of vegan activism and—indeed—animal activism in general. In the context of animal activism more broadly, visibility politics has a long history (Kean, 1998: 39–69). As touched on previously, some of the earliest modern animal rights movements (and animal rights legislation) emerged in the UK during the Victorian period, where animal activism was also entangled with other political concerns such as women's suffrage (French, 1975; Elston, 1987). One of the biggest controversies in the nascent animal rights movement, for instance, took place at the turn of the nineteenth century when two students, Louise (Lizzy) Lind af Hageby and Leisa Schartau, took physiology classes at University College London in order to ascertain whether uses of vivisection were adhering to regulations.[1]

The testimony produced by the two women yielded a book (*The Shambles of Science*) and fed into a number of speeches and documents by activists, which were subject to legal action (Mason, 1997). Eventually these events resulted in what was known as the Brown Dog Affair, where the first memorial dedicated to laboratory animals—a statue of the little brown dog whose treatment the women had documented—was erected (Garlick, 2015). The statue itself drew still higher levels of attention, even resulting in riots after medical students' attempts to remove it were met with local resistance (in part due to consternation over the intrusion of middle- and upper-class students into the working-class area of Battersea; see again Mason, 1997).

While the emergence of various media technologies might have changed, with cameras displacing (or at least supplementing) testimony (McCausland, O'Sullivan and Brenton, 2013), and social media used in addition to speeches and pamphlets (Giraud, 2019: 118–41), the centrality of revealing what is ordinarily hidden has remained a central tactic for animal activism and vegan politics in particular. Again, in drawing attention to this history of visibility politics, I am not saying that vegan activism is synonymous with other forms of animal activism, such as anti-vivisectionism. I do, nonetheless, suggest that it is useful to recognize that historically there have been overlaps between those involved with these different strands of protest, especially in relation to issues such as animal research and the live export of "food" animals (Munro, 2005). Early writings by vegan activists, moreover, explicitly included laboratory animals in definitions of what veganism is (Batt, 1964). In addition, and perhaps more significantly, a tactical emphasis on visibility has remained an important aspect of vegan political practice, in order to combat a series of sociohistorical developments that have meant aspects of animal agriculture are often hidden from view (Philo and McLachlan, 2018).

Historians, literary theorists, and animal geographers have long noted a transformation that took place throughout the nineteenth century, when the spaces in which animals were sold and slaughtered were gradually removed from public view (Philo, 1995; Fitzgerald, 2010; Geier, 2017; McCorry and Miller, 2019). For example, Chris Philo (a key figure in establishing contemporary animal geographies as an area of study in its own right) has traced how animal markets were the focus of public anxiety during the nineteenth century. This anxiety was often intensely classed and Philo provides some remarkable archival materials that reconstruct a popular discourse asserting that "livestock animals should be kept 'at a distance' from the normal spaces of the 'refined city' for the good of the 'public morals'" (1995: 670). As reflected by these sentiments and in line with stigma that was popularly attached to the urban working class from this period, which intensified during the Victorian era, there was a widespread belief that working classes would be especially susceptible to the negative influence of animal behavior. Shifting markets and slaughterhouses out of cities were not only seen as a means of negating animals' influence, in other words, but also the influence of those who worked with livestock, who were stigmatized as unclean and potentially violent due to the nature of their work (Eisenman, 2016).[2]

This social and cultural backdrop informs many of the concerns that have been central to vegan theory and practice. Work within critical animal studies (CAS), for instance, has argued that vegan praxis needs to be coupled with anti-capitalist politics if it is ever to meaningfully dismantle systems that tie together human and animal oppression (Stephens Griffin, 2014). In ecofeminism, moreover, these processes of dismantling enmeshed oppressions have been explicitly connected with questions of visibility. As touched on previously, Carol Adams's theory of the absent referent (2000 [1990]) suggests that animal lives are systematically rendered invisible in ways that foreclose ethical questions about the different oppressions bound up with industrialized animal agriculture. As a means of combatting this process, a large body of academic work has aspired to bring animals back into the frame to *foreground* their lives and perhaps more notably deaths (e.g., Stewart and Cole, 2009; Cudworth, 2011; Hamilton and Taylor, 2013; Fitzgerald and Taylor, 2014; Almiron, Cole and Freeman, 2016, 2018; Cole and Stewart, 2016; Potts, 2016; Gillespie, 2018). By working to make animal lives and deaths visible, these scholars have sought to unsettle the norms, categories, and practices that naturalize the use of animals for human benefit.

Theories of cognitive dissonance (Festinger, 1957) are also routinely applied to animal product consumption, to suggest that it relies on individuals making ethical justifications for aspects of their behavior that sit uneasily with their broader ethical commitments (e.g., Loughnan, Haslam and Bastian, 2010, 2014). This sentiment, for instance, underpins Melanie Joy's conception of carnism in *Why We Love Dogs, Eat Pigs, and Wear Cows* (2011), which begins with a description of the presumed reader attending a dinner party and relishing the smells of cooking, only to find out the dish in question is golden retriever. The reader's initial reaction of disgust, Joy suggests, likely changes to acceptance on being told by the host that this is just a joke and they will actually be served beef, due to different cultural perceptions of which animals are seen as friends and which are food. This example offers a starting point for Joy to argue that differences between species are not natural but ideological, with the rest of the book working to unpick the logic of carnism that, she alleges, enables people to rationalize culturally contradictory relationships with animals.

Yet the assumption that making something visible, or highlighting presumed ethical contradictions, necessarily instigates change is not without problems, with long histories of academic and activist reflections showing that this is not the case in practice (e.g., O'Sullivan, 2011; Stallwood, 2014; Taylor, 2016). As Richard White and Simon Springer put it:

> What is painfully obvious though is that the process of conscious-raising, and articulating the hidden "truth" about the appalling death and violence that is constantly revealed through transgressing these spaces, has not resulted in more wide-spread action to boycott animal products. Regrettably in a speciesist consumerist society, the desires not to confront the violent geographies of meat, but to be reassured by the convenient myths (welfare standards, appropriate monitoring), quickly reassert themselves. Thus, in itself, it is important to confront the question: if the truth is not enough, what then? (White and Springer, 2018: 175)

The stakes of these varied arguments about whether revealing the "truth" of animal suffering alters the way animals are perceived and classified can be explored on turning to an especially prominent tactic in vegan activism: exposés that have emerged in the wake of undercover filming.

Exposing Violence

Although visibility politics and hidden filming more specifically might have long histories, as with other forms of citizen journalism, circulation of such footage has intensified with the rise of the internet and social media (Mummery and Rodan, 2017). In contemporary contexts of vegan activism, shock tactics that involve the circulation of imagery revealing suffering within animal agriculture are routine (for a critical overview, see Wrenn, 2013). Sometimes these images can take the form of exposés, where particular incidents are documented in order to draw attention to abuses: as with infamous images of workers on Bernard Matthews UK turkey farms hitting the birds with baseball bats for amusement

(BBC, 2006) or footage of un-sedated calves from cows whose milk is destined for Nestlé ice cream, being punched and kicked before having hot irons pressed to their heads to prevent horn growth.[3] Groups such as Anonymous for the Voiceless have attempted to take this tactics to the streets, promoting veganism with a tactic they describe as a "cube of truth" wherein a group of activists in Anonymous masks stand in a square holding signs with "truth" in large font while others hold television screens depicting what they describe as "graphic and powerful footage of animal exploitation" (Anonymous for the Voiceless, ND).

Numerous problems have been associated with these instances of activism (and activist groups), but the danger associated with such approaches from a "vegan studies lens" (to use Wright's turn of phrase, 2019) is that this type of imagery runs the risk of framing suffering as an exception to the norm, which should be dealt with through better adherence to welfare guidelines. Shock tactics, in other words, can inadvertently strengthen the legitimacy of the system itself. In the context of veterinary agriculture, for instance, horn removal is portrayed as necessary to prevent cattle injuring one another (and the humans who work with them), while removal via hot irons is depicted as less painful than other forms of removal (though breeding out genes that produce large horns is seen as the most desirable outcome of all) (Laven, 2010). Activist critiques of de-horning can thus be undermined by reframing the problem as being *how* de-horning is executed, as opposed to a food system in which de-horning is necessary. Similarly, exposés that depict individual acts of violence run the risk of invoking a "carceral veganism" that not only, again, deflects attention away from systems and toward individuals but "relies on and perpetuates a surveillance and detention framework to 'solve' systemic issues connected to animal cruelty" (Activist History Review, 2020). These tactics can thus shore up problematic institutions that activists might be otherwise critical of, such as criminal justice systems (and the racialized and classed inequalities these systems are often bound up with).

Perhaps a more productive tactic can be found in other imagery used in activism, which works not through exposing the exception or foregrounding individual action, but by questioning *routine* components of contemporary food systems. Typical imagery used in these campaigns, for example, includes unwanted male chicks who are superfluous to egg production tumbling down conveyor belts like inanimate rocks (as incorporated into Franny Armstrong's documentary *McLibel*, 2005), distressed dairy cows being separated from calves (such as contemporary footage posted on YouTube from groups such as Mercy for Animals), or thirsty, disoriented pigs being transported to slaughterhouses (as with the Save Campaigns, see the following section).[4]

Rather than drawing attention to practices that fall outside of the norm, tactics that throw norms themselves into question are designed to reframe the routine as violent. This approach, I suggest, could potentially be an important site where attention to systems and overlapping forms of oppression are "held in view," in a manner that unpicks the rationalization and normalization of these systems: as pointed to by valuable scholarship such as Timothy Pachirat's visceral slaughterhouse ethnography *Every Twelve Seconds* (2011) or Kathryn Gillespie's

ethnographic research into the dairy industry in *The Cow with Ear Tag #1389*.
The potential to disrupt processes of routinization by reframing them as ethical
concerns can be illustrated on looking at an example of systemic critique in more
depth: footage taken by Craig Watts, a US farmer who appeared in *Eating Animals*
(dir. Quinn, 2017), a feature-length documentary based on Jonathan Safran Foer's
(2010) book of the same name.

Watts rose to prominence after allowing activists to film chickens in his own
barns to expose the conditions in which Perdue Farms Corporation forced him
to keep the animals. The argument central to the film version of *Eating Animals* is
that US agriculture now occurs on such a scale that individual farmers have little
control over animal husbandry on their own farms; birds, feed, and distribution
networks are all managed by large corporations, with the farmer receiving
chicks that their responsibility is to rear for only a few weeks before being sent
to slaughter. In the documentary itself Watts walks through dark, chicken-filled
sheds, pointing to birds who cannot stand or walk due to congenital conditions
and intensive breeding, in order to bring the consequences of this form of farming
to the fore. The uptake of Watts's footage saw it gain attention in the mainstream
media (e.g., Kristof, 2014; McKenna, 2015), as well as being utilized by activists
and civil society groups (Compassion in World Farming, 2015; Whistleblower
Lawyer Team, 2016), in addition to his story being a central thread in *Eating
Animals*. Crucially, these campaigns reveal scope for new alliances between
communities of farmers and activists who are normally framed as locked in battle
due to irreconcilable ideological differences.

Debates surrounding Watts's case, however, also highlight a number of
challenges that have to be navigated when considering the ethical and political
significance of tactics that centralize suffering as a shared concern between those
with otherwise different commitments. Critical disability studies scholar Sunaura
Taylor (2017) points out that—due to widespread, ablist assumptions about what
forms of life are worth living—a focus on suffering needs to be careful to avoid
falling into a similar trap to exposés: where the problem is attributed to individuals
rather than systems. As Taylor suggests, a focus on suffering caused by inbreeding
or injuries created by crowded living conditions can be co-opted in support of the
argument that it is *more* humane to kill individual animals suffering from these
problems, to avoid prolonging this suffering (2017: 38). This approach, she argues,
can thus reinforce long-standing prejudices about which sort of lives are worth
living. Indeed, Taylor's warnings seem apt when turning to industry responses
to Watts's footage. An investigative report on the case by Maryn McKenna (who
later wrote a popular book on contemporary chicken farming; McKenna, 2017)
gathered responses from an expert panel that attributed the problems Watts
identified in his own husbandry:

> Chicks with congenital or development defects, such as a twisted leg or a crossed-
> beak are expected given the fact that more than nine billion chicks are hatched
> annually in the U.S. Usually chicks with congenital defects are euthanized at
> the hatchery and never sent to the farms. Those that are missed or develop an

anomaly after placement at the farm are supposed to be humanely euthanized by the farmer. (In McKenna, 2015)

In addition, experts argued that a lack of movement on the part of the chickens was normal in light of the fact that they were genetically selected to maximize breast growth, thus were disinclined to move due to finding it too much of an exertion (McKenna, 2015). This rhetorical framing echoes Taylor's arguments: through the act of pathologizing the bodies of individual chickens, industry narratives could deflect responsibility away from routine agricultural practices and toward Watts. In order to contest this logic, Taylor argues, the commonplace activist tactic of emphasizing suffering is not sufficient and—in some instances—can contribute to broader pathologizing discourse about bodies that fall outside socially prescribed norms (2017: 42–3). Instead, Taylor explores an alternative option: extending a social model of disability to animals.

In the context of disability activism, a social model of disability has resulted in vital political change by shifting away from a medical model that "position[s] the disabled body as working incorrectly" (2017:13) toward the understanding that "disability is not caused by impairment, but the way society is organized" (13). What Taylor is pushing for, in other words, is to shift the focus from individuals to *systems* in order to ask how less-disabling ways of organizing social life could emerge. This drawing together of critical disability studies and animal studies is increasingly important in a context where activism and academic work (beyond but including animal studies and activism) have been criticized for centralizing notions of visibility, holding in view, and other ocular metaphors that can themselves inscribe ablist assumptions (Becerril, 2018).

Reading Taylor's arguments against the Watts case also points toward an additional aspect of hidden filming that is politically and conceptually significant, which relates less to the footage itself and more how it is received and debated. What is notable about whistleblowing cases is that they do not just highlight the conditions of animals, but expose the *mechanisms* through which violence is transformed into nonviolence through virtue of being treated as routine. It is such transformations that Dinesh Wadiwel dissects in *The War Against Animals* (2015), where he employs a biopolitical framework to make sense not just of animal death but the intricate processes through which animal life is regulated in order to optimize its value.

As responses to Watts's footage illustrate, unlike more overt abuses, the ethical significance of routine practices is often interpreted in radically different ways by those with contrasting political commitments. As Wadiwel emphasizes, routinized practices within the biopolitical management of animal populations (such as de-horning as touched on earlier, or, to use his own examples in the context of chicken slaughter, live hanging, electrified water baths, and defeathering tanks; 2015: 1–2) are often not depicted *as* violent and seen as standard from an industry perspective, or even necessary in ensuring the health of the population as a whole. This clash between what is seen as violent from an activist perspective and standard from an industry perspective has been a persistent obstacle to activist narratives

from the birth of the contemporary animal rights movement. These dynamics
have often proven detrimental to activists because, when industry definitions act
as dominant frames within the mainstream media, activist perspectives are by
extension framed as falling outside the norm and portrayed as overly sentimental
(Giraud, 2019: 98–117). What Wadiwel points out is that this marginalization of
activist perspectives is not just reinforced through normative *discourses* about
human-animal relations, but also commonplace industry *practices*, pointing to
two specific processes that he argues are central to transforming violence into
nonviolence.

First, Wadiwel argues that contemporary human-animal relations deploy a
range of violent processes to regulate animal life. Integral to these processes is
the incorporation of resistance on the part of animals, as the efficient large-scale
manufacture of animal products relies on recognizing moments of resistance
(such as bodies moving, thrashing, and generally not behaving in ways that
allow them to be easily processed by humans and machinery) and re-shaping
systems in response to this agency. Resistance is thus constantly acknowledged
in order to "find ways to make the slaughter of animals smoother, more efficient
and less 'fricative'" (2015: 13). This reduction of friction through creating new
technological systems and techniques to manage animals gives rise to the second
stage of the process of transformation Wadiwel describes: its *epistemic* dimension,
or how the routine treatment of animals informs and perpetuates specific cultural
understandings of animals.

The smooth, systematic nature of practices that occur in sites such as
slaughterhouses, large-scale dairy and battery hen farms, or indeed in non-food
sites such as fur farming, do not just make the manufacture of animal products
easier, Wadiwel argues, but normalizes assumptions about animals as "lower
beings," to the point that actions that would be interpreted as "violent" in other
contexts (if they were used against animals such as pets who are subject to different
cultural classifications) are not interpreted as such. For Wadiwel this process of
transformation is politically significant, because "If violence can be smoothed in
such a way that it does not appear as violence then the process of converting an
animate sentient into a 'thing' is complete, and resistance and war become hidden
under a veneer of peaceability" (Wadiwel, 2015: 13).

As these arguments illustrate, from a vegan studies perspective it is thus not just
a matter of *exposing* routine practices of animal agriculture but *reframing* practices
that are routinely seen as peaceable, yet this is not always a straightforward task. By
re-articulating routine practices as part of a wider war against nonhuman animals,
Wadiwel is making a deliberate provocation that counters industry narratives.
Due to anthropocentric assumptions associated with conceptions of violence, and
war in particular, however, his work has to dedicate substantial time to working
through the complexities that allow the concept of warfare to be applied to animals.
In activist contexts, such a reframing is arguably even more of a challenge not just
due to its sheer complexity, but because of the criminalization of tactics such as
hidden filming that seek to document routine practices (as with famous examples
such as "ag-gag" laws in the United States; Adams, 2018: 16). As discussed in more

depth in the next chapters, awareness campaigns by large NGOs have proven particularly poor at articulating the treatment of nonhuman animals as violent in context-specific, sensitive ways, often relying instead on crude comparisons between human and nonhuman animal suffering that reinforce rather than contest other oppressions (Deckha, 2008b; Kim, 2011; Harper, 2010b; Ko, 2017a).

In addition to practical, legal challenges for activism that focuses on visibility, what is highlighted in these discussions of exposés, hidden filming, and whistleblowing is that visibility politics is far from straightforward. As Emilia Quinn puts it, bound up with an emphasis on visibility is the sense that making animals visible can give rise to social transformation, as "typified by the popular maxim that 'If slaughterhouses had glass walls, everyone would be a vegetarian'" (Quinn, 2020: 915). Alongside this assumption that change accompanies visibility is a positioning of "veganism [as] an awakening to, and recovery of, hidden knowledge," while "meat-eating is posited . . . as an acquiescence to a speciesist culture reliant on the concealment and obfuscation of reality to sustain itself" (Quinn, 2020: 915). As touched on earlier, however, and as Quinn asserts, it is important to avoid the assumption that revealing something that is assumed to be hidden will necessarily instigate change.

Although veganism has achieved growing prominence in popular culture, this has gone hand in hand with a rearticulated carnism where animals are increasingly made visible through a "happy meat" discourse (Gillespie, 2011; Stanescu, 2014). Indeed, even the rise of veganism itself has come alongside a normalization and intensification of meat consumption, with the United Nations predicting global meat production to increase by 19 percent by 2030 (FAO, 2018: 14). Tobias Linné's (2016) analysis of dairy marketing also foregrounds how visibility is often used strategically in the marketing of animal products, with particular aspects of farming highlighted (such as animals wandering around in green fields) while others are hidden (calves being removed from mothers, the industrialized dimensions of agriculture).

These developments in the wider media landscape point to some of the complexities associated with visibility politics, as activists have to work within, and against, an existing media environment that challenges or undermines their tactics by offering competing representations of animals (see Parkinson, 2019, discussed further in Chapter 5). The difficulty, in other words, is reframing what are socially treated as nonviolent practices—due to happening to other species—as violent, in ways that not only cut against standard industry practices but media discourse. As discussed in the next chapter, what is often seen as integral to this task is unsettling categories such as "livestock" themselves, in order to include animals within the ethical community, but this tactic is insufficient without also unsettling the infrastructures that perpetuate these categorizations. Before moving onto more fundamental debates about infrastructural change, here I turn to activist groups who have approached this task of ethical inclusion in a very specific way: reframing animals as subjects whose deaths are worth mourning, rather than livestock that can be routinely slaughtered. These tactics could again be seen as a form of visibility politics, but this time as exposing norms rather than suffering to scrutiny.

Exposing Norms

A recent development that has attracted attention within both the vegan community and vegan scholarship is the Save Movement. Originating in 2010 in Toronto, Canada, Save has since grown to over 500 autonomous chapters worldwide (Lockwood, 2018: 107). The central activity undertaken by the movement are vigils held outside slaughterhouses, where activists gather to commemorate the deaths of animals; an approach that has attracted substantial media attention and controversy (e.g., McMahon, 2019). Save, therefore, are a movement who actively work to disrupt the sorts of biopolitical logics identified by Wadiwel; in explicitly framing animals as ethical subjects, slaughterhouse processes cannot be "smoothed" over as "peaceable" relations. As I argue in this section, however, the way Save achieve this disruption generates additional complications that relate to the broader social implications of reframing standard industry practices as violent.

Scholar-activist Alex Lockwood has written extensively about Save (e.g., Lockwood, 2016b, 2018, 2019a, 2021) and highlights four key characteristics of the movement. First, their focus on "collective witnessing," second, the attempt by activists to offer temporary solace to animals wherever possible (e.g., through offering fruit and water), third, the way the protests work to make the spaces where animals are slaughtered visible, and, finally, the creation and dissemination of written testimony and visual recordings of the events (2018: 109). Through these actions, he argues, Save "mak[e] visible . . . already exiting embodied entanglements with farmed nonhuman animals, suggesting a form of 'active witnessing' that offers opportunities for radically reimagined relationships with those species we identify as food" (2018: 107).

Lockwood offers rich accounts of the emotional experience of the protests, as these events do not only involve bearing witness to suffering but are punctuated by affective encounters with the animals themselves. At a particular pig save, for instance, he describes a moment when "the animals shuffle over, take water and watermelon, and sniff our fingers with the snouts they push through the air vents" (2018: 111). Through these activities, activists not only work to include animals as ethical subjects who are worthy of mourning but, Lockwood suggests, are able to foster a felt sense of responsibility toward animals that go beyond abstract sympathy toward a sense of *feeling* part of the same ethical community (a theme developed in further depth in Chapter 5).

As well as constructing a more expansive ethical community, the vigils also work to actively combat the spatial arrangements discussed in the previous section wherein the slaughter of animals has systematically been removed from public space and made physically inaccessible to the public. Protestors, for instance, frequently use banners to label vigil sites as slaughterhouses—combatting their invisibility— or create art-work that dramatizes and commemorates animals, thus preventing their deaths from being treated as routine (Lockwood, 2021). This physical act of intervening in the spatial arrangements that separate humans from animals is significant in light of Wadiwel's arguments that the inclusion or exclusion of actors within a particular ethical community is not just created through the sorts of classifications pointed to by Joy, but material arrangements and practices that are entangled with categorization (or *dispositifs* to use Foucauldian terminology; see also Wolfe, 2012).

Though much of the analytic focus has been on the experience of participating in Save protests, awareness-raising is also an important component of the movement; indeed, some of the imagery generated by the vigils can be read in line with Kevin DeLuca's concept of "image events" (1999): a term he uses to describe moments when activists place their own bodies in vulnerable positions to (metonymically) draw attention to the vulnerability of the environment. A particularly prominent incident at a Save Vigil in Toronto, for instance, saw founder Anita Krajnc facing prosecution for offering thirsty pigs drinking water (Kassam, 2017; see Krajnc, 2016 for further discussion). Although she was eventually found not guilty, this incident blurred the boundary between commemoration and awareness-raising, because it transformed Krajnc's initial ethical act of relieving suffering into an image that was circulated more widely: articulating the sense of shared vulnerability between human and animal bodies, and attendant ethical inclusion of animals, beyond the immediate activist context.

Further questions need to be asked, however, about the relationship between the vegan ethics enacted by Save and other pressing social justice issues that are entangled with intensive animal farming. Animal agriculture is not only a site where animal death is smoothed over but where it intersects with a number of other social inequalities (including labor and environmental concerns, as brought to the fore in Watts's case). In contexts such as the United Kingdom and the United States where farm labor is also classed and racialized, the problem of how to include nonhuman animals in the ethical community without inadvertently excluding marginalized humans is critically important.

It is notable that the need to negotiate this problem was *not* ignored by protestors. Lockwood describes instances of activists working to combat these divisions, as when activists shared food with one another to foster solidarity during the protests and invited farm laborers to participate. These attempts, unfortunately, were often unsuccessful and it is important to reflect on possible reasons for these barriers to food-sharing. Despite embedding tactics designed to foster solidarity with workers, protests such as Save, that challenge the categorization of animals as livestock, mark a clash of two competing—and perhaps irreconcilable—versions of reality, which correspond to different ways of categorizing, cutting up, and understanding the world. The act of situating animals as subjects worthy of mourning, and reframing their treatment as violent, necessarily renders those who work with the animals as perpetrators of this violence in a manner that puts them at odds with activists. Finding ways to unpack tensions that stem from what is, or indeed is not, seen as violent in particular social contexts is thus a task that is both difficult to realize but necessary to confront moving forward.

Other initiatives written about and engaged with by Lockwood have grappled with similar problems. The years 2018–19 have often been seen as the era of the New Climate Movements, with the rise of initiatives such as #FridaysforFuture (the global network of school strikes, initiated by Swedish teenager Greta Thunberg) and the Extinction Rebellion protests. Though treated broadly positively in the mainstream media, Extinction Rebellion (XR) has also been subject to staunch critique, due to a number of factors. Issues have ranged from the problematic role of its founder, its use of arrest as a disruptive tactic (which ignore issues of racialized privilege), accusations of imposing totalizing, neocolonial narratives of environmental activism, and its preoccupation with *human* extinction (Doherty, de Moor and Hayes, 2018; Hayes and Doherty, 2019; Slaven and Heydon, 2020). In 2019 Animal Rebellion was instigated in response to a further problem associated with the anthropocentrism of much contemporary environmentalism— particularly the lack of discussion about animal agriculture's contribution to climate change that persisted within Extinction Rebellion—but the sister movement also sought to learn from the other critiques that had been leveled at the wider XR movement, as well as criticisms leveled at animal activism more broadly.

A key tactic undertaken by Animal Rebellion was occupying Smithfield: the largest and most prominent meat market in the UK. Rather than simply blockading the market, however, activists spoke with stall-owners beforehand and made clear they would not disrupt business, leading to positive headlines, such as "Traders Welcome Vegan Activists Occupying Smithfield Market," even in the conservative British press (Ball, 2019). Though the occupation was initially met with some hostility, over the course of the protests a greater degree of solidarity was eventually developed with farmers: some of whom voiced agreement with protestors' aims and one of whom even went on to sell plant-based food, the first time this had ever occurred in this site (Lockwood, 2019b). Working as a media spokesperson, Lockwood was clear in articulating that the problem pointed to by activists was structural and required institutional change, stating for instance that "The meat industry is on its knees, but there are still no subsidies to help farmers who want to transition to a plant-based food system," "we're not at Smithfield to disrupt ordinary people from their work," and "we're here to send a message to the Government: this industry at the heart of the climate emergency has to be helped transition to a plant-based food system, with just processes in place to ensure workers can still feed their families, while properly tackling the climate catastrophe" (in Francis, 2019).

The choice to occupy the market and focus on constructing a media narrative that highlighted enmeshed oppressions, rather than blockading the site and encouraging members to draw attention to climate change by getting arrested, also meant the group ameliorated some of the classed and racialized inequalities surrounding who was able to participate in Extinction Rebellion. This is not to say, again, that the movement should be treated uncritically; the wider XR movement remains the focus of heated debate, while the tactics engaged in by Animal Rebellion themselves have been heavily debated, even within the vegan community (Lockwood, 2019c). At the same time, it is important to reflect on the insights that can be gained from activism which draws together environmental and animal ethics concerns, particularly movements that have attempted to create solidarities across difference and reflexively modify their own practice in light of criticisms.

As both Save and Animal Rebellion illustrate, despite potentials in these forms of activism, sometimes reasserting the subjectivity of animals and temporarily disrupting existing infrastructures might not be enough to instigate lasting change. Instead, it is vital to create new political solidarities and alternative media frames that challenge the idea that human and animal rights are at odds. Though this assertion has been central to activist aspirations (such as the well-known animal activist slogan "one struggle, one fight, human freedom, animal rights"), developing initiatives that negotiate these relationships in meaningful ways has proven difficult in practice. The rest of the chapter turns to activism that has moved toward this task, by pushing for a wholesale transformation of systems that support structural inequalities and creating alternative infrastructures that prefigure desired multispecies futures.

Enacting Alternatives

A particularly informative campaign that sought to tie animal rights, labor, and environmental politics together was the International Campaign of Action Against McDonald's, which was at its peak in the 1990s but remains an important precursor to more contemporary activism. The campaign emerged after McDonald's took advantage of repressive UK libel laws in 1990, issuing libel writs to a small group of activists who had published a five-page "Fact Sheet" critical of the corporation, which was distributed outside London branches of the store during the 1980s (Vidal, 1997).

At the time, libel laws in the UK placed the burden entirely on defendants. Those accused of libel were, first, denied legal aid and, second, had to prove everything they were claiming was correct, while those suing did not have to provide evidence that this information was incorrect (Nicholson, 2000). The complexity of McDonald's as an organization, coupled with the resources it was able to spend on legal costs, meant that, prior to the case, in the UK a large number of media organizations who had raised criticisms of the corporation had been forced to issue public apologies for fear of being sued. McDonald's took a similar tactic with the activists, initially asking five of them to publicly apologize or be sued (including an activist who was since discovered to be an undercover policeman, or "spycop," see Stephens Griffin, 2020). However, two of the activists refused to say sorry, in an act that resulted in the longest trial in British legal history (as dramatized in Armstrong's *McLibel*, 2005). The trial's length and its depiction as a "David and Goliath" battle between activists and the corporation (Downey and Fenton, 2003: 196) drew huge levels of mainstream media attention and is generally seen as a public relations disaster for McDonald's due to creating a high-profile platform for activists' critique (Hilson, 2016).

The campaign eventually became a transnational initiative, oriented around the McSpotlight website that was established in 1997—before McDonald's launched their own site—and included mirror sites in different countries (to avoid censorship), a web-forum, and an overview of problems caused by McDonald's in a range of national contexts (see Pickerill, 2003). Although McSpotlight served as a hub for this information, it also encouraged de-centralized protest by containing anti-McDonald's pamphlets translated into a range of languages and instructions on how people could "adopt" their own McDonald's to picket (Giraud, 2019: 21–45). The McLibel case is striking in itself, but from a vegan studies perspective the trial and attendant support campaigns are significant due to being a high-profile example of how vegan politics could be connected to other social and political issues. In the original anti-McDonald's campaigns animal welfare issues were linked to environmental concerns such as waste and deforestation, as well as human rights issues such as the forced removal of Indigenous communities from agricultural land, outsourcing of labor in the production of happy meal toys, and problematic employment practices within McDonald's branches (Vidal, 1997). Although the activists did not win the trial overall, they caused huge embarrassment to McDonald's, which meant the corporation never collected the £40,000 they were eventually awarded after spending 10 million pounds in legal expenses.

In addition, activist claims were judged to be accurate in crucial aspects of the trial, such as animal welfare. As analyses of the legal implications of McLibel have argued, various problems with existing welfare legislation were highlighted, which revealed that the industry was effectively setting its own standards, because in the current legal system "any practice in accordance with common modern farming or slaughter practices [was] acceptable to the law, even if it [was] cruel" (Wolfson, 1999: 20). The judge, however, ruled that just because a practice is normative does not mean it is ethically acceptable, pointing out that economic drivers make it untenable for the industry to self-regulate (Giraud, 2019: 35). Significantly, the final verdict emphasized corporate responsibility for setting agricultural norms, with the judge ruling that, as the largest purchasers of beef in the world, McDonald's were actively responsible for the conditions of animals slaughtered for their products.

Akin to debates surrounding Watts's footage, therefore, the trial underlined the specific role of corporations in establishing the norms that regulate animal treatment, in order to push for systemic change. What was distinctive about McLibel, however, was that it drew attention to the way that particular human populations were *also* a target of behavioral intervention. For instance, a crucial aspect of the trial was demonstrating not just that McDonald's paid their workforce "low wages" but had "depressed wages in the catering industry as a whole" (Vidal, 1997: 312). A key way McDonald's accomplished this was through translating Fordist principles of the factory assembly line—wherein each worker is responsible for a specific task in order to produce cars as cheaply and easily as possible (a system itself derived from slaughterhouse organization, see Shukin, 2009)—to the restaurant. These practices aimed to create a workforce that could be easily managed, to both enable the smooth running of the restaurant and ensure that specialized skills were not required, thus allowing expenditure on staff to be kept to a minimum. As revealed during the trial, just as the food industry justified commonplace agricultural practices by arguing they were normative—without taking responsibility for setting these norms and while deflecting questions about whether they were ethical—similar logic was at play in discussions of workers' rights. For instance, McDonald's justified staff wages on the basis that it was unskilled labor, without acknowledging that kitchens had been deliberately designed to minimize skill levels involved in food production (Giraud, 2019: 34). Labor, moreover, was just one issue that was addressed during the trial, which also sought to situate animal ethics within a broader critique of the social and ecological consequences of globalized capitalism, as symbolized by McDonald's.

Its attempts to connect different issues to enact a critique of corporate power meant that McLibel was not just significant in itself, but an important precursor to anti-capitalist activism that gathered force throughout the 1990s and 2000s and in which veganism continued to play a role: not just as something promoted but enacted. Anti-capitalism is a complicated label (Chatterton, 2010: 1205–6), which is often applied in a range of different ways in reference to everything from anarchism to more formal left-leaning political parties who have a socialist emphasis. As with my previous work, here I use the term in reference to nonhierarchical, leaderless, groups of activists who seek to craft grassroots spaces and lifestyle practices that are alternatives to capitalism (Giraud, 2018: 130; see also Pickerill and Chatterton, 2006). One of the hallmarks of these movements is that they often engage in prefigurative politics on a collective level, developing practices and infrastructures that prefigure desired anti-capitalist ways of living (Brown and Pickerill, 2009; Maeckelbergh, 2011).

Informative examples of how tensions in prefigurative politics are negotiated can be found in sites such as protest camps (Feigenbaum, Frenzel and McCurdy, 2013; Brown et al., 2017). One such example is the construction of Horizone, a protest camp developed in response to the 2005 G8 Summit, which was held at the Gleneagles resort in Scotland. The term "G8" refers to the "group of 8" (Canada, France, Germany, Italy, Japan, Russia, the United Kingdom, and the United States) who were gathering to discuss transnational trade agreements. From 1999 (where the World Trade Organization's meeting in Seattle had been subject to large-scale protests, known as the Battle of Seattle) the G8, and similar summits, had been the target of protest (Juris, 2007). As a result, these institutions had moved to increasingly isolated locations to make them difficult for protestors to access; protest camps such as Horizone offered a solution to this problem (Harvie et al., 2005). Horizone was a temporary eco-village, which not only served as a convergence site for activists but a place where alternative forms of social organization were experimented with. In a very practical sense, a number of infrastructures had to be created to support those attending the camp: ranging from media (Feigenbaum Frenzel and McCurdy, 2013: 69–112) to sewerage systems (Starhawk, 2005). These infrastructures were not just designed to get the job done, but to show how anti-capitalist principles such as nonhierarchy and sustainability could be embedded into everyday life.

Similar principles were true of food provision; activist narratives about the camp, for instance, describe the painstaking way that activists tried to craft connections with the local context (Anarchist Teapot, ND; Morganmuffel, 2005).

Although the decision was made for all food to be vegan, this in itself was not seen as offering "moral solace" (in the manner that some theoretical critiques of veganism have suggested, see Chapter 3). Instead, effort was made to enact a vegan praxis that embodied other nonhierarchical and environmental principles (Giraud, 2019: 86–9). Rather than using their normal suppliers, UK-based caterers sought to build relationships with local farmers and food outlets to source organic vegetables and staples such as bread and flour. Organizational hierarchies were perhaps more difficult to negotiate, as particular activist groups owned equipment or had substantial catering experience and familiarity with UK catering legislation (such as well-known vegan campaign caterers Veggies and the Anarchist Teapot), while others—often collectives coming from other countries—lacked these resources.[5] However, through tactics such as skill- and equipment sharing, and by working to ensure other groups had access to resources they needed, the UK-based caterers sought to ensure that catering was as de-centralized as possible. As other accounts of creating Horizone's infrastructures suggest, moreover, caterers also worked with other activists to ensure that waste was disposed of in a sustainable manner (Starhawk, 2005). Overall, therefore, even though the process was not easy, there was a concerted effort to enact food provision in a way that connected eating with a range of environmental and labor issues as well as animal ethics.

The sense that connections between vegan politics and other social issues need to be crafted has been concretized by other long-standing social movements. From the 1980s, for example, Food Not Bombs (a group originating in the United States but since establishing chapters worldwide) have gathered food that was destined to be thrown away and collectively prepared vegan and vegetarian meals to share in city centers (Heynen, 2010; Sbicca, 2013). Often food giveaways have been established to deliberately challenge policies such as no-loitering laws designed to exclude homeless people from public space (Mitchell and Heynen, 2009) and "contest the way contemporary public spaces promote uninterrupted modes of consumption and circulation" (Spataro, 2016: 193). In Food Not Bombs protests while vegan and vegetarian ethics is taken as a benchmark, the movement simultaneously works to feed hungry people and draw attention to food waste, inequality, and the corporatization of public space (Winter, 2015).

As I have discussed in previous work focused on food giveaways (Giraud, 2013a, 2015, 2018, 2019: 89–97), the very public nature of food distribution (in the context of both Food Not Bombs and other vegan campaigning) creates space for members of the public to discuss, debate, and sometimes challenge activist values. Vegan food giveaways, for instance, were incorporated into anti-McDonald's protests in the UK in the late 2010s, with vegan burgers cooked and distributed for free outside of the chain in order to offer a performative counterpoint to the restaurant itself (see Giraud, 2015, 2018). In comparison with regular pickets of McDonald's in the wake of the McLibel trial (which had tended to focus more on the distribution of pamphlets that were often discarded by members of the public), food-sharing created space for debate, dialogue, and even contestation.

Finding ways to ensure vegan politics is enacted in nonhierarchical ways, however, is not straightforward and research about these movements indicates a range of barriers (often social and economic) that prevent these ideals from being realized. Research about Food Not Bombs, for instance, foregrounds how food-sharing can, in certain political contexts, reinforce barriers between activists and hungry people who need food (e.g., Sbicca, 2013). In US cities where food-sharing was criminalized, moreover, those whose social standing meant they were less vulnerable if they were arrested were happy to face legal action while others were forced to drop out. Activists also have to negotiate the danger of co-opting hungry people into a spectacle: where food is shared to make a political point that interpellates those who need it. Parallel concerns emerged in the context of food giveaways used in UK anti-McDonald's protests, where various initiatives were again developed to negotiate hierarchies between activists and members of the public (such as inviting people to be involved in the action by taking part in cookery skill-shares and taking part in producing food for the giveaways), but these had varying degrees of success (see Giraud, 2015 and 2019: 89–95).

Despite all of these tensions, both protest camps and food giveaways share certain attributes that help to complicate narratives of veganism as a single-issue cause or rigid moral imperative, by instead showing the role vegan ethics can play in prefiguring alternative worlds (cf Giles, 2018). First, these initiatives work not only to highlight but also to *enact* the relationship between vegan politics and other social issues. Food giveaways and protest camps both disrupt existing patterns of consumption and prefigure alternative infrastructures to support new norms. What is also important, second, is that these forms of activism involve constant experimentation to ensure that new consumption norms are not rigid, but responsive to context. In food giveaways and protest camps, veganism in itself is not treated as sufficient, instead constant experimentation with new ways of organizing are engaged with to ensure that food is sourced, produced, and distributed in ways that are responsive to the local environment and political setting. Third, the way vegan politics is materialized in these examples creates space for activist norms and assumptions to be contested, by enacting them in public and highly visible ways.

This ideal of connecting vegan politics to other social justice issues, of course, is not always realized in practice. Although activist histories offer rich insight into the challenges of recognizing and responding to enmeshed oppressions, even in these contexts experiments with nonhierarchical vegan politics are not always successful. As long-standing debates about the persistence of informal hierarchies in activism suggest, however, similar tensions persist in a diverse range of activist groups (Freeman, 1984; Nunes, 2005). While it is important to reflect on the problem of hierarchies within vegan activism, therefore, singling it out as *especially* problematic is potentially misleading as such problems need to be situated as part of a wider range of issues that "nonhierarchical" activist groups need to confront. In addition, while internal commentaries and critiques of veganism from within activist communities might point to tensions in vegan politics, they also demonstrate that veganism does not function as a universalizing norm even in activist contexts where it is regularly practiced. Instead, vegan politics is routinely reevaluated, contested, and renegotiated.

Conclusion

The tactics I have focused on throughout this chapter show how prominent forms of vegan activism have striven to be more than a diet or identity marker, and indeed more than an intervention in consumption practices, by instead offering a challenge to the systems that normalize contemporary human-animal relations and render them "peaceable" (to use Wadiwel's terminology). To conclude I will reiterate two major concerns that emerge when turning to activist practice.

First; at a moment when veganism is gaining increased social prominence it is important to ask serious questions about what can be learned from specific social movement histories, in terms of the pitfalls and problems created by particular tactics, as well as their potentials. To echo concerns raised at the end of the previous chapter, further questions need to be asked in the present moment about whether the reflexive, experimental modes of politics that characterize (some of) the instances of activism I have discussed here are being undermined by the rise of veganism's popularity. In particular, the identification of vegans themselves as a market who can be co-opted has transformed the landscape vegan politics that operates within. Can acts such as distributing vegan food outside fast-food restaurants remain counter-hegemonic if vegan food is also being served *within* these sites, for instance? Or, if plant-based eating is seen as an end in itself, does this undermine scope to create connections with other issues and foreclose more expansive conceptions of veganism?

The second significant concern is that, just as it is important for vegan activism to learn from movement histories, this is also important for *Vegan Studies*. In my previous work I have argued that learning from activist histories—and the tensions and challenges associated with particular tactics—is not just politically but conceptually informative. For instance, the tactics described here have included visibility politics that seeks to expose animal suffering and the contestation of structures that perpetuate animals being treated as resources, as well as grassroots activism that highlights connections between human and animal oppression and, in some instances, crafts alternative, less oppressive, infrastructures. Developing an understanding of the challenges and struggles of implementing these approaches in practice is significant not just in practical terms. As the title of this chapter suggests, a better grasp of tensions associated with some of the tactics I have discussed here is also valuable in complicating academic research that has made similar claims to activists about the power of visibility, connection-making, and acts of disrupting classifications, in creating less anthropocentric ways of inhabiting the world.

Chapter 5

ANIMAL SUBJECTIVITY AND ANTHROPOMORPHISM

As hinted at in the previous chapter, one of the most notable aspects of vegan activism has not historically been food or dietary politics per se, but, rather, veganism's more far-reaching attempts to trouble classifications and practices that depict animals as "lower beings" who can be used for the benefit of particular groups of humans. This chapter provides a more in-depth exploration of tensions that can surround attempts to extend a sense of ethical community beyond the human, turning to campaigns that aspire to unsettle the classification of animals into categories such as "livestock" or "pets."

The bulk of the chapter contrasts three case studies: vegan poster campaigns that draw comparisons between human and animal suffering, virtual reality videos that encourage a more embodied and empathic identification with industrially farmed animals, and sanctuaries that aim to foster alternative—and less exploitative—multispecies communities. Each case illustrates some of the challenges, as well as the potentials, that come with framing animals not as objects but subjects with their own needs, desires, and agency. Before turning to these examples themselves, though, it is useful to contextualize all three cases in relation to a wider set of criticisms that have been leveled at cultural and philosophical frameworks which have historically treated humans as "exceptional" and deserving of special privileges over other beings.

Rethinking Human Exceptionalism

Both vegan campaigns themselves and scholarship in fields such as Vegan Studies (as well as animal studies and the environmental humanities more broadly) have sought to unsettle distinctions between humans and other animals, in order to craft less anthropocentric ways of understanding the world. To give an everyday example of attempts to disrupt human exceptionalism: use of the term "nonhuman animals" is a deliberately political gesture. This label is employed frequently by activists and critical scholars, serving as a reminder that humans *are* animals and part of "nature." The term "nonhuman animals," therefore, works to contest the logic that portrays homo sapiens as exceptional and holding dominion over the so-called natural world.

Uses of language such as "nonhuman animals" is just one of a myriad of activist and academic attempts to extend ethical responsibility beyond the human by unsettling the notion that humans should have special privileges. As the previous chapter illustrated, the tactic of rendering-visible relationships between humans and nonhuman animals, that seem violent from a vegan perspective, might not have the desired transformative effect if this tactic is undercut by notions of animals as lesser beings for whom different social norms apply. Often exceptionalist logic functions implicitly, simply meaning that particular uses of animals are treated as natural and beyond question (as with Chapter 4's discussion of norms surrounding animal agriculture). At other times, the exceptional status of humans is appealed to explicitly as a means of defending particular uses of animals. Notions of a great chain of being—where humans are at the top—for instance, are regularly drawn upon to naturalize uses of animals for human benefit (for critical analyses of the philosophical lineage of this logic, see Tyler, 2003, 2006, 2012; Wolfe, 2003, 2010; Calarco, 2008; Khandker, 2014, 2020; Jackson, 2016, 2020). In the context of campaigning work, however, questions about *how* to unsettle human exceptionalism have opened up some heated debates and two problems in particular complicate attempts to extend ethical obligations beyond the human.

The first problem relates to the concept of human exceptionalism itself. This concept and notions of speciesism, more broadly, have sometimes caused friction between animal liberation and social justice activism that contest the marginalization of particular groups of people, such as anti-racist and feminist movements. As Aph Ko (2019: 19–38) describes, tensions between different forms of activism exist, in part, due to insensitive campaigns by groups such as PETA (who are often erroneously conflated with veganism writ large), where crass comparisons have been made, for instance, between factory farming and slavery (see also Harper, 2010b; Kim, 2011). In addition, Ko and other thinkers delineate more fundamental problems with notions of human exceptionalism or, at least, how this concept is commonly engaged with in the context of activism.

The problem with assuming that humans are "exceptional," and that this exceptionalism lies at the root of the oppression of other species, is that it is not just animals who have historically been positioned on the lower rungs of a great chain of being (Jackson, 2016). The relationship between processes of racialization and animalization (Kim, 2015), or connections between the devaluation of nature and patriarchal social relations (Adams, 2000; Wright, 2015), has meant that particular people have also historically been—and continue to be—excluded from access to certain political and social rights (see also Chapters 2 and 6). Syl Ko (2017) foregrounds, therefore, that if concepts of human exceptionalism are not used carefully, in a manner that acknowledges more complex relationships between human and animal oppression, this can erroneously infer that human lives are always consistently placed above animals. Indeed, one of the major points of tension between anti-racist and animal activism has stemmed from the level of public outcry related to the deaths of specific animals—such as Cecil, the lion whose killing by a trophy hunter in 2015 caused an outcry—who are perceived to receive *more* media attention than routine acts of police violence or structural discrimination toward people of color (Ko, 2019: 23).

The attention afforded to animals such as Cecil intersects with a second problem associated with activism that seeks to challenge human exceptionalism: campaigns that make overly simplistic comparisons between human and animal lives. One of the key tactics for extending ethical value beyond the human has been to understand animals not as entities that can be objectified, but as subjects who have their own agency: a tactic often achieved through emphasizing affinities between humans and animals (e.g., Castricano, 2008; Weil, 2012). In this regard, the role of anthropomorphism—or the attribution of human characteristics to animals—has held an especially uneasy position (Serpell, 2003).

Attempts to engage with questions of animal subjectivity by emphasizing affinities with humans (be this through a shared capacity to suffer or to experience joy) have often been criticized for relying on anthropomorphic imagery that centers on particularly "charismatic" animals (Lorimer, 2007, 2015). Such approaches might seek to extend ethical responsibility beyond the human but are argued to do so by imposing notions of rights onto animals, often valuing creatures who possess qualities that resemble human(ist) understandings of subjectivity (such as sentience or the capacity to suffer). The use of anthropomorphic imagery, from this perspective, is self-defeating and even shores up hierarchies between species by extending rights to "certain privileged others" (Lorimer, 2013: 12), that is, animals humans can easily identify with, while neglecting less-charismatic species as well as other forms of nonhuman life. Anthropomorphism, it is argued, often reinforces *anthropocentric* ways of seeing the world and perpetuates the very hierarchies between humans and nonhuman animals that vegan politics is trying to contest.

As Parkinson (2019) points out, however, the politics of anthropomorphism is far messier in practice than commonplace criticisms give credit. Although in certain contexts anthropomorphism can reinforce hierarchies between species, in other contexts it can create political and ethical opportunities to *challenge* these hierarchies. It is thus important, Parkinson argues, to move beyond simply seeing anthropomorphism as a bad thing and instead reflect on the more subversive work that it can accomplish in specific settings.

One such context is Sea World or, more specifically, critical media texts about the theme parks, such as the film *Black Fish* (dir. Cowperthwaite, 2013) that documents controversies surrounding Tilikum, a killer whale who became infamous after the death of a trainer. What is striking about Sea World's case, Parkinson argues, is that it reveals the ambivalence of anthropocentrism. Yes, theme parks such as Sea World anthropomorphized whales and, yes, these processes of anthropomorphism were integral to generating profits and perpetuated exploitative socioeconomic relationships. But, at the same time, anthropomorphism also facilitated conditions for political change: creating a level of emotional and ethical investment in whales by different publics, which led to a barrage of criticism over keeping orca in captivity and eventually triggered a radical overhaul of legislative frameworks. Sea World's emphasis on the intelligence and charisma of whales, in other words, is what ultimately led to a broader rethinking of the relationship between humans and marine life.

Parkinson's recognition of the productive ambivalence of anthropomorphism speaks to longer activist histories wherein the act of emphasizing similarities between humans and animals has both been valuable in contesting particular uses of animals for human benefit and served as a site where academic work and political practice have historically intersected. Peter Singer's *Animal Liberation* (2015 [1975]), for example, centralized questions of animal suffering as the basis for fostering human responsibility toward animals and challenged the idea that sentience was a purely human quality. It is important to note that his core argument—that what matters is animals' ability to suffer—has since been heavily contested, both on the part of those seeking to move beyond animal liberationist frameworks (e.g., Haraway, 2008) and those who aim to further normative animal ethics (e.g., Taylor, 2017 and ecofeminist work; see Chapters 2 and 4 for a more in-depth explanation). At the same time, Singer has been an undeniable influence upon animal activist movements, offering a framework that justifies activists' attempts to expand the ethical community beyond the human in his emphasis on a shared capacity to suffer that transcends species boundaries. Whether movements have engaged explicitly with Singer or not, the legacy of his emphasis on suffering has pervaded vegan campaigns; as discussed in the previous chapter the tactic of depicting animals in pain and distress is frequently used within vegan activism, in contexts ranging from poster campaigns by large NGOs such as PETA or Viva to high-profile awareness raising films including *Earthlings* (dir. Monson, 1995) and *Cowspiracy* (dir. Anderson and Kuhn, 2014).

Yet suffering is not the only tactic that activists use to engender a sense of affinity with nonhuman animals. Other appeals to animal subjectivity—including depictions of animals experiencing emotions commonly thought of as uniquely human, such as joy, curiosity, and affection—are routinely foregrounded in vegan campaigning work. As discussed in more depth later, appeals to charismatic animals are also often employed to raise funds for sanctuaries that home ex-farm animals, as with the high-profile *Peaceable Kingdom* films (2004 and 2009, dir. Stein) or the social media accounts of grassroots animal rescue centers.[1] While such tactics are often critically read as anthropomorphism, a number of scholars have sought to reassert the value of empathy and care as manifested in such texts: particularly in the context of ecofeminism (Fraiman, 2012; Probyn-Rapsey, O'Sullivan and Watt, 2019).

Perhaps the most prominent recent instance of care ethics being developed in support of vegan practice is found in Lori Gruen's *Entangled Empathy* (2015), a text which is rooted in ecofeminism while also building on the posthuman argument that humans are—by necessity—entangled with other species (see Chapter 2). Gruen argues that traditional ethical theories, grounded in reason, often fail to move people to behavioral change.[2] In contrast, she offers an ethics of "entangled empathy," a theory Gruen illustrates by drawing on her own transformative relationship with a chimpanzee, Emma, to elucidate how ethical change can arise in practice. The insight generated from this encounter, for

Gruen, was that close engagements with nonhuman animals can "fundamentally alter one's perception" and generate empathy that traverses species' lines while avoiding anthropocentrism (2015: 75). As Gruen continues in a later essay: "Not many people have this sort of relationship with chimpanzees, but many of us have deep relationships with companion animals that help us to try to figure out what it means to live well as someone very different, like a dog or a cat or a turtle" (2020: 42). Gruen suggests, in other words, that relationships with animals can give rise to new forms of understanding that, in turn, generate empathy, care, and a desire to improve relationships with nonhuman companions, which go beyond anthropomorphic presumptions about particular species' needs.

In sum: a range of ethical and political frameworks have offered ways of understanding animals as subjects rather than lower beings who can be used and killed without reflection, though these approaches have also generated frictions. While animal rights and liberation approaches (following Regan and Singer) have tended to appeal to reason and shared attributes between humans and animals (see Milburn, forthcoming), ecofeminist and critical media studies research has questioned the efficacy of utilitarian approaches to animal rights and liberation and reasserted the politics of emotion or even (critical) anthropomorphism. As underlined by Jackson (2020), however, regardless of their conceptual grounding, critiques of human exceptionalism should not be deployed in broad-brush, universalizing ways. Instead, it is important to ensure any arguments about human dominance over animals are carefully situated in relation to specific geographical, historical, and institutional contexts.

In the rest of this chapter I focus on three contexts that illustrate how theoretical debates about animal subjectivity speak to vegan campaigning work. First, I examine the ways in which animals have been analogously likened to humans within some especially criticized campaigns, those undertaken by perhaps the most famous NGO working in vegan campaigning: PETA. Next, I engage with a campaign produced by Animal Equality, which invites audiences to try and see things from the perspectives of animals instead, via uses of virtual reality headsets and YouTube videos that are filmed as though looking at the world through a given animal's eyes.[3] The chapter then shifts to a very different form of representation: the joyful, but still ambivalent, reworking of what a multispecies family could look like, which is found in the home of Esther the Wonder Pig, before opening into a wider discussion of the community-making found in ex-farm animal sanctuaries.

Comparing Suffering

Some of the most (in)famous examples of attempts to unpick the human/animal dichotomy can be found in the work of PETA: a group, who have routinely—and dramatically—used human bodies as stand-ins for animal bodies. Campaigns that have garnered particular controversy include billboards that use fat-shaming to encourage a reduction in animal products, depictions of semi-naked women hanging from meat hooks, uses of holocaust imagery, and comparisons between factory farming and slavery (Kim, 2011).[4] While PETA are routinely criticized within the media, however, their tactics are often justified by spokespeople who take the stance that the end justifies the means. A 2016 campaign centered around women's testimonies about sexual assault—only to reveal that these testimonies were not referring to the personal experiences of the women speaking, but practices in animal agriculture—for instance, was defended in a manner that, notably, evoked Singer's emphasis on suffering: "Every decent person abhors and denounces sexual abuse of women but we cannot blithely accept the sexual abuse of other females who happen not to be human but have the same vulnerability to pain" (Newkirk in Shapiro, 2016).

These campaigns have been criticized widely within the popular media, but it is important to note that criticism of PETA is not restricted to those who disagree with their ideology and that scholarship sympathetic to veganism has also condemned their approach (e.g., Deckha, 2008b; Harper, 2010b; Glasser, 2011; Polish, 2016; Pendergrast, 2018). Corey Lee Wrenn has pointed to a range of problems with the institutional politics of PETA, from questioning the efficacy of shock tactics for fostering engagement with veganism (Wrenn, 2013) to criticizing the labor politics associated with PETA for being reliant on the emotional work of young women (Wrenn, 2015). Laura Wright is similarly critical of PETA's "ends justify the means" stance, and elucidates the self-defeating nature of its tactics through analyzing a well-known campaign image of actress—and famous vegan—Pamela Anderson. In the image, Anderson's body is marked as though it is cuts of meat (including "rump" and "breast" printed on corresponding parts of her anatomy). The intended message of this campaign is clear: if those viewing the image find the treatment of a woman's body as though it is cuts of meat offensive or at least distasteful, then why can animal bodies be treated in this manner without ethical reflection?

The problem, as Wright (2015: 137) points out, is that women's bodies *are* routinely consumed without question—not, of course, in a literal sense, but through their objectification within the media. Because the shock to thought that PETA's image is intended to offer can only work if it depicts human bodies that aren't already routinely objectified, rather than denaturalizing meat consumption the image simply feeds into preexisting, narrow conceptions of what constitutes a sexually attractive body in the United States (Wright, 2015: 137). Wright's claims are grounded in Carol Adams's theory of the absent referent, which, as described previously (see Chapter 2) argues that the persistent association between women and animality feeds into a discourse that allows women to be objectified in ways that strip them of subjectivity and agency. Adams's *Sexual Politics of Meat* (2000 [1990]) focuses in particular on the use of sexualized imagery in the marketing of animal products and her book contains an overwhelming number of—sometimes bizarre—advertisements, including bikini-clad pigs batting their eyelashes at would-be consumers. Viewed through the lens of the absent referent, PETA's campaign necessarily fails in its attempts to foreground and contest the objectification of sentient animals. Because such uses of sexualized imagery are so objectifying, for Adams (and Wright) this means that rather than emphasizing animal subjectivity these campaigns simply have the effect of reproducing the erasure of women's subjectivity. It is important to note that labeling such imagery of women straightforwardly as "objectification" is an argument that has not gone uncontested (for an important critique, see Hamilton, 2019: 24–30), but the fundamental point remains: because different inequalities entangle and intersect, it is not only undesirable on its own terms to compare human and animal oppression but also self-defeating.

A. Breeze Harper's *Sistah Vegan* (2010b) makes allied arguments in its opening pages, where Harper critiques the use of racially loaded imagery in PETA's work. Uses of such imagery, she argues, infer that "the exploitation and torture of nonhuman animals come from the same master/oppressor ideology that created atrocities such as African slavery, North American genocide, and the Jewish Holocaust" (xiv). It is necessary to underline, moreover, that PETA are not novel in problematic comparison-making; as Claire Jean Kim points out: "the US animal liberation movement has for generations evoked Holocaust and slavery analogies as a way of characterizing the treatment of nonhuman animals" (2011: 312). The problem, Harper points out, is that unlike scholarship that has tried to understand the relationship between human and animal oppression in situated, sensitive, and historically contextualized ways, the simplistic comparisons that have been used by certain animal liberation movements both undermine their own aims and exacerbate tensions between these groups and anti-racist movements. In Harper's words, "the wounds and scars of United States's sordid history of violent racism, in which Black Americans were derogatorily categorized *as* animals within a racist colonial context . . . need to be addressed and reconciled on a national level" as, if not, comparisons between racialized humans and animals will continue to feed into these oppressive dynamics (Harper, 2010b: xiv–xv).

It is important to reiterate, however, that Harper is not dismissing *all* attempts to consider the relationship between human and animal oppression; the act of critiquing crude comparisons between different forms of suffering is not the same as disavowing the existence of more complex intersections between oppressions. Instead, as Syl Ko has underlined, the problem is that comparisons are often made "too late in the game and for disingenuous reasons" (2017: 84), for instance, to deflect criticisms leveled at animal activism for focusing on other species amid so much human suffering, or to garner media attention for particular campaigns. Aph Ko argues, moreover, that comparisons between factory farming and human suffering not only flatten differences between historically specific forms of oppression but also fail to address the shared roots of these oppressions:

> When we examine animal oppression, we need to look at factors other than just the obvious or surface-level symptoms, such as factory farming or speciesism. Factory farming is not the cause but the result of something else horrible that's occurring . . . Black experiences with zoological racism (racism anchored to the human/animal binary) should not be treated as an inconvenience to animal rights theory; it should be used to bolster our understanding of both what

"animal" means and how the category of *Homo sapiens* does not necessarily provide refuge from zoological terrorism. (2019: 29)

Again, therefore, what Ko's arguments underline is that iterations of vegan ethics that uncritically evoke human oppression for the purpose of drawing attention to the plight of animals are both problematic and ineffective. At the same time, the abundance of *criticism* regarding such tactics offers a glimmer of hope and illustrates that critiques of single-issue politics already play an important role in vegan scholarship. Indeed, a key characterization of Vegan Studies, as it has evolved to date, is its criticism of vegan politics that perpetuates other oppressions. Some vegan initiatives, however, carry tensions that are perhaps less obvious than PETA campaigns and in the rest of this chapter I think through the dynamics of slightly messier and more ambivalent appeals to animal subjectivity, turning first to "iAnimal."

Embodying Suffering

Animal Equality's "iAnimal" series of films offer a high-profile attempt to go beyond simplistic comparison-making between species, and instead bring animal subjectivity to the fore. In addition to its high profile, the reason why iAnimal is an especially informative campaign to examine is twofold: first, Animal Equality's films illustrate the potentials and limitations of commonplace approaches used in animal activism to encourage emotional identification with other species. Through applying a body of theoretical work to these texts, which holds more complex understandings of animal subjectivity and empathy, I work to bring these issues into relief. My aim, though, is not just to conduct a critical analysis of iAnimal but to, in turn, complicate theoretical arguments that have framed embodied ethics as more radical than other animal rights and advocacy frameworks.

Currently three iAnimal films are available, each of which promises insight into the life experience of intensively farmed animals, with a focus on pigs reared for meat, dairy cows, and broiler chickens. In addition to being available online, Animal Equality tour virtual reality versions of these short films that they claim offer a "360-degree immersive experience," which enables audiences to "get a unique perspective into the lives of farmed animals" (Animal Equality, ND). These films thus seem, at least on a surface level, to offer a counterpoint to PETA's attempt to denaturalize animal product consumption by likening women to meat. As described previously, Anderson's campaign was paradoxical due to being, on the one hand, anthropocentric (suggesting people should value animals because they are somehow like humans), while, on the other hand, contributing to the objectification of women (via zoomorphism). What this campaign failed to do, in other words, was unsettle the functioning of the category "animal." In contrast, rather than mapping animal bodies onto humans, the "iAnimal" films encourage viewers to foster a sense of sympathy toward animals by seemingly sharing *their* embodied experiences.

Mike Goodman's work, for instance, has focused on *iAnimal: Pig Farms in 360°* (see also Giraud, 2019: 142–70). This film starts with a view of a sparse room that is partly obscured by the metal bars of a cage, with the scene then contextualized by actor Peter Egan's voice-over: "you don't know what you're in for, but you're behind bars. Looking around you see countless others like you, your neighbour on the left tries to comfort you and seek comfort from you" (Animal Equality, 2016).[5] Four minutes in, the imagery becomes more graphic—as the film progresses toward the moment of slaughter itself—when "you" are prodded along a narrow tunnel, accompanied by loud noises of other pigs squealing in what appears to be fear. The overwhelming noise and disorientation of this scene abruptly comes to an end as the camera switches to a third-person perspective, which captures a line of pigs being stunned and strung up by one leg before having their throats slit. Despite this shift in viewpoint, Egan's voice-over still encourages identification with a particular pig and—after the others have been hung up—states "it's your turn," with the final sequence shifting viewpoint to dwell on the thrashing body that audiences are encouraged to think of as "theirs," a body whose front legs make a cycling motion that slowly ceases, as the kill-floor is hosed down to remove their blood.

While *iAnimal Pigs* is especially graphic, all of the iAnimal films share similar aesthetic and emotive qualities that are utilized to encourage identification with particular animals. Each film, for instance, spends substantial time evoking the animal in question's enclosed, austere, living environment and works to recreate a sense of bewilderment and fear (via noise or obscuring the viewpoint of the camera). The violent nature of these films, alongside Animal Equality's positioning of them as an "immersive experience into the lives of farmed animals" (Animal Equality, ND), seems to reflect the logics of shock and revelation that have been criticized from both critical and mainstream animal studies perspectives for evoking horror in audiences but ultimately failing to support sustained change (e.g., Wrenn, 2013; Lorimer, 2015; Ramussen, 2015).

A different aspect of the films—their focus on the bodily—however, complicates the way viewers are encouraged to engage with shocking imagery. iAnimal does not just work to make animal lives visible in order to foster sympathy, but attempts to generate more empathic relations through conveying what it *feels* like to be a particular animal. Through their choice of perspective and use of VR headsets, the videos do not just depict images of suffering but claim to recreate the animal experience itself. It is in this shift in register from sympathy to empathy that is experienced on a bodily level, which resonates with theoretical work that has seen embodied relationships with animals as fostering ethical responsibility more effectively than abstract frameworks of animal rights. The iAnimal films, moreover, seem to address the major practical barrier associated with embodied empathy: its emphasis on "proximity (being within touching distance)" to animals (Greenhough and Roe, 2011: 62).

Within the prominent body of scholarship focused on bodily ethics, closeness is often held up as one of the major ways people develop a felt sense of animals' needs: as with Gruen's encounter with Emma the chimpanzee. As Gruen points out, though, most of the time it is impossible to be in close proximity with animals who are under threat. By allowing access to spaces of slaughter and production that are ordinarily distanced from consumers (Philo, 1995; Pachirat, 2011; see previous chapter), the iAnimal films thus appear to circumvent these barriers to embodied empathy. Overcoming the problem of distance is also politically important because, historically, the act of associating physical closeness to nonhuman animals with ethical understanding has fed into long-standing hierarchies between those who work directly with particular species and those who are perceived to only have abstract understandings of their needs (Giraud, 2019: 98–117). For example, critical-activist arguments have routinely been excluded from debates about vivisection on the basis of their alleged sentimentalism and irrationality in comparison with scientific expertise about animal physiology—a problem that has persisted from the Victorian origins of the anti-vivisection movement to the present day (Michael and Birke, 1994; Giraud, 2019: 98–117). Similarly, stereotypes about anti-hunting campaigns often portray critics as ignorant urban activists with no knowledge of the countryside (see Cassidy, 2019).[6] The iAnimal initiative, in part, therefore, could offer a response to a political landscape where distance from animals has been used to delegitimate people's ethical concerns.

Further attention needs to be paid, though, to persistent anthropocentrism in the way that embodied relationships with animals are constructed in the films. A pull quote displayed on the iAnimal website from actor Evanna Lynch, for instance, states: "You don't know what it's like to be in a room designed to kill you" (Animal Equality, ND), in order to position the videos as filling this gap in experiential knowledge. However, the voice-overs of the videos frame these experiences via an anthropomorphic framework: using language that frames nonhuman animal kin networks in line with human familial structures (referring to mothers and children, and describing behavior in relation to emotions, e.g., "happy," "scared," that are intelligible from a human perspective). While a degree of anthropomorphism in animal advocacy is perhaps inevitable and, as Parkinson (2019) points out, can sometimes do productive work, the dangers of iAnimal's approach can be drawn out upon turning to theorists who share Gruen's emphasis on the transformative potential of embodied ethics but have slightly different conceptions of how this mode of ethics unfolds in practice.

Like Gruen, Vinciane Despret (2016) argues that a felt understanding of animals' needs emerges through situated encounters, where those interacting with one another learn to interpret one another's bodily cues. Although this process of co-learning might create space for humans to impose their obligations onto animals (as when humans learn about dog behavior in ways that make subsequent training easier), Despret argues that it also creates room for animals to impose their obligations on humans (as when a dog refuses to do something because their needs have not been recognized; see also Haraway, 2008). Central to Despret's arguments is that situated encounters with animals generate ethical responsibilities that are driven by animal agency rather than by what humans *think* animals want.

To illustrate these arguments, Despret's work is animated by a range of beautiful examples derived from both historical case studies and ethnographic work. These examples serve to unsettle reductive notions of animal agency that position other species as being emotionally or cognitively "lower" than humans. One such example is the case of "clever Hans," a horse who rose to fame in Germany in the early twentieth century, for his apparent ability to count and answer basic mathematical sums by tapping his hoof the correct number of times (Despret, 2004). Hans, however, was actually sensing when he needed to start and stop counting by interpreting the body language of his trainer, rather than demonstrating awareness of basic arithmetic.

The case of Hans is routinely held up as illustrating biases that affect attempts to assess animal intelligence, where the actions of the experimenter are a distorting variable that influences results in misleading ways. Even the Wikipedia page on Hans, for instance, states that the "Clever Hans effect" is "used in psychology to describe when an animal or a person senses what someone wants them to do, even although they are not deliberately being given signals," noting that "[i]t is important to take this effect into account when testing animals' intelligence." Despret, however, suggests that this framing of the Clever Hans effect as something negative or problematic reinforces an anthropocentric notion of what intelligence *is* (an ability to count) while neglecting the more radical potentials inherent in Hans's relationship with his trainer:

> Yes, it was a beautiful case of influence, but it was moreover a wonderful opportunity to explore a fascinating question. Indeed, the horse could not count, but he could do something more interesting: not only could he read bodies, but he could make human bodies be moved and be affected, and move and affect other beings and perform things without their owners' knowledge. (2004: 113)

From Despret's perspective it is thus important to move beyond seeing the (in-)ability of animals to achieve tasks (such as counting) as being reflective of intelligence, because such markers privilege aspects of behavior that are intelligible in line with humanist knowledge while neglecting a whole host of other capacities that could be specific to particular species. How, for instance, was Hans able to "read" his trainer correctly and how, more significantly, was he able to teach those interacting with him to communicate accurately without even realizing they were being taught? These questions feed into a broader argument across Despret's work: in many instances, stereotypes about animal capacities—such as sheep being "stupid" (Despret, 2006)—can actively foreclose the capacity to notice animal agency and abilities that are radically different from, and sometimes exceed, human capacities. To overcome anthropocentric bias, she argues, it is vital to cultivate a "politics of attention" (Despret and Meuret, 2016: 26). By taking an interest in how species relate to their co-constitutive ecology, Despret suggests, space is created to be affected by animals, foster a sense of their needs, and allow animals to impose their own distinct obligations upon humans, which go beyond anthropocentric perceptions about what particular species are or require.

If the embodied empathy fostered by iAnimal is analyzed in light of Despret's arguments, its limitations become explicit; simply put, the films fail to move beyond anthropocentric interpretations of how nonhuman animals experience the world. For Despret empathy with other species "is not experiencing with one's own body what the other experiences," but a slow process of learning how other species experience their environment differently to humans (2013: 85). What is neglected by the iAnimal films are precisely these differences between human and animal sensoria, differences that are particularly important in the context of slaughterhouses, because details that might seem innocuous to humans are often distressing to other animals: "A little plastic water bottle lying harmlessly, a shiny reflection, a yellow jacket hanging on a fence, all those turn out to be, in their world, wrong details; a fan's blades slowly rotating creates flicker, a shadow on the ground becomes a deep cliff, a dark spot turns out to be a bottomless pit" (Despret, 2013: 58). In light of Despret's arguments, therefore, it would be easy to interpret iAnimal as *almost* developing an ethics beyond anthropocentrism, but failing at the last hurdle.

A slightly different interpretation of iAnimal is, however, also possible; while the insights offered by Gruen and Despret help to illustrate the limitations of such texts, certain aspects of the videos can—in turn—highlight the limits of ethical approaches that centralize bodily entanglements and empathy. To close this section, I will reflect briefly on two of these limitations. First, it is important not to overstate the transformative potential of empathy gained through bodily encounters— particularly its capacity to lead to structural change. For instance, Gruen and Despret's work (as well as thinkers informed by Despret such as Haraway) shares a similar emphasis on the role of embodied relationships with animals in fostering care and ongoing ethical responsibility. Yet these thinkers arrive at very different conclusions about what *sort* of ethical responsibilities will emerge from embodied entanglements. The sheer existence of these points of difference between key theorists of embodiment serves to trouble neat conclusions about the power of embodied ethics to radically transform preexisting relationships between humans and nonhuman animals.

In an essay entitled "What Motivates Us to Change What We Eat?" Gruen argues that entangled, bodily empathy will "move us toward more conscientious ethical reflection and engagement" and that "[r]elationships of exploitation or complete instrumentalization, which is how we might characterize the bulk of our relationships with other animals at the moment, are precisely the sorts of relationships that should change" (2020: 42). In contrast, although—like Gruen— Despret and Haraway claim that embodied, entangled relationships give rise to new awareness of animals' needs and open up ethical obligations to respond to these needs, they apply these arguments to contexts including animal laboratories, slaughterhouses, and domestication practices. Though both Despret and Haraway's work persuasively shows how bodily entanglements with nonhuman animals have led laboratory and slaughterhouse designers to reshape these spaces to reduce stress, this reshaping does not result in a fundamental questioning of the institutions themselves.

The second challenge to embodied empathy that iAnimal highlights relates to the capacity for insights gained through this approach to be *co-opted*. As sketched out in Chapter 2, an emphasis on the agency that animals have to shape knowledge and care practices has been an important theme in posthumanist animal studies. This observation has supported the argument that animals express agency even in instrumental settings, thus disrupting narratives of human mastery over other species. If cows signify their needs in slaughterhouses or mice express resistance in laboratories, then this undermines notions of animals as just being passive tools. The process of gaining felt responsibility of animal needs in otherwise instrumental spaces has also been characterized (perhaps paradoxically) as less anthropocentric than abstract frameworks, such as animal rights, due to actively responding to animals' behavioral triggers and ethological requirements as opposed to anthropomorphic projections of these requirements (see Haraway, 2008; Despret, 2013). Theory that has emphasized the ethical potentials of embodied empathy on a micro-sociological level, however, tends to neglect the wider contexts in which these encounters take place (see Johnson, 2015), sidestepping the more fundamental critiques of animals being treated as resources that are present in vegan ethics. It is important, therefore, that recognition of animal agency does not deflect attention from the instrumental settings in which particular encounters with animals unfold and the (often violent) processes through which more disruptive forms of agency are eliminated, molded, or constrained to fit with human requirements in these settings.

As discussed in the previous chapter, in *The War Against Animals* (2015), Dinesh Wadiwel details how developing a sense of animals' behavior and needs does not always perform a benevolent function: with the expression of animal agency often playing an important role in the biopolitical management of animal agriculture. Resistant expressions of agency, he describes, are frequently taken into account and learned from in order to inspire re-designs of technologies to manage and regulate animal behavior more effectively and minimize chances of future disruption (2015: 12–13). My own research with Gregory Hollin, in the context of the historical standardization of laboratory beagles, showed similar patterns of researchers learning from individual animals' resistance and agency in order to transform the dogs into more compliant experimental subjects. Turning to the first large-scale experimental beagle colony, which was funded by the Manhattan Project to test the effects of radiation on a living population, we illustrated that close attention was paid to the dogs' ethological needs throughout the life span of the colony, which resulted in these needs radically reshaping everything from cage design, to floor surfacing of kennels, and how long caretakers spent with the animals (Giraud and Hollin, 2016). Yet, as with the sorts of slaughterhouse redesign described by Wadiwel, here too the careful consideration of animal agency ultimately served to deter beagle behavior that was disruptive and enhance qualities that were compatible with the needs of experimenters. On one level, embodied understanding and empathy was transformative of the living space of the animals and the way they were treated, but the reach of these changes did not ultimately question the institutions at stake and ultimately fed into the status quo by strengthening human capacities to instrumentalize beagles (with insights gained in these experiments also going on to inform subsequent experimental designs). These processes might have alleviated the beagles' immediate stress, but they also enhanced beagles' compliance as experimental subjects in both the short and long term. Both slaughterhouse and laboratory design, therefore, illustrate how felt understanding and empathy can improve animal welfare and even lead to the construction of more animal-centered built environments, but does not always lend itself to an ethics that questions the instrumentalization of animal life in a more fundamental way.

Overall, while theories of embodied and entangled empathy point to some important limitations of texts such as iAnimal, the opposite is also true and the films can be used to highlight dangers in pinning too much hope on this form of ethics as a motor for wider change. Though bodily entanglements with animals can, in some contexts, generate a sense of ethical responsibility toward their needs, it is also important to pay attention to settings in which these entanglements do the opposite and prevent alternative, less instrumental, relationships from emerging. The need to engage with structural factors that constrain the agency of nonhuman animals is emphasized still more sharply, and perhaps unexpectedly, by the final example I turn to in this chapter: Esther the Wonder Pig and other sanctuaries for ex-farm animals.

Creating a Multispecies Community

The examples discussed so far have all aimed to raise awareness by drawing attention to death. In the final case study discussed in this chapter, however, I turn to a very different example, one that does not just seek to criticize existing human-animal relations but rework them: the story of Esther the Wonder Pig. Esther is a celebrity pig whose escapades are documented on various social media platforms (with dedicated Facebook, Instagram, Twitter, and YouTube accounts), as well as her personal website. She rose to fame after her human companions, Steve Jenkins and his partner Derek Walter, began to document her story and everyday activities online. What emerges when examining the phenomenon of Esther is another ambivalent picture, which highlights the work that (critical) anthropomorphism can accomplish but, again, confronts the limitations of this tactic.

Esther could be situated as part of a burgeoning vegan cultural industry, where influencers and campaigning groups utilize social media to promote animal welfare while simultaneously generating income streams (DeMello, 2018). Resonating with fictional cultural precursors such as *Babe* (dir. Noonan, 1995)—whose lead actor James Cromwell famously became a vegan environmental activist after working on the film—what emerges across Esther's transmedia story is a multispecies community that troubles the classifications pointed to in Joy's *Why We Love Dogs, Eat Pigs, and Wear Cows* (2011). Videos of Esther splashing around in paddling pools, eating cupcakes, and having a "tantrum" after her breakfast was slightly late one morning, might open revenue streams for Jenkins and Walter, but—in doing so—they also open questions as to why certain animals are treated as companions and others consumed. The need to generate income from Esther, in this context, cannot be disentangled from the project of unsettling the classifications that underpin carnism. Esther's story is thus not simply an instance of humans profiting from an especially charismatic animal, the reason why this funding was needed was in order to transgress the boundaries that would ordinarily relegate Esther to agricultural spaces and construct her as "meat."

"Pork" production has been seen as an industry that holds particular environmental and welfare implications (as dramatized in Lockwood, 2016b; see also Blanchette, 2020; Neubert, 2020). Against this backdrop, Esther has received attention for illustrating the capacity of social media content that seems trivial, or even silly, to perform a more subversive role than it might appear (Jevesejevas, 2018): here offering an alternative vision of how to relate to pigs. As Mary Trachsel (2019) suggests, commonplace media framings of pigs are often those established by "the industrial pork story"; a story that, as Brett Mizelle (2011) notes, is reinscribed through the popular cultural veneration of foods such as bacon. Recent years, however, has seen alternative "pig stories coming from a proliferation of farmed-animal sanctuaries, from the social media presence of 'celebrity pigs' like Esther the Wonder Pig and Priscilla, and from tourists in the Bahamas who tell stories about swimming with the 'Pigs of Paradise'" (Trachsel, 2019). Yet although "alternative pig stories" might disrupt specific anthropocentric classifications, the wider critique of anthropocentrism that they enact is more limited.

Esther's particular "origin story," for example, is documented on her website and a series of YouTube videos, as well as books *Esther the Wonder Pig: Changing the World One Heart at a Time* (2017), *Happily Ever Esther* (2018), and children's picture book *The Adventures of Esther the Wonder Pig* (2018). She began to live with the couple after Jenkins received a Facebook message from a (now former) friend, asking if he would like a "micro-pig" that would grow up to 70 lb and be approximately the size of a domestic cat (Esther The Wonder Pig, 2019: "About"). Even in the early days of this narrative, Esther's story begins to trouble species hierarchies; a report about her life in *The Guardian* newspaper, for example, explicitly counters the categories foregrounded by Joy, wherein dogs are objects of love and pigs cast as edible, with Jenkins describing how Esther neatly settled into the household: "When the dogs got up to do something, she'd follow, and she soon became part of their pack" (Jenkins, 2017). On taking Esther to visit the vet, however, these multispecies relations came under threat when, on noting her cropped tail, the vet informed him that she was a commercial sow rather than a micro-pig. By this point the "friend" who was Esther's original owner had made a swift exit, but Jenkins and Walter had become so attached to Esther that they were reluctant to give her up, eventually transforming their home into the Happily Ever Esther Farm Sanctuary.

Esther's narrative speaks to a growing body of work that suggest vegan ethics "queers" human-animal boundaries by troubling normative assumptions and categories that underpin everyday life (Stephens Griffin, 2017: 21). In particular, Esther's depiction resonates with Emilia Quinn's (2020) account of "vegan camp," a concept Quinn develops to encapsulate visual and material culture wherein the emphasis on visibility and revelation that often characterizes vegan campaigning (see previous chapter) is replaced with a more humorous interrogation of carnism. As Quinn puts it, despite not offering an overt mode of critique, "vegan camp nonetheless offers a productive means of recognizing the ways in which humor and parody can diffuse the seeming triumph of an anthropocentric culture over the nonhuman animal" and, as such, offers a "reorienting of perspective that reveals the utopian longings, community identification, and humor that can productively exist alongside ethical awareness" (Quinn, 2020: 915). In the case of Esther, for instance, kitschy images of her eating gaudy cakes, donning fancy dress, and disrupting the lives of Jenkins and Walter in humorous ways hold a more serious function. This imagery might gain clicks, shares, and likes, but it also articulates a sense of hoped-for community amid the backdrop of industrial agriculture where this community is routinely denied (a point underlined by a section of Esther's website entitled "the darker side" which contains a series of images of mistreated pigs accompanied by the caption "Unfortunately, not all pigs are treated as well or are as lucky as Esther. Her brothers and sisters have a much different life").

Through adopting the visual rhetoric of vegan camp to unsettle carnist norms, Esther speaks to theoretical work that has called for a more expansive notion of what notions of kinship might mean (which go beyond biologically determined or heteronormative conceptions of the family). Reworking understandings of kin, for instance, has been central to Haraway's *Staying with the Trouble* (2016), which uses the slogan "make kin not babies" to call for less focus on the human and more caring relationships with other species at a time of mass extinction and environmental crisis. Though perhaps not quite what Haraway had in mind, a particularly memorable video on Esther's Facebook speaks to this push for multispecies kin-making. The video depicts Esther slumbering on a mattress, while Jenkins lies adjacent to her, head propped up on her side as he watches a video on his laptop.[7] Partially lying over Jenkins is Shelby, a more conventional canine companion (who alternates between dozing contentedly and licking Jenkins's leg). Rather less contented is a third family member, Cornelius, a large turkey who enters from the right while Jenkins and Walter begin to giggle as he forces himself in front of the camera and tries to climb on the mattress by any means necessary (even if he disturbs the others' sleep). After Cornelius actively tries to push Jenkins over, he has to put down his laptop and sooth the turkey with a hug.

Something subversive is at work in Esther's story, beyond simply expanding the human family unit to include nonhuman animals. Due to the sheer difficulty of including Esther within the household, the multispecies community that she is part of reveals not only shared emotional attachments but also the shared labor involved in making-kin. The act of foregrounding this labor is particularly important in light of criticisms that have been leveled at Haraway's calls to expand ideas of kinship beyond the human. What Haraway means by "make kin not babies" is that instead of focusing on reproducing the human species by any means necessary, it is important to re-discover mutually beneficial ways of cohabiting the planet with other species (2016; see also Clarke and Haraway, 2018). Her formulation of this slogan, however, and particularly the refrain *not babies*, has been accused of evoking racially problematic Malthusian narratives of overpopulation (Lewis, 2017) and, in a context where environmentalism is routinely leveraged in support of blood and soil nationalism, appeals to such narratives are dangerous: no matter how carefully articulated (see Chapter 6).

Sophie Lewis's own exploration of these themes (2018, 2019) offers an alternative approach, which reasserts the importance of understanding kin-making as a form of labor. These arguments again speak to aspects of Esther's life. To an extent Esther neatly maps onto long-standing feminist calls to recognize that domestic work in the home is just that: work. To put it bluntly, the sheer size and shape of fully grown pigs mean that everyday acts of caring—such as bathing or feeding— are depicted in exaggerated form. As one video points out: in the summer Esther is bathed every day and getting her into the bath, let alone washing her, is not always easy. By illustrating the labor involved in making Esther kin, in other words, these videos also highlight everyday forms of care- and advocacy-work that are often devalued and hidden (for more on the work behind animal advocacy, see jones, 2014; Coulter, 2016: 97–138).

Yet Esther also foregrounds the difficulties of expanding what "kin" means in a slightly different way. From Lewis's perspective, transforming what kinship means is not something that can be done by changing patterns of thought but requires "work[ing] through the preconditions and likely strategies for achieving (non-) reproductive justice politically" (Lewis, 2017: NP). Although there is no scope to explore Lewis's arguments in depth here, what is critically important about this point is that it foregrounds how existing gendered and racialized social relations often *constrain* the possibilities for "making-kin." In order to transform what kin means and who can be kin, particular constraints and inequalities need to be contested. The life of Esther the Wonder Pig brings these issues into stark relief; though her household might disrupt commonplace notions of "kin," her story also illustrates how structural constraints can limit alternative ways of kin-making to those in positions of privilege.

Reclassifying Esther from "livestock" to "pet," for instance, was not something that occurred simply by Jenkins and Walter changing how they felt about pigs through entangled empathy. Aside from the practical difficulties of homing a 650 lb pig in a domestic dwelling, doing so was prohibited in legal terms: illustrating how classificatory systems are always bound up with material arrangements that hold them in place, such as technological infrastructures and legislative norms (Star, 1991; Bowker and Star, 2000). In the case of Jenkins and Walter, the only way of shifting Esther's status was to intervene in the built environment by creating an animal sanctuary where humans and animals could cohabit: a task that required funding and resources that they were able to obtain through securing Esther's status as an influencer. Even now, preventing Esther from being classified as "livestock" requires work to fend off various socio-technical arrangements that constantly function to re-categorize her as "food." When she had surgery to remove a tumor, for instance, Jenkins and Walter were informed that, if the cancer had spread, Esther would not be able to get further treatment—such as chemotherapy—in the same way as other companion species, with the couple claiming that this was due to Canadian Food Inspection Agency ruling it is illegal to administer particular medical interventions to "food" animals (Appia, 2018).

Even though distinctions between "food animals" and "pets" might be arbitrary or at least culturally specific, therefore, changing minds is not enough unless the infrastructures that perpetuate how particular species are categorized are also transformed. The resources required to accomplish these changes, however, can make transformation difficult to achieve in practice without the necessary resources or media nous. Indeed, as Jonathan Turnbull, Adam Searle, and William Adams (2020) show, animal sanctuaries are increasingly reliant on savvy uses of social media to generate the necessary revenue to survive. The need for such revenue streams can lead to a paradoxical situation wherein the creation of alternative multispecies communities—outside of systems that treat animals as resources—is reliant upon revenue gained through anthropomorphic influencer work.

This brings things to other, perhaps more fundamental, points of tension associated with the specific construction subjectivity found across Esther's social media. Even though Esther's website draws attention to the plight of other pigs, it is difficult to deny that her influencer status is contingent on emphasizing how special she is as an individual. The signifiers of this specialness—including the food she is given, clothes she wears, and living arrangements—could also be criticized for mischaracterizing the needs of an adult pig and the same argument applies to other animals inhabiting Esther's household. In the aforementioned Facebook video, for instance, when Cornelius the Turkey disrupts family downtime he is recast from livestock animal to jealous child (or "Mr Jealous Pants" as the caption for the video reads). While this framing might unsettle Cornelius's classification as a "livestock," it also obscures the relationship between his actions and specific attributes of turkeys as a species (that make them likely to exhibit such behavior). Esther's family, therefore, speaks to the political ambivalence of anthropomorphism more broadly. Critical engagements with anthropomorphic imagery can be used to unsettle classifications that frame animals as resources, but these tactics struggle to articulate what less anthropocentric way of relating to animals could look like moving forward. The wider sanctuary movement, however, has offered routes into answering this complicated question.

North America is perhaps home to some of the most well-known ex-farm animal sanctuaries, such as Farm Sanctuary, but even in this context there is a huge degree of heterogeneity with sanctuaries characterized by different models of community-building (Donaldson and Kymlicka, 2015). The complexity of the US movement itself is aside from considering sanctuaries in other national contexts, as well as allied initiatives such as rescues that re-home mixtures of "domestic" and "livestock" animals, retired working animal sanctuaries, and wider rehoming networks for ex-battery hens and laboratory animals. Through rehoming farm animals, sanctuaries create a community for beings whose lives would ordinarily be radically truncated. Sanctuaries often also engage in vegan outreach as well as fundraising to support their work. Although all sanctuaries contain ambivalences stemming from inevitable power asymmetries between human workers and animals, many explore radical ways of centering the species-specific needs of their residents (see jones, 2014). While sanctuaries' approaches might vary, then, their commitment to finding new ways of living alongside ex-farm animals offers a practical exploration of another common question asked of veganism (that is often, though not always, expressed as a "gotcha moment"!): What will happen to former "livestock" once such categories no longer exist? Sanctuaries have been seen as holding hopeful potentials for responding to such questions by posing, as Kathryn Gillespie argues, "a possibility for exploring other nonnormative ways of creating liveable spaces for formerly farmed animals that do not reproduce farming models of social segregation, farm-based practices of care, and highly uneven power relationships between human caretakers and animal residents" (2018: 127). Indeed, emerging research has begun to explore initiatives such as "microsanctuaries"— which might only care for a small number of ex-farm or laboratory animals—as a viable means of extending sanctuaries' principles of multispecies community, care, and solidarity beyond larger institutions (Narayanan and Gillespie, 2020).

In addition to their practical significance, initiatives such as sanctuaries complicate theoretical criticisms of veganism that have emanated, in particular, from posthumanism. These critiques have framed veganism as a denial of complexity that fails to recognize that human and animal lives are often so entangled it is impossible to fully separate them and revert to some "pure" state before human interference (see Chapter 3). Sanctuaries offer a rich, multifaceted tradition that illustrates how these problems have long been recognized and responded to in practice. In addition, theoretical work about sanctuaries is just one example that shows how interdependencies between species—far from being unacknowledged—have been a central concern in vegan scholarship.

As Sue Donaldson and Will Kymlicka put it in *Zoopolis* (2011), notions of "wildlife" and noninterference are no help for developing new, nonexploitative ways of living alongside "deliberately bred domesticated animals that have become dependent on us" (6). These arguments pave the way for Donaldson and Kymlicka's broader exploration of how to reorganize social relations with animals who have very different types of relationships with humans and, as such, pose different ethical obligations. On a similar note, Kendra Coulter's (2016) research foregrounds how acknowledging animals as workers needs to go beyond simply recognizing that animals have agency (as sometimes occurs in posthumanist literature) to instead ask what obligations this agency might impose on humans in order to *improve* these working conditions. Rather than just highlighting limitations imposed by particular cultural classifications of animals, or how these classifications are reinforced within specific institutional settings, therefore, these authors offer ambitious visions for alternative forms of social organization that could come in the wake of unpicking a great chain of being that is shaped by exclusionary conceptions of "the human."

Conclusion

Collectively, the examples described in this chapter illustrate how the emphasis on animal subjectivity that is often central to vegan campaigning generates more complex conversations about how animals are classified within particular cultural contexts. These conversations can, in turn, give rise to broader interrogation of the infrastructures and social relations that need to change in order to find new ways of living with animals who have codependent relationships with humans, once these animals are no longer treated as resources or tools. Yet, as the case of PETA in particular illustrates, complexity can also be shut down if campaigns offer a narrow focus on shocking imagery or uncritical anthropomorphism that focuses on encouraging changes in individual consumer behavior. In addition, campaigns that neglect the enmeshment of oppressions (as with the tactic of drawing simplistic or disingenuous comparisons between human and nonhuman animal suffering) not only fail to extend ethical responsibility beyond the human but can serve to reinscribe existing social inequalities (Harper, 2010b; Kim, 2011; Ko, S. 2017; Wright, 2018, 2019; Ko, A., 2019). I elaborate on these arguments in the next chapter, but before doing so it is useful to draw out one final concern that emerges when considering the range of campaigns discussed in this chapter and the academic debates that surround them.

As described in the first chapters, in formulating initial ideas for Vegan Studies, Wright points to a need to bring different disciplinary insights together. To an extent this chapter reasserts these arguments, highlighting a need to engage in careful analysis of—often messy and contradictory—cultural texts, using tools from literary, media, and cultural studies, as well as empirically-focused sociology. Moving forward, however, further attention is needed to how audiences themselves engage with and make sense of mediated appeals to animal subjectivity, in recognition of one of the central tenets of media studies: that just because texts are designed to convey a particular meaning does not mean that this is the interpretation audiences themselves will have.[8]

At the same time as noting the need for further interdisciplinary engagement in relation to how animal subjectivity is understood by audiences of vegan campaigns and initiatives, I want to reiterate Chapter 1's note of caution about the way interdisciplinary work is approached. In animal studies and the environmental humanities more broadly, fields such as ethology, zoology, psychology, and the life sciences are increasingly being drawn upon to depict animals as subjects and support theorists' ethical commitments. Haraway, for instance, argues that the "best biologies" are beginning to erode species' boundaries in *Staying with the Trouble* (2016: 30). More critical narratives make similar claims; Singer's emphasis on sentience, for instance, has meant that finding ways to *evidence* this sentience has long been central to work that has sought to extend ethical frameworks beyond the human (e.g., Noske, 1997). Literary, cultural studies and philosophical research have, likewise, routinely drawn on ethologists such as Marc Bekoff to support their ethical arguments (as with Despret's partial affinities and Gruen's more critical account of entangled empathy). While such approaches can be productive, care needs to be taken with how different disciplinary knowledges are brought together.

As this chapter has shown, a key tactic for vegan ethics and politics—in both academic and activist contexts—has been to highlight and contest classifications which are ordinarily used to classify animals in general as "lower beings" and corral certain species into problematic categories (such as "livestock") that carry markedly different ethical obligations to others (such as "pets"). At the same time as recognizing the historical contingency of classifications, however, it is important to historicize human emotional responses. As touched on in the previous chapter and elaborated on in this one, vegan praxis can carry assumptions about what is needed to foster behavioral change: whether this is making animal suffering visible, or identifying shared cognitive abilities and emotional responses across species. Such assumptions are often lent support by academic research, such as Joy's focus on how to change psychological responses to animals or Gruen's appeal to neuroscience to support discussions of embodied empathy. However, it is important to tread carefully when drawing on these resources.

To take psychology and neuroscience more specifically as a case in point; over the past decade in social and cultural research more broadly, a number of thinkers have highlighted dangers associated with ethical theories that have engaged in "strange borrowings" (Papoulias and Callard, 2010) from popular neuroscience to support understandings of the human mind (with particular criticisms leveled at affect theory, see Leys, 2017). These analyses illustrate how taking studies from one discipline to support claims in another can be problematic in multiple ways. Appeals to popular science in the humanities and social sciences often run the risk of misrepresenting scientific research (treating studies as representative of fields as a whole when they are not), falling into the trap of a pick-and-mix approach where only work that fits particular conclusions is cited (and contradictory work discarded), or neglecting the problematic social and cultural context of particular studies. Some of the most high-profile popular accounts of empathy that are touched on in animal studies contexts, for instance, have emerged from autism neuroscience, which has been heavily criticized by neurodiversity activists for portraying certain groups of people as incapable of engaging in particular emotional and social relations (see Hollin, 2017 for analysis of this problem).

Social scientific, historical, and philosophical research has also charted the way that behavior and cognitive abilities have been interpreted in different ways over time in the context of particular sciences. Human emotions have distinct histories, with what it means to be "happy" or sad, for instance, being tightly bound to particular sets of cultural norms and values in ways that are deeply political (Ahmed, 2014). Work in the philosophy of science and history of emotion, likewise, has charted numerous points at which the cultural context of ethological research has led to misreadings of animal behavior. Historically, in the context of the life sciences, assertions have been made about animals that relate to everything from dominance hierarchies (Haraway, 1988), to stress (Ramsden, 2011), to suicidal tendencies (Ramsden and Wilson, 2014) and the evolutionary sophistication of particular species (Khandker, 2020: 169–89), with many of these claims saying more about the cultural context of the research than about animal lives and feelings themselves.

Rather than creating universal narratives about human and animal subjectivity or about the cognitive processes through which change toward veganism occurs, therefore, it is again necessary to situate attitudes toward animals within particular historical, geographical, and institutional contexts. When reflecting on possibilities for social change, similarly, it is important to avoid generalizations and ask instead how the socio-technical relationships in a specific context could be changed in order to disrupt whatever manifestation of anthropocentrism arises in that site. As I go on to discuss in the next chapter, this sort of situatedness is important not just in confronting the material conditions that erase more complex understandings of animal subjectivity in society, but in avoiding universalizing narratives about human exceptionalism in vegan discourse that fail to consider the way that—historically—it is not just nonhuman animals but particular groups of people who have been denied status as full political subjects.

Chapter 6

INTERSECTIONAL VEGANISM(S)

Combatting oppressions that are not single-issue but "enmeshed" (Wright, 2018, 2019) is a difficult task. As this and the next chapter highlight, the challenge of unpicking the relationships between different forms of inequality has only intensified in the wake of veganism's popularization. In vegan campaigns it is all too easy to slide into simple, attention-grabbing messaging and single-issue politics, which places the emphasis on "going vegan" without attending to inequities related to race, class, gender, disability and other factors that might complicate this process. Popular depictions and stereotypes of veganism often serve to compound such problems in portraying vegan practice as individualistic purity politics (whether or not this is the case in practice, see Chapter 3).

These two chapters confront the difficulty of negotiating enmeshed oppressions in contexts where veganism has moved from the margins to the mainstream. The next chapter delineates some of the overarching characteristics of popular veganism(s), characterizing recent developments as a "post-vegan" sensibility where veganism's status as a social movement has been overshadowed by more individualistic modes of plant-based capitalism. This chapter approaches things from a slightly different angle. Here I zoom in on perhaps the most prominent— and urgent—set of tensions associated with popular veganism that has been highlighted in recent years, which relates to the work of activists and scholars (and indeed scholar-activists) calling for veganism to directly confront overlapping forms of inequality rather than existing as a single-issue mode of ethics (e.g., Harper, 2010a, 2010b; Brueck, 2017, 2019; Ko and Ko, 2017; Wrenn, 2017a, 2019). These thinkers have argued not just for further attention to the way animal exploitation intersects with allied oppressions but have pushed for veganism itself to go beyond single-issue politics by forging connections with other social justice movements.

Though this chapter touches on a range of contexts and debates, its main aim is to highlight two forms of erasure that have been discussed in vegan scholarship and emerged across notable instances of popular culture. The first type of erasure is associated with veganism itself or, more specifically, the cultural phenomenon that has come to be known as "white veganism." This conception of vegan praxis has coded it as a privileged, middle-class, lifestyle politics that is only accessible to those who have the time, resources, know-how, and perhaps even cultural capital to access it (Polish, 2016; Hamilton, 2019: 168–78). Worse, this brand of veganism operates in a landscape which fails to recognize or trivializes socioeconomic inequalities that might make certain ethical lifestyles difficult to access (Harper, 2012). The second type of erasure is slightly messier and relates to exclusions bound up with the act of conflating white veganism with all veganism (cf Greenebaum, 2017, 2018). Recently concerns have emerged that, in some settings, critiques of veganism's whiteness can be performative: centralizing a version of vegan practice that cuts away other, "non-Westernized" traditions of plant-based food. Put differently, critique can sometimes exacerbate precisely the problems it is critical of. In order to understand how erasure arises in both vegan practice itself and critiques of it, it is necessary to first revisit debates that surround intersectional veganism.

Intersectional Veganism

As discussed in Chapters 1 and 2, some of the most important early work in vegan studies emerged in the wake of calls to apply a critical race lens to critical animal studies (CAS). Most prominently, A. Breeze Harper (2010a) used vegan practice as a case study to show that contesting one problematic aspect of eating— animal product consumption—does not equate to being "cruelty free." Along with Harper, other critical voices have since argued there is a need to develop an approach to animal studies that engages with questions of race and racism (Kim, 2015; Boisseron, 2018; Jackson, 2020), with this line of argument also extended to veganism more specifically (Brueck, 2017; Ko and Ko, 2017; Ko, 2019).

A vegan politics that engages with questions of racialized social inequality has, however, been understood and described in different ways by different thinkers. Perhaps the most well-known terminology is "intersectional veganism," a concept engaged with by scholars such as Harper who have pushed for animal activists and scholars to move beyond single-issue politics to focus on unpacking the way that different oppressions intersect. While sharing Harper's commitment to interrogating the relationship between different axes of inequality, another key figure in Vegan Studies, Aph Ko (2019), instead uses the term "multidimensional oppressions" to characterize the way that different oppressions do not just intersect but actively co-constitute one another. As touched on previously, ecofeminist work has also reflected on the complex relationships between veganism and "enmeshed oppressions" (Wright, 2018, 2019). The important differences between these approaches are explored in further depth later in the chapter. For now, it is just useful to underline that although these theorists have different conceptual orientations and frameworks, what they share is a rejection of simplistic comparison-making between human and animal suffering—such as the tactics enacted by certain strands of animal activism (see Chapter 5)—while also insisting that connections do exist between oppressions. These connections, however, need to be understood in a more nuanced and context-specific way than is often the case in either animal studies scholarship or activist practice.[1]

Arguments about intersectional veganism have tended to unfold in North America, due to the explicitly racialized inequalities associated with foodscapes in this setting and the United States in particular: most notably food deserts (Harper, 2010b, 2012). The influence and significance of debates related to intersectionality are such, however, that they have implications beyond an American context, with calls for both an intersectional Vegan Studies and CAS spreading (e.g., Castricano et al., 2016; Nocella and George, 2019). These developments have led to a number of scholars extending intersectional frameworks to reflect on the varied ways that human and animal oppressions are knotted together in a range of global contexts. Thus, although it is important not to draw universalizing conclusions from insights gleaned from specific nations, the issues raised by intersectional veganism have purchase beyond their North American origins. To summarize Harper (2012), *all* food spaces are classed and racialized and it is important to reflect on the implications of these processes for the political and ethical possibilities that can be realized in specific contexts.

What makes things difficult is that, echoing what Patricia Hill Collins (2015, 2019) describes as the wider "definitional dilemmas" of intersectionality, there are sometimes differing understandings of what intersectionality is and means: a problem that is especially acute in relation to vegan praxis. Kimberlé Crenshaw's (1989) initial coining of the term "intersectionality" built on legacies of Black feminism (notably the work of bell hooks and Audre Lorde) to develop an engaged-theoretical framework in order to identify—and contest—forms of oppression that could not be accommodated by single-issue frameworks alone. In her influential 1989 article, Crenshaw elucidates the limitations of single-issue approaches by focusing on a series of legal rulings; in the context of *DeGraffenreid v. General Motors*, for instance, she illustrates how the car company was able to defend itself against discriminatory employment practices when it was sued by five Black women, via the defense that they already hired both women and African-American men. By treating oppressions in isolation, the company was able to avoid legal repercussions. In Crenshaw's words, a single-issue approach thus means that "Black women are protected only to the extent that their experiences coincide with those of either of the two groups. Where their experiences are distinct, Black women can expect little protection as long as approaches, such as that in *DeGraffenreid*, which completely obscure problems of intersectionality prevail" (1989: 143).

Crenshaw's focus on the specific forms of oppression that emerge when race and gender intersect and complicate one another has led to some scholars reading intersectionality in a similar light to ecofeminist explorations of overlapping or enmeshed oppressions between women and animals. A number of thinkers have, for instance, drawn affinities between intersectionality and CAS's conception of total liberation, or the concept of "consistent anti-oppression" (cf Brueck and McNeill, 2020). A notable body of work, in addition, has suggested that an intersectional approach could be expanded—or "posthumanized" (Twine, 2010: 13)—by reflecting on the role of species as an additional axis of oppression, and (building on posthumanist thinkers such as Wolfe and ecofeminists such as Adams) perhaps the underlying mode of exclusion that sustains others. From the perspective of this body of research, divisions between species that treat animals as lesser beings can contribute to other forms of oppression by creating a label that is then projected onto particular groups of humans: portraying certain people as more "animal-like" and less deserving of legal, political, and ethical recognition. Contesting the logic of species, it is argued, can contribute to a broader project of dismantling other enmeshed oppressions (for elaboration of these arguments see Chapter 2).

Others, such as Harper, have situated intersectionality more directly in its original lineages. While recognizing connections between racism and species, these thinkers have not seen veganism as a straightforward solution to overlapping oppressions and pushed for further recognition of how specific inequalities might complicate how both vegan activism and consumer politics should be enacted. Veganism, for instance, has itself been taken to task for failing to address its imbrication in other inequalities. As Julia Feliz Brueck argues:

> Within communities of color, veganism has garnered an image of being a movement solely for privileged white communities, untouched by the realities that affect marginalized peoples . . . while loudly proclaiming veganism is "easy"; that nonhuman lives are of more importance than oppressed humans ("Nonhumans first!"); and that anyone who doesn't adopt a vegan lifestyle simply "doesn't care." (2017: 11)

What intersectional veganism refers to in Brueck's work, then, is a veganism that refuses to take its connections with other social justice issues for granted. Instead, veganism should explicitly engage with the voices of people facing multiple forms of marginalization, in order to develop collective responses to contesting different modes of oppression.

While the engagements with intersectionality outlined here in relation to veganism are not entirely removed from one another—and thinkers sometimes use different understandings of the concept simultaneously—it is nonetheless important to highlight a difference in emphasis in key uses of intersectionality, which can sometimes result in confusion or lead to people speaking past one another. On the one hand is the argument that echoes vegan ecofeminism and CAS approaches which position veganism as a response and perhaps even a solution to intersecting oppressions, due to animal agriculture lying at the nexus of a number of other problems. From this perspective, the act of becoming vegan can help to address inequalities in the distribution and production of food and move toward climate justice, as well as tackling animal exploitation. For thinkers adhering to these arguments, the difficulty at the moment is that people often fail to understand or recognize the connections between human and animal exploitation; the task for activists and scholars is thus to highlight veganism's intrinsic links to other social issues, in order to encourage the more widespread adoption of veganism that is necessary to prompt wider change.

Others have argued that although links between veganism and other social justice issues *can* exist (as with some of the social movements outlined in

Chapter 4 who sought to craft such relationships, for instance), these links are not inevitable. As Brueck asserts: "Vegans must reject the idea that veganism upholds human rights by default—that just by going vegan, one immediately stops partaking in human oppression or exploitation" (2017: 4). Indeed, as other essays in Brueck's edited collection show, at times certain manifestations of veganism can contribute to other forms of oppression, as when commitments to animal liberation have resulted in ethnocentric stereotyping of Indigenous communities (Robinson, 2017) or cultural appropriation (Ganesan, 2017). Rather than seeing the widespread uptake of veganism as a motor of change in itself, the form of intersectional veganism espoused by Brueck is marked by the recognition that the transformation of (food) systems is what lies at the root of a more widespread uptake of vegan practice. Or, put differently, what makes this body of work so valuable is that it pinpoints what needs to be contested at a systemic level in order to fully shift vegan praxis to the mainstream, foregrounding the importance of dialogue between different social movements.

The aim of the rest of the chapter is to elaborate on issues related to intersectional veganism, reasserting the value and significance of work that has called for vegan and animal activism to more actively make connections with other social justice issues, in a cultural landscape where these connections are often neglected or even erased (see Ko, 2019: 19–38). Before turning to a series of examples from popular culture that further these arguments, I am going to dwell briefly on some of my own interview materials. When I began writing this book, I felt that one of the most important issues to grapple with were persistent concerns about the elitist implications of veganism's popularization in a context where ethical consumerism is often only available to the few (echoing Shotwell, 2016). In the process of gathering documents about veganism and speaking to interviewees, however, I realized I needed to reframe some of my assumptions, finding my own thoughts about the relationship between veganism and inequality severely wanting.

Taking Care with Intersectionality

There is growing recognition that it is not enough to assert that connections exist between different forms of oppression, but to understand how—as Zakiyyah Iman Jackson puts it (2020:10)—these oppressions "braid together" under specific social and cultural conditions. The need to develop carefully situated understandings of how oppressions shape one another, in ways that move beyond generalized assertions that they do so, has become increasingly central to debates about veganism. Questions about how to make, as Syl Ko (2017) puts it, the "right" connections between different types of oppression, which do not perpetuate the logic of insensitive activism that draws analogies between human and animal suffering (as with campaigns that have likened animal agriculture to slavery, see again Harper, 2010b), are not straightforward to address. This challenge is compounded by issues emerging from different understandings and usages of the term "intersectional veganism," the stakes of which become clearer still when turning to reflections on the part of people I interviewed.

One of the most notable arguments was found in comments by white, or white-passing, vegans about whether they should be using the term "intersectional veganism" at all, in light of the risks of misuse and appropriation due to their own privilege. One academic interviewee, for instance, described her choice to focus on ecofeminist vocabulary to characterize the relationship between human and animal oppression, rather than intersectionality: "I think that intersectionality is such a useful term, and so useful for thinking about the ways that oppressions overlap and are engaging and mutually reinforcing. . . . But like I've said, I'm sort of trying to not appropriate that term in terms of my own work simply out of respect" (Wendy, vegan nineteen years). Others shared these concerns, emphasizing the importance of intersectionality while reflecting on whether it was "their" term to use in the context of veganism. Another interviewee, for instance, stated that "intersectionality as a body of theory and activism is hugely important and you know is a wake-up call for everyone, not just vegans," pointing to the need to avoid centering white, middle-class, male voices in both social movements and academia. At the same time, due to concern over *being* one of these voices, he described feeling "uneasy about" using the term itself and "appropriating the language of Black feminism" to think about vegan ethics (Chris, vegan fourteen years).

The backdrop to these reflections is wider concern about increasingly heterogeneous uses of intersectionality, not all of which lend themselves to progressivist agendas for social change (Collins, 2019). In relation to veganism specifically, certain thinkers have accused pro-vegan work of misappropriating and depoliticizing intersectionality; in an essay for the *Vegan Feminist Network* (founded by Corey Lee Wrenn), for instance, Michele Martindill (2015) traces the emergence of controversy in the wake of a high-profile blog post that criticized abolitionist veganism for appropriating the language of intersectionality without recognizing its Black feminist roots. The blog argued that animal liberationist groups were increasingly using intersectionality as shorthand for "all oppressions are connected" in a manner that goes, as Martindill puts it, "perilously close to the white-centered claim that all lives matter." She continues: "When anyone in the animal rights movement claims they are practicing intersectional veganism, defining it merely as wanting justice for all and being against all exploitation and oppression, they are operating under a misguided act of cultural appropriation." It was in recognition of the need to avoid this problem of inadvertent appropriation that interviewees suggested that perhaps alternative terminology from ecofeminism or CAS—which have purposefully been developed in relation to animals—would be a way of showing sensitivity to these issues.

These tensions were parsed in a thoughtful way by another interviewee. After stating that intersectionality is a "term that a white cis fellow like me shouldn't be chucking round" without care, he delved into *why* this was the case in a way that was reflexively critical of his own previous actions: "I've stopped using that term because . . . in recent years I feel like there's been more of an acknowledgement that this is something that came out of Black feminism and that, I've been totally guilty of this, has been used opportunistically and removed from that context" (Graham, vegan twelve years). What emerged in this discussion, in particular, but was a common theme across the majority of my interviewees' reflections is the sense that, as Graham put it, intersectionality is not "old wine in new bottles." Intersectionality, in other words, isn't just another means of describing "entangled" or "enmeshed" oppressions (Nibert, 2002; Wright, 2018, 2019) and thus shouldn't be used interchangeably with concepts such as "total liberation" in ways that neglect intersectionality's specificity and origins. At the same time, Graham wondered whether his own worry about whether to use the term "intersectionality"—due to concern about "staying in [his] lane"—could itself be a problem if it resulted in disengaging with the issues raised by intersectional feminist thought. Put differently, the roots of intersectionality mean that it is not interchangeable with other terms that describe the connectedness of oppressions, but resisting the *mis*-use of intersectionality is not the same as avoiding its use entirely. The stakes of this argument are brought home by another interviewee:

> Whilst I can call myself intersectional vegan being a Black person using a term made by a Black woman and I know that the work that I do is intersectional across the board, there is a problem with white vegans using the term intersectional in a way that kind of appropriates and almost hijacks a movement and in doing that they're erasing and ignoring the voices of Black and Brown people . . . to be able to use this term that gives them kind of like this credibility but they're not doing any of the work behind that to make these movements inclusive and intersectional. (Ali, vegan twelve years)

Ali's response is worth dwelling on here as it speaks to the challenges opened up by intersectionality's different usages; here Ali is decisively *not* using the term synonymously with the idea that all oppressions are entangled but in reference to developing a vegan politics that works not just to recognize but dismantle oppressions: including inequities veganism itself might be complicit in. The term "intersectional vegan," Ali argues, becomes problematic when it is used as an individual identity marker or "badge" for people to feel like they're opting out of human and animal oppression through virtue of being vegan, because: "when you put that with a white person feeling like they're not a fucking racist or whatever all of a sudden the badge gets bigger and bigger and bigger and they want to wear the 'I am an intersectional vegan' thing whereas actually intersectional veganism is the thing they should be promoting rather than being an intersectional vegan." Again, these arguments speak to a backdrop of wider debates about the popularity of intersectionality's use as an identity marker, or individualizing label to express allyship, rather than a tool to describe intersecting relations of oppression that then need to be actively unpicked (Crenshaw, 2017; for a more sympathetic critical appraisal of the term's expanded usage, see Nash [2018]).

In a blog post responding to these sorts of controversies, Harper (2018) herself offers an informative response about whether intersectionality should be rejected in the context of veganism, asking: "do I abandon 'intersectionality' now just because it is being 'co-opted' more and more by a status quo that uses it in a 'trendy' way but still doesn't truly want to demolish capitalism and covert-systemic forms of white supremacy"? Concluding the piece with a resounding "no" she continues:

> The goal is not to get "stuck" in swirling around in making a game out of how *"everything is connected"* . . . . You just can't learn about intersectionality as some fun exercise to analyze the world or make fun connections like a puzzle game. Now you have learned that it's all connected to the wheel of neoliberal capitalism/neo-colonialism you need to take [the] next steps . . . to be something *outside of neoliberal capitalist solutions.* (Harper, 2018)

Together, therefore, these critical narratives about the usage of "intersectionality" are helpful in pointing to the danger of intersectional veganism being reduced to a label or marker of particular political commitments. By extension, rather than assuming that veganism intrinsically offers a response to intersecting oppressions in all contexts, it needs to be understood as an ongoing practice that has to negotiate a number of structural barriers if it is to realize this aim.

Not all interviewees straightforwardly echoed these arguments, however, and before moving on, it is useful to engage with the words of participants who made slightly different points. In an early interview I made an attempt to discuss the relationship between veganism and whiteness in what—at the time—I thought marked recognition of my own complicity in structural inequalities. However, when I raised this line of questioning with my interviewee, Benny, he felt I was creating erasures of my own: in this instance sidelining *his* experiences as a Black, UK vegan. In response to a question about what he thought about stereotypes of veganism being a white, middle-class practice, for instance, he warned: "You've got to be careful, that's quite an absolute statement, you've got to ask who's perpetuated that claim, whose benefit it might serve" (Benny, vegan twenty-four years), before engaging in a longer discussion of the dangers of this inference. This response echoes other vegan research where interviewees who faced inequalities voiced discomfort and anger, or even felt patronized, by perceptions of veganism as something white and middle class (Greenebaum, 2018) or inaccessible (Stephens Griffin, 2017: 87–8).[2] It is, of course, important to carefully contextualize such responses. Benny, for instance, is based in the UK, a setting which has an especially problematic relationship with racialized inequalities. Despite commonly framing itself as not sharing the same problems as the United States, a number of scholars have pointed out that racism in the United Kingdom is simply easier to deny due to being the seat of empire but not having to confront its colonial legacies in the same way as North American nations (e.g., Bhopal, 2018). Yet, while this national context is critically important, it is also necessary to recognize that the specific dynamics of the UK means that tensions surrounding *food* politics are manifested slightly differently.

Although strands of veganism are still coded as middle class and elitist, the particular legacies of British colonialism mean that some of the UK's largest diasporic communities have distinctive plant-based food traditions. For instance, restaurant culture associated with South Asian communities in cities such as Leicester have seen it labeled the vegetarian capital of the UK, Rastafari Ital cuisine is common in Afro-Caribbean food outlets, and some of the earliest "celebrity vegans"—most notably Benjamin Zephaniah—were explicit about their anti-racist commitments.[3] The relationship between plant-based food and whiteness, therefore, has historically been messier in the UK than in other national contexts. In this environment, the coding of vegan praxis as a white, individualistic form of politics was perceived by Benny as a *break* with veganism's more radical roots and an act of cutting away alternative narratives and experiences: including his own.

Similar concerns were raised by other interviewees. Karima (vegan twenty-two years), for instance, discussed racism in animal activism extensively throughout her interview, reflecting in particular on the problem of comparison-making between different oppressions and the danger of taking "imagery from the history of race relations and then applying them to animals, other animals, other species, without being aware of . . . the offence that would cause. Even if you're the person who says 'I don't think being called an animal is an insult', the fact is historically it has been an insult!" In addition, at the end of the interview, when I asked if she had any other comments or reflections, she revisited these themes in a slightly different context: "One of the unsolved problems in the animal rights movement is addressing racism. And I've seen it, I keep seeing it, it's still there." In particular, Karima was concerned with the assumption that it is somehow "other cultures" (particularly China) who are culpable for cruelty, and the persistence of these tropes of Othering within activism. Karima's critical reflections are significant in themselves, but it is notable that—like Benny—she also hints at diametrically opposing forms of erasure. While animal activism more broadly might have a long history of using problematic imagery, she argues that it is important to avoid neatly conflating these issues with vegan practice again describing discomfort at the assumption that veganism is a white middle-class movement: "This friend of mine just made this comment about middle class people going vegan is not an adequate solution to environmentalism and I just thought 'is she talking about me'?! And actually that's *not* my background and that wasn't . . . . It's very culturally specific isn't it?" For Karima this point about cultural specificity is critically important because

> It's fair enough if one is trying to analyze veganism within certain countries . . . . But if you're making a general statement about what veganism is, what the history of veganism is, then, you know, yeah I think well: my motivations for becoming vegetarian and the opportunities, or the accessibility of vegetarian food, for me is not a problem because Middle Eastern and Asian cuisine is very . . . is full of vegetables, you don't have a piece of meat as the center of a meal necessarily, so making that transition is not the same, it's not difficult, or not as difficult . . . . I just think: are you talking about a specific population, because the story's much bigger than that!

It is important to underline that questions of classed and racialized inequality should not be swept aside on the basis that they jar with the experiences of specific individuals (especially in light of problematic histories of tokenization in the animal rights movement; Brueck, 2017: 100). At the same time, both Benny and Karima's reactions highlight the need to ensure that critique of certain iterations of veganism does not itself foster exclusions. It is these two types of erasure—which occur in both veganism that neglects intersections with other social justice issues and in critiques of veganism—that I focus on in the rest of this chapter, by turning to a range of examples from popular culture.

Post-race Food Ethics and White Veganism

As these interviews suggest, it is important to distinguish between the lived experience of veganism, which varies significantly between national contexts in terms of accessibility, feasibility, and the norms associated with it, and mediated depictions of veganism that create universalizing narratives about who is a "typical vegan" or perpetuate racist tropes. It is these mediated narratives that I focus on now, to develop a clearer sense of why veganism has attained a problematic status even if this does not mesh with individuals' personal engagements with vegan practice.

If any recent phenomenon illustrates why veganism has been associated with classism, whiteness, and gentrification, it is the infamous blog and recipe book series *T*** Kitchen* (TK), an initiative that has been subject to censure in both vegan scholarship and the wider blogosphere (Harper, 2014; Wrenn, 2014; Wright, 2015: 150; Priestley, Lingo and Royal, 2016).[4] TK originated as a blog that posted recipes using cheap, accessible ingredients, accompanied by a liberal sprinkling of profanity. The tagline of the website was "eat like you give a fuck" and website navigation tools were given labels such as "older shit" (rather than, for instance, "previous recipes"). The recipes themselves had a similar tone, with the summary at the start of a recipe for roasted tomato soup, for example, stating:

> THIS FLU SEASON AIN'T FUCKIN AROUND AND YOU SHOULDN'T EITHER which is why you need a big bowl of our roasted tomato soup bc that canned soup ain't nothin but spoonfuls of sodium.

It was not just that the site used slang or profanity, but that the specific sentence structures, terminology, and linguistic features of the site and books corresponded with the characteristics of African-American Vernacular English (AAVE), leading readers in a certain direction of who the authors might be (Priestly, Lingo and Royal, 2016). This impression was compounded by the book's opening pages, which included the torso of an African-American man skateboarding while holding a canvas bag with the "eat like you give a fuck" slogan. Recipes themselves were accompanied by generic imagery associated with poorer urban areas such as graffiti, cracked pavements, and even shoes on a wire.

Initially, the TK phenomenon was seen in positive terms as a lighthearted means of making healthy eating accessible. On initially engaging with the website, for instance, author of recipe book *Vegan Soul Kitchen* (2009) Bryant Terry describes how TK seemed—at least superficially—to resonate with his own views:

> As an African-American activist and author working to excite people to eat more healthfully (and create more access to fresh affordable food in communities most impacted by food injustice), I have long thought about the important role of pop culture and online media in changing people's attitudes, habits and politics around food. (Terry, 2014)

Terry describes, however, how he grew increasingly discomforted by the blog as time passed, finding its humor—and uses of stereotypes—increasingly problematic. Discomfort shifted to something more profound after food blog *Epicurious* revealed that far from being poor, working-class people of color, TK was written by two middle-class white people, Matt Holloway and Michelle Davis (Priestley, Lingo and Royal, 2016). This revelation was especially problematic in light of the site's title; as Harper explains, the term

> "thug" can be triggering for thousands of Black people in the USA, in light of Oscar Grant, Trayvon Martin, and Michael Brown's murders. Please understand, this is all within a USA context in which the term "thug" has been racialized to mean "a threatening Black male who deserves preemptive strike against just for walking around while Black." This change in the social/racial meaning of "thug" has happened within the past decade, with great significance. Many have argued, "thug" is the PC way to call a Black male the n-word. (Harper, 2018)

In light of the authors' identities, TK's use of language thus shifted from being interpreted as irreverent humor that re-appropriated racially changed stereotypes to something that actively reinscribed racist tropes.

Alexis Priestley, Sarah K. Lingo, and Peter Royal (2016) engage in a sustained critique of TK in their chapter in *Critical Perspectives on Veganism*, focusing on its use of language in further detail. While, building on Harper, the authors underline the need to engage with the blog from an intersectional vegan perspective, they also highlight issues related to its emphasis on accessibility. As Priestly et al. point out, the book and blog appear to offer a means of making veganism financially and technically accessible, in promoting quick, easy, recipes with "regular" ingredients. Yet this promise of accessibility is repeatedly undercut by TK's appeal to ingredients such as "no added ingredient nut butter" that might—as the authors describe—be full of "less shit" than normal peanut butter, but is often inaccessible to those on a budget (Priestley, Lingo and Royal, 2016: 356). This failure of the recipes to enact their promise is significant because many of the ingredients—and even the jokes— used on TK construct certain ways of eating as unhealthy without acknowledging that many of the "healthy" ingredients described are expensive or difficult to access. It is precisely this erasure of the inequalities that shape access to healthy food, which Harper (2012) describes as the defining characteristic of "post-race" alternative food landscapes; the sense that race, class, and other inequalities don't matter and dietary choices are just down to the individual.

It is important to note, however, that while staunchly critical of TK itself, Terry is careful to differentiate between the brand of appropriative white veganism it offers and veganism writ large, arguing that "The worst offense here is the misrepresentation" (a phrase Priestly et al. borrow for their chapter title). Elaborating on what he means by this, Terry states: "African-American cuisine may suffer from the stigma and stereotype of being based in fatty pork-based dishes and butter-heavy comfort foods, but in truth, that kind of meat-heavy, indulgent decadence was scarce for millions struggling under the oppression of segregation before the industrialization of our food system." For Terry, in other words, the problem with TK is not simply misappropriation and racist stereotyping, but in grounding its humor in conceptions of an alternative food landscape that exclude people of color. As Terry puts it, this revelation highlights the deep-rooted problem with TK's humor and its reliance upon "The contrast drawn between the consciously progressive dishes shown and the imagined vulgar, ignorant thug." This joke, he argues,

> only works if the thug is the kind of grimy person of color depicted in the news and in popular media as hustling drugs on a dystopian block, under the colorful glow of various burger stands, bulletproof take-out spots or bodega signs. "Those kind of people," the visual gag suggests, intimidating you into . . . preparing arugula or tempeh? How absurd, how shocking, how hilarious! (Terry, 2014)

While pointing to the symbolic violence wrought by white veganism itself, therefore, these debates also illustrate the importance of ensuring that criticism of texts such as TK does not inadvertently perpetuate these erasures, resonating with concerns raised by Benny and Karima's interviews.

Due to so much controversy surrounding TK it would be easy to write it off as a problematic exception, but it is vital to resist this conclusion and recognize the complex ways that exclusions can manifest themselves in vegan discourse and practice more widely. While TK has been held up as a particularly egregious example of white veganism, as described in the previous chapter, other instances of popular veganism create problems not through neglecting the connections between oppressions but by making connections in disingenuous ways. To deepen understanding of the problems this sort of comparison-making creates, it is informative to return to a more recent PETA campaign.

In February 2020, PETA released a campaign advertisement that they claimed had been "banned" from live broadcast during the Super Bowl. The advertisement itself depicted a series of animated woodland animals humming the Star-Spangled Banner while kneeling solemnly, before fading to the tagline "Respect is the right of every living being" and "#endspeciesism." The menagerie in question was more expansive than might be expected; as well as bears and bees, it included animals such as snakes, fish, and—of course—a bald eagle. While involving animals who don't actually have knees might have been intended to disrupt the type of speciesist distinctions pointed to by Joy (2011; see previous chapter); this relentless series of images created a semiotic excess that appeared to parody Take a Knee's original meaning.

The proposed placing of the advertisement—to be broadcast during the Super Bowl—alongside the act of taking a knee itself, was in direct reference to the series of symbolic protest acts that spread across the US National Football League from 2016 in support of Black Lives Matter. PETA suggested their work was a marker of "respect" for figures such as Colin Kaepernick who had initiated the protests, while also offering a "lighthearted approach to a very serious subject: the abuse of animals killed and raised for food" (PETA, 2020). As highlighted in the previous chapter, however, a number of commentators have pointed out that such imagery is not only disingenuous but doomed to failure, due to working within the parameters of cultural discourses that already treat some humans as having fewer rights than others (Kim, 2011). In this context, rather than unsettling human/animal distinctions, such tactics simply perpetuate the construction of preexisting inequalities. Here, in addition, the unexpected species taking a knee, combined with PETA's framing of the campaign as "lighthearted," couches the imagery in postmodern irony to the extent that it is difficult to gain critical purchase on it (a tactic routinely used to deflect criticism of deliberately offensive texts by positioning those harmed by them as failing to get the joke, see Chapter 7).

As outlined in Chapter 5, PETA's detrimental connection-making between humans and animals is not new (Harper, 2010b), but the ramifications of these tactics have gained heightened significance over the course of the past decade due to parallel forms of appropriation by white supremacist groups who have deliberately used slogans such as #alllivesmatter to depoliticize questions about the specific violence created by institutional racism. While uses of similar slogans by animal advocacy groups might not have intended to reinforce racist rhetoric, even taken on face value as referring to the intrinsic value of all life, this sentiment perpetuates the notion that society has entered a "post-race" era.

The concept of post-race refers to dominant discourse in society, which "insists that the legacy of racial discrimination and disadvantage has been waning over time, reaching a point today where, if existing at all, such discrimination is anomalous and individually expressed. It is not structural or socially mandated" (Goldberg, 2015: 2). As with similar cultural phenomena such as postfeminism (Gill, 2007, 2017; see the next chapter), post-race discourse portrays anti-racist work as no longer required because society has already attained equality, at least in a technical sense. Such perspectives do not necessarily deny that racism (or indeed misogyny, classism, and homophobia) exists, but attribute racism to individual "bad apples" rather than seeing it as something structural or institutional that requires profound social change. Although policy initiatives that "yok[e] antiracist discourses to colour-blind denials of racial privilege and stigma" have a history dating back to the 1940s (Mukherjee, 2016: 49; see also Crenshaw, 1997), contemporary post-race discourse is more commonly associated with the Obama era. As Roopali Mukherjee argues, the existence of a Black president is routinely evoked to illustrate that race no longer matters in a manner that "re-envisions the scriptures of colour-blindness by firmly acknowledging a specified range of racial differences that serve to disavow any vestige of their consequence for anyone—of any race—who can fashion themselves as properly neoliberal subjects" (Mukherjee, 2016: 50). This concept of post-race, in other words, speaks to a broader constellation of developments in which different forms of inequality are reframed as individual rather than social problems. It is this series of developments that David Theo Goldberg is referring to when describing the neoliberalization of race (Goldberg, 2009).

Post-race is a critically important concept for making sense of tensions surrounding contemporary veganism both within and outside of the United States, as evidenced not just by parallel arguments made in the United Kingdom (e.g., Bhopal, 2018) but the transnational visibility afforded to these phenomena as they are circulated, particularly online. Harper, for instance, describes her *Sistah Vegan Project* website explicitly as "a critical race feminist's journey through the 'post-racial' ethical foodscape and beyond." Harper's criticisms here speak to the way that, in the context of vegan advocacy, notions that race, class, gender, and other inequalities are irrelevant are sometimes used to justify sweeping these concerns aside to get the job of animal advocacy done (e.g., Harper, 2010a, 2012). Aph Ko (2017a) offers an informative illustration of how these discourses operate in practice, in an essay that details responses to her curation of a list of influential Black vegans—#BlackVegansRock—as a means of combatting white-dominated depictions of vegans in the mainstream media. When the list was posted on the Vegan Society's social media accounts, it generated a large number of critical comments, which are revealing in terms of how post-race discourse and veganism can come together. These responses ran the gamut of accusing Ko of reverse racism to lamenting that race shouldn't matter, vegan outreach shouldn't be complicated by bringing up other forms of discrimination, that it is more important to focus on the truly voiceless: the animals, and that the hashtag should instead be #AllVegansRock (see Ko, 2017a: 13–19).

Ko's essay, though, also points to dangers that can arise in commonplace criticisms leveled at veganism. The reason Ko published the list was because even though dominant discourses about veganism centralize whiteness, this is not the same as saying all vegans are white. As Ko puts it, "Vegans of color were [already] doing the work, but there wasn't any serious infrastructure in place to ensure they were receiving the visibility and support in the global advocacy movement they deserved" (Ko, 2017a: 14). Her initiative, in other words, was designed to counter the marginalization of vegans of color in mainstream depictions of veganism, which, in contemporary contexts, often consists of a celebrity culture of white, heterosexual vegans promoting vegan ethics as a lifestyle that is oriented around purchasing the right products (Harper, 2012; Doyle, 2016). These perceptions are, of course, against a backdrop of exclusionary narratives propagated by phenomena like TK or disingenuous comparison-making within PETA campaigns. Such exclusions, however, do not just exist in popular vegan discourse but can also be reinforced by criticisms of veganism that continue to perpetuate stereotypes about who a typical vegan might be. To gain purchase on the significance of this, very different, form of erasure, it is useful to reflect on responses to another prominent event from early 2020: Joaquin Phoenix's speech for his best actor Academy Award.

Phoenix's speech fostered controversy by drawing connections between different social justice issues, with Phoenix stating that "whether we're talking about gender inequality or racism or queer rights or indigenous rights or animal rights, we're talking about the fight against injustice. We're talking about the fight against the belief that one nation, one people, one race, one gender, one species, has the right to dominate, use and control another with impunity." This speech received high-profile criticisms for being perceived to flatten out distinctions between different forms of suffering. A high-profile article in UK newspaper *The Independent* by journalist Harriet Hall, for instance, described Phoenix's attempts to connect different social justice issues as a "galling juxtaposition" that "highlights Phoenix's already startling male privilege" (Hall, 2020). Hall's critique, however, was itself condemned by author and researcher Christopher Sebastian, who expressed unease at the idea of conflating "bad" connection-making (such as PETA's) with all attempts to create connections, arguing that this conflation sidelines existing work by high-profile anti-racist, queer, and feminist activists who have a long history of more sensitive and complex connection-making (see also Ko, S. 2017). Hall's arguments, Sebastian argues, make exactly the same rhetorical "white savior" moves that she attributes to Phoenix: leveraging certain forms of discrimination to dismiss others in what Sebastian describes as "dishonest virtue signaling at best, and willful weaponizing of oppression at worst" (Sebastian, 2020).

These arguments are part of a long-standing set of concerns articulated by Sebastian in a series of essays appearing on his website. Another think-piece—"If Veganism is Racist and Classist, Bad News for Nonveganism" (2018)—for instance, focuses on important criticisms of veganism for failing to grapple with problems such as food deserts. Though these criticisms are vital, Sebastian suggests that they become dangerous when articulated by those who are neither "living in a food desert themselves" nor "experiencing the type of economic hardship that would preclude them from limiting their participation in human and animal exploitation." Inequalities, he argues, should not be deployed by those unaffected by them to dismiss environmental and animal ethics.

However, even as Sebastian is critical of the "weaponization of oppression" he doesn't leave veganism itself off the hook and his work also makes a series of incisive criticisms of "single-issue vegans" who shame particular communities who face conditions that might make veganism a challenge.[5] Sebastian, moreover, is not alone in adopting a critical stance toward both exclusionary forms of veganism *and* critiques that perpetuate these exclusions, with his work forming part of a broader counter-discourse that takes aim at both modes of erasure. For instance, while Mi'kmaq scholar Margaret Robinson (2017) foregrounds problematic attitudes toward Indigenous people that she has encountered in animal activism, she has also criticized patronizing and essentializing assumptions on the part of those who "project white imperialism onto vegans" in order to "bond with Aboriginal people over meat-eating" (2013: 190). Brueck, likewise, reiterates that while it is important to be critical of vegan praxis that contributes to or ignores other forms of oppression, the conflation of white veganism with *all* veganism carries its own erasures:

> It IS possible to work towards anti-speciesism while being pro-intersectional and anti-oppression. Don't use your solidarity with marginalized humans to reject veganism, even if those marginalized humans cannot go fully vegan at the moment due to access, mental health, or other issues. Your commitment to social justice of any kind should not be contingent on the individual or societal circumstances of others. (2017: 22)

Brueck's arguments echo the interventions made by Ko's #BlackVegansRock initiative and Harper's *Sistah Vegan* (2010b): which critique post-race food cultures, while also providing a platform for engagements with veganism by people of color who are marginalized from mainstream depictions of veganism as white and middle class.[6] Subsequent research by Harper (e.g., 2012) has continued to highlight the complexity of vegan practice and representation: of the need to acknowledge the imbrication of food systems in classed and racialized inequalities, and how this might delimit ethical praxis, while also recognizing the erasures that arise on neglecting non-Westernized ethical, cultural, and religious traditions where the elimination of animal products is commonplace. The simultaneous need to address veganism's exclusions and the challenges in doing so can be brought to the fore when turning to the conflicting narratives that surround global veganism.

Global Veganism(s)

One of the biggest sources of tension associated with contemporary veganism relates to the relationship between modes of vegan politics that have been popularized in settings such as the Global North and industrialized, urban South, and those that have emerged in the Majority World. Different arguments have emerged, which resonate with the forms of erasure described in this chapter. Veganism has been accused, for instance, of positioning itself as the first type of cultural movement that has sought to eliminate animal products. This narrative has been criticized for contributing to the erasure of other food traditions that have long encouraged abstention from animal products. A number of popular commentaries argue that the positioning of Donald Watson as "founder" of veganism, for instance, runs the risk of erasing other contexts where animal products have been eliminated for religious and cultural reasons: such as Rastafarianism, Hinduism, Jainism, and Buddhism (e.g., Shah, 2018).[7]

Redressing the problem of exclusion, however, is something that requires care, especially due to the complications posed by post-race discourses about lifestyle ethics. Some commentaries suggest that decentering an Anglo-European narrative about veganism simply requires recognizing the existence of vegan practice that preceded and continues to run alongside its contemporary "Westernized" iteration. What matters, however, is *how* these stories are told. Two dangers emerge in particular; first, there is a risk of creating well-intentioned narratives that are designed to be inclusive and decenter white, Westernized notions of plant-based lifestyle politics, but inadvertently achieve the opposite by homogenizing a range of dietary and cultural practices as proto-iterations of what has come to be understood as "veganism" in the Vegan Society sense. Second, it is important to situate debates about global veganism within a popular cultural landscape dominated by post-race narratives about food culture, wherein the act of highlighting the existence of plant-based foods in a variety of global contexts has sometimes been used to *defend* veganism against criticisms of whiteness and cultural insensitivity. Thus, while it is vitally important to develop more pluralistic, expansive notions of veganism—which refuse to cut away vegan histories and cultural contexts that have very different origins to the stories and representations that are usually centralized—it is also important to carefully situate these narratives.

When reading articles, blogs, and popular commentaries to research this book, for instance, a recurring theme emerged in critical narratives. Many texts attempted to go beyond culturally specific understanding of "veganism," that centralize the UK Vegan Society, by pointing out that vegan food has long existed in contexts outside of Europe, prior to the coining of the term "vegan" itself. Broad references to Hinduism and Buddhism were commonplace, as were commentaries pointing out that vegan staples—from hummus and falafel to tempeh, tofu, and mock duck—are "non-Western" in origin. Indeed, as Cole (2014: 205) points out, the founding documents of the Vegan Society itself recognized that plant-based dietary practice did not originate with them, or even with the formalized emergence of vegetarianism in the nineteenth century.

On one hand, tracing these longer histories is important in recognizing that an ethos of refusing to treat animals as resources does not begin and end with North American and Western European practices (in line with Harper, 2012). It is valuable, in other words, to recognize that abstention from animal products in specific religious and cultural contexts does not neatly map onto contemporary "veganism" (e.g., Avieli and Markowitz, 2018; Barstow, 2017; Valpey, 2020). On the other hand, as well as complicating "Westernized" histories of vegan practice, more expansive narratives about veganism also complicate *critiques* of vegan practice. As described earlier, criticisms of veganism are often grounded in a wariness of universalizing modes of ethics, which do not acknowledge their positionality within specific, often economically privileged, contexts. The danger of these critiques is that they can themselves centralize a version of veganism as a privileged, "Western" phenomenon, which perpetuates monolithic understandings of what veganism is and means. Indeed, it is even dangerous to suggest that the current manifestation of "plant-based capitalism" (see Chapter 7) is somehow a phenomenon restricted to North America and Western European contexts. In South Korea, for instance, there is a burgeoning industry that has emerged around commodifying Buddhist temple cuisine. Seoul restaurant Balwoo Gongyang holds a Michelin star, while literature distributed to diners eating in Sanchon describes how the owner (a former Buddhist monk) holds a PhD in business for his research exploring how to commercialize temple food.

It is necessary, therefore, to trace continuities and affinities between different contexts where uses of animals for human benefit have been eliminated, in order to complicate and decenter normative narratives about veganism that have been articulated both in support of vegan practice and in order to criticize it. At the same time, it is also important that pro-vegan perspectives resist presuming a homogenous overarching narrative about veganism as some sort of global phenomenon. Dietary, lifestyle, or spiritual practices from different global contexts might bear superficial similarities to one another, but do not necessarily hold identical meanings or implications, because they are shaped by radically different religious or ethical commitments and in some instances by socioeconomic necessity. Research about Buddhism and plant-based food, for example, has pointed out that these ideals often come into conflict with cultural realities that create differences between theory and practice (Barstow, 2017); an analysis that challenges the way that Buddhism is sometimes evoked as a straightforward counterpoint to critical narratives about the "Western-ness" or privilege of veganism.

My own initial, conflicted response to reading narratives that made claims about global veganism was informed by personal experience. My father is Lebanese and was brought up in the Middle East. Some of my fondest memories are of Dad's excitement at realizing that foods from his background were "accidentally" vegan and of us making a mess of the kitchen as we charred the skins of aubergines for dishes like baba ghanoush (particularly the time when he forgot to pierce an aubergine and it exploded during cooking). Yet while these experiences underline that plant-based cuisine is not a recent phenomenon, the associations Dad and I have of these foods are slightly different. On his part, for instance, baba ghanoush is an everyday staple with no specific ethical connotations, whereas on my part it has often been a special veggie menu option that is rooted in a particular food politics. It is not straightforward, in other words, to situate certain foods as part of some global vegan narrative. Indeed, the conflation of all dishes that happen to be plant-based with veganism is not only misrepresentative but can inadvertently contribute to post-race understandings of food. Such narratives can point to foodstuffs that happen to be vegan in different global contexts, in order to foreground the universality of vegan practice while neglecting the very different contexts and meanings behind these foods.[8]

More subtly problematic tensions can be found in narratives that infer that there are intrinsic connections between particular ethnicities or religions and veganism: even if this move is intended to de-centralize Westernized narratives about its origins. Rama Ganesan's essay in *Veganism in an Oppressive World*, for instance, expresses frustration at speaking to yoga-loving vegans who infer some intrinsic connection between Hinduism and veganism. She points out not only that this is a misinterpretation of Hindu interpretations of human-animal relations but also that "the beef ban in India is a form of oppression by a nationalistic government and that vegetarianism is a form of upper class purity—which is, in fact, a direct contradiction to intersectional vegan advocacy" (2017: 66). Indeed, other research has not only pointed to the role of vegetarianism in purity narratives that support Hindu nationalism, and its attendant Islamophobia, but also suggests it has played a constitutive role in the Indian caste system (following Ambedkar, 2020).[9] It is important, therefore, to recognize the complexities of how different oppressions are enmeshed in an Indian context. Yamini Narayanan's critical appraisal of cow protectionism, for instance, argues: "To meaningfully advocate for animals, the Indian animal advocacy movement needs to clearly reflect upon the sectarianism, casteism and speciesism inherent in cow protection, or it consciously and/or unreflectively becomes complicit in sustaining oppressive discourses" (2018: 349). This argument offers a warning to animal activists to resist tactically using cow protectionism as a means of popularizing their aims. At the same time Narayanan suggests that an animal advocacy which takes the riskier approach of campaigning for *all* animals could play a more productive role, both in settling cow exceptionalism and the hierarchies the ideology is entangled with.

Again, these debates are too complex to do justice to here, but the debates Narayanan sets out productively highlight and unsettle different forms of erasure. As her work underlines, while the eschewal of animal products is not a "Western" phenomenon, this does not mean that it is possible to straightforwardly transplant narratives about entangled oppressions that have been developed in specific contexts and apply them to other settings (see also Narayanan, 2017). It is, in other words, necessary to pay careful attention to context and history in order to situate narratives about *veganism*, but the same situatedness is equally important when analyzing—and making claims about—how shared *oppressions* between humans and animals manifest themselves.

Wright's *Vegan Studies Project* helps to foreground the importance and complexity of situating narratives about enmeshed oppressions. At the start of the book she suggests that stigma attached to veganism in the United States is not just due to its nonnormative status, but the product of specific discourses emerging from the war on terror that have stigmatized diets perceived as "un-American." In Wright's words: "Veganism, as a nonnormative dietary choice in the United States, represented as an ideology at odds with an increasingly authoritarian regime . . . became associated with protest, dissent, Muslim dietary dictates, and terrorism, and had to be covertly monitored" (2015: 41). As discussed previously, Wright's work is important in picking apart the situated ways that vegan identity is constructed in US culture. However, something about the particular set of linkages evoked in this framing of enmeshed oppressions sat uneasily with me when first reading these lines.

My response was initially a visceral one. Although my family background is Muslim and I have close family who are not from the UK and racialized in particular ways, I am non-practicing and pass as white. Many of my childhood memories involve realizing my privilege as I was able to pass through securitized spaces—most notably airports—far more smoothly than family members (and I have no doubt on many other occasions I was oblivious to this privilege). These personal experiences stand in stark contrast with the relentless, everyday racism and Islamophobia endured by family and friends, thus any inference that my own experiences of exclusion at being vegan is anything like these structural forms of discrimination made me automatically wary. As Shazia Juna points out, moreover, there is no neat linkage between Islam and veganism; far from being associated with Muslim dietary practices Juna instead details having to navigate tensions between "personal ethical choices and sociocultural norms" (2017: 59)—including resistance from family members—in her own negotiation between her Islamic background and veganism.

It is important, however, to try to make sense of these frictions in a manner that goes beyond my initial, knee-jerk reaction. First, my experiences are UK-based and the discourses described by Wright are in the United States where hostility to lifestyles deemed nonnormative—particularly beyond the coastal regions and certain large cities—is more pronounced. Moreover, Wright is tracing a specific discourse wherein the label "animal" is both used to justify ongoing violence toward animals and serves a label that can then be applied to particular groups of humans, as a means of excluding them from ethical consideration (Wright, 2018). Yet these debates are complex. Although connections between anti-vegan and nationalist discourses are commonplace—as with uses of milk symbolism or the derogatory epithet "soyboy" by white supremacist groups (Gambert and Linné, 2018b; see Chapter 3)—other far-right discourses make very different connections that sometimes shade into a pro-animal stance. Criticism of Halal (and Kosher) meat, for instance, is also often deployed by far-right political organizations in the UK to denigrate religious and ethnic minorities (Clark et al., 2008); indeed, one of the ways it is easy to tell if a particular group's animal rights credentials are simply dog-whistle racism and anti-Semitism is if they begin and end with a criticism of particular slaughter methods.

It is important not to conflate racially motivated criticism of particular forms of animal slaughter with veganism, as sometimes occurs, because these far-right discourses usually consist of appropriative uses of animal rights language that focus on very specific dietary practices (namely those associated with religious or ethnic minorities in particular national contexts). In contrast, human-animal relationships that might be oppressive but conform to certain nationalistic norms are valorized (paralleling Narayanan's work on Hindu nationalism in an Indian context). What *is* still necessary to reflect upon, however, is whether appropriations of pro-animal discourse by the Right complicate assumptions that veganism is always a response to—and way out of—enmeshed oppressions. In many instances, the oppression of animals and particular groups of humans *does* align in nationalist state-building projects: as typified by Jair Bolsonaro's removal of Indigenous and environmental protections in Brazil, for instance (Gillespie and Narayanan, 2020). In other instances, pro-animal rhetoric runs the risk of placing different social justice issues at odds with one another. Esther Alloun points, for instance, to instances of "veganwashing" where concern for animals has sometimes been used to support settler-colonialist projects, by delineating between those deemed "civilized" and "uncivilized," and charts the complex ways that both Palestinian and Israeli activists seek to negotiate and overcome these tensions (Alloun, 2020; see also Alloun, 2018). The way different oppressions are configured, in other words, might vary dramatically across and within national contexts. Correspondingly, the means of unpicking enmeshed oppressions can be radically different and demand attention to specific histories, social contexts, and institutional arrangements (echoing Cudworth, 2014).

Conclusion

Through assembling a range of texts that typify the problems of "white veganism" and elucidating how complex it can be to create global narratives about vegan practice, without either misappropriating or cutting away plant-based food cultures with longer histories, this chapter has highlighted different forms of erasure. In addition to foregrounding well-documented problems associated with white veganism itself, as manifested in issues discussed by interviewees and examples from popular culture, I have sought to centralize counter-discourse pushing for a veganism that engages with the relationship between the oppression of humans and nonhuman animals. While being staunchly critical of particular iterations of vegan lifestyle politics, activism, and media culture, these thinkers have shown that overly general critique of vegan practice can serve to undercut anti-oppressive aims by fostering erasures of its own: centralizing white, middle-class conceptions of veganism at the expense of other experiences. What is also underlined by the academic-activist interventions that I have focused on in the chapter is the importance of avoiding appeals to either "the global" or "cultural difference"—and all of the ethnocentric assumptions attached to these generalized labels—as rhetorical footballs to legitimize either pro- or anti- vegan arguments. Indeed, even across different European contexts (Aavik, 2019a, 2019b) or within the same North American contexts (Harper, 2010b, 2012; Robinson, 2013), vegan practice and experience is far from homogeneous: a point again underlined by interviewees.

A particularly difficult question raised by these debates is whether it is possible to articulate a more situated understanding of veganism without descending into a relativism that maintains a sense of animals as Other. As argued in this chapter, resources for addressing this question can be found in work by thinkers *already* working at the nexus of different forms of inequality, who are not only trying to trace but—in Harper's (2018) terms—dismantle these relationships by recognizing oppression as something multidimensional (Ko, 2019). Yet even as the thinkers drawn on throughout this chapter have centralized intersecting and multidimensional oppressions, they have done so without reinforcing anthropocentric hierarchies or excluding animals from consideration.

Some of the most promising work that has trod the difficult line of exploring relationships between oppressions, without homogenizing these relationships, can be found in dialogue between cutting-edge cultural theory and more public-facing theoretical work: such as Aph Ko's engagement with the work of Zakiyyah Iman Jackson and Claire Jean Kim. Jackson argues that a common way of understanding the relationship between racism and speciesism is that "animal" is an exclusionary label, which has historically been projected onto people of color to deny them of human rights (a perspective that is sometimes shared by key texts in Vegan Studies and strands of animal studies, notably posthumanist approaches; see Chapter 2). What this analysis misses, Jackson argues, is the way that concepts of animality and race have shaped one another from the start: with the origins of contemporary understandings of both "species" and "the human" having their roots in projects of colonial expansion that gathered force during the European Enlightenment (Jackson, 2020: 3; see also Jackson, 2015, 2016; Kim, 2015).

For Ko, the insights offered by this theoretical rethinking of the relationship between human and animal oppression have significant bearing on activism. At present, she argues, wider uptake of narratives of intersectional veganism (especially beyond their original context in Black feminism) runs the risk of adding "speciesism" as another axis of oppression that people need to reflect on: something that can just serve to add to the burden of those who are already struggling to attain social justice (Ko, 2019: 26). For this reason, Ko is wary of vegan activism that simply tries to encourage people of color to become vegan. Instead, she emphasizes the need for a "multidimensional" perspective on oppression, which both situates a critique of animality as part of—rather than a distraction from—anti-racist activism while also illustrating the need for animal and vegan activism to engage more meaningfully with questions posed by race and racism.

Responding to the challenges opened up by recent academic and activist interventions looks set to be a complicated task and, as I have reflected on at various points throughout this chapter, even the desire to enact a politics that recognizes the relationships between oppressions can inadvertently do the opposite, especially when coming from a place of privilege. I certainly do not exempt my own perspective from this problem, informed as it is by being a white-passing woman based in the UK. Echoing Polish (2016), this chapter has sought to centralize the voices of those already engaged in vegan praxis that centralizes the relationships between oppression and who have raised vital criticisms of contemporary veganism while also showing paths forward.

Some informative lessons about how to engage with these sorts of sympathetic critiques of veganism can be learned from examining similar dynamics between second-wave feminism and the interventions made by women of color throughout the 1970s and 1980s, which gave birth to intersectional feminism. Theoretical work has argued that attending to the complexities of feminist narratives is vital in opening up the stories that are told about second-wave feminism, which are often misrepresented as suggesting that critique of a specific iteration of white feminism should result in the dismissal of feminism writ large (Hemmings, 2005; Wiegman, 2012). These thinkers are *not* engaging in a wholesale defense of second-wave feminism, but instead arguing that entirely conflating it with white feminism sidelines the role of Black feminist thought: rendering it merely as something that critiqued, rather than that actively complicated and contributed to, feminism.

When telling stories about veganism, likewise, it is vital to recognize the plurality of stories that can and need to be told. Broad-brush dismissals of vegan practice often frame sympathetic critiques—which have drawn attention to systemic inequalities, problems associated with particular forms of activism, or even tensions within animal studies as an academic field—as merely criticism of, rather than contributing to, veganism's rethinking of human-animal relationships. This narrative is dangerous. The power of engaging with activism and critical social theories—including critical race theory, Black feminism, the social model of disability, and queer studies—is that such approaches offer an important space for confronting material questions about how to decolonize strands of vegan praxis that fail to recognize the imbrication of particular social arrangements in racist, classist, and ablist inequalities. The risk of using sympathetic critique of vegan practice to dismiss veganism outright is that such a dismissal can inadvertently sideline the urgent, concrete, and complex questions opened up by this body of work: avoiding, rather than grappling with, the task of how to respond to these vital interventions.

Chapter 7

POST-VEGAN?

THE RISE OF PLANT-BASED CAPITALISM

This book began by suggesting that an important, burgeoning, area of research about veganism relates to tensions that have emerged in the wake of its ongoing popularity. As discussed previously, while the popularization of veganism is seen by many as worthy of celebration, popularity also creates challenges. Certain developments have made it easier to maintain vegan practices, including broader cultural awareness of what veganism is, the fashionability of veganism (at least in certain contexts), and the increasing accessibility of vegan food, alongside a flourishing internet culture of vegan communities and support networks. These developments, however, have been accompanied by friction generated by the attendant commercialization of veganism, which troubles its potential to be more than a diet. Questions are arising, for instance, about whether activist-vegan ethics—which rethink human-animal relationships beyond food and seek to engage with other anti-oppression movements—are being displaced by a "lifestyle veganism" that is "uncoupled and detached from related actions relevant to inter-species social justice" (White, 2018). In other words, rather than offering a more fundamental rethinking of how particular humans relate to other beings, the popularization of certain aspects of vegan practice (and not others) has brought the political emphasis back onto food.

This chapter identifies some of the major tensions that have emerged in the wake of veganism's (partial) move to the mainstream, with a focus on messy distinctions that have begun to emerge between popular veganisms and grassroots vegan practice stemming from a more radical tradition. Or, put differently, the difference between a veganism that is concerned with interrogating human-animal relations in a range of contexts and as part of a wider analysis of "enmeshed" and "multidimensional" oppressions (Wright, 2018, 2019; Ko, 2019) and what I refer to here as "plant-based capitalism" that centers around eating. The label "plant-based capitalism" itself is inspired by the reflections of interviewees who I have engaged with in my own wider research exploring what "long-term" vegans (who have engaged in vegan practice for at least ten years) think and feel about its recent popularization.

A recurring theme across these interviews was criticism of the label "plant-based," which people saw as a depoliticizing term that referred solely to food and, as such, was emblematic of broader challenges surrounding veganism's popularity. Although "plant-based" was not perceived as intrinsically problematic in its own terms, interviewees were wary about the routine way this label was used instead of, or sometimes conflated with, veganism in contexts such as restaurant menus and food marketing, as well as within popular culture more broadly. In particular, people were concerned that labeling foods as plant-based marked an attempt to detach certain products from the longer histories of veganism; even speculating this was a deliberate act of distancing on the part of food manufacturers to take advantage of growing markets without engaging with the ethical connotations of veganism.

Events in early 2020 help to bring home the stakes of these developments, when a high-profile employment tribunal in the UK ruled that an employer (anti-blood sports charity The League Against Cruel Sports) had discriminated against one of its employees for being an "ethical vegan" by dismissing him after he raised concerns about its pension investments in companies involved with animal research (Kay, 2020). The judge deemed ethical veganism to be a protected characteristic under the 2010 Equality Act in a move that, on one level, appeared to be an important legislative development for vegans. As Kate Stewart and Matthew Cole (2020) point out, however, the danger is that the addendum "ethical" reframes values that have historically been an integral component of veganism to instead being a fringe concern, relevant only to a specific type of vegan practice. Describing the explosion in plant-based foods as a new "green rush" for multinational food corporations, they warn: "This massive increase in the number (and popularity) of products without animal ingredients, frequently described as 'vegan', doesn't necessarily reflect the ethics of the movement that invented the word" (Stewart and Cole, 2020). It is in light of such social and legislative developments that terms such as "plant-based" assume more profound meaning, epitomizing tensions between, on the one hand, a desire for veganism to become more widespread and, on the other hand, concern that the *way* this mainstreaming is happening is detrimentally narrowing the meaning and connotations of eliminating animal products by stripping vegan practice of its fundamental ethical significance. These arguments are rapidly evolving and some thinkers have argued that the meaning of "vegan" should be stripped down to a simple definition as a dietary practice, for the purpose of maximizing inclusivity and clarity (Dutkiewicz and Dickstein, 2021). Yet, though such interventions are both valuable and thought-provoking, the social and cultural affordances that veganism is assuming in the present moment illustrate potential risks in detaching the "ethical."

This chapter unpacks some of the tensions surrounding the new "green rush" (Stewart and Cole, 2020) of plant-based capitalism, drawing on insights from my interviewees alongside a range of examples that form the backdrop of popular vegan culture (including social media, blogs, recipe books, marketing materials, agricultural reports, and pro-vegan campaigns). Building on the approach taken in the previous chapter, which sought to centralize and learn from scholarship from a critical race studies perspective that has interrogated the dangers of post-race alternative food landscapes, this chapter engages with complementary work that has criticized *postfeminist* media discourse. By reading developments in popular veganism against this body of feminist research, I identify several emergent themes that constitute what can be thought of as a "post-vegan" sensibility within popular vegan culture; a sensibility which places the emphasis on individual (consumer-oriented) action as opposed to structural change. The developments that characterize post-veganism, however, are perhaps more ambivalent than postfeminism (which, as I outline in more depth later, is itself a highly complex cultural phenomenon), and also carry hopeful potentials that complicate a straightforward reading of post-veganism as entirely apolitical.

Learning from Postfeminist Critique

As touched on previously, veganism is not the only social or political movement that has had to negotiate problems associated with its popularization. In the contemporary political landscape, a number of other social movements—most prominently strands of environmental activism—have seen an uptick in popularity along with concern about the potentials and pitfalls this popularity could engender (Doherty, De Moor and Hayes, 2018). Perhaps the most prominent movement that has had to negotiate tensions associated with its mainstreaming, however, is feminism. These parallels mean it is useful to offer a sketch of existing tools and debates within feminist media and cultural studies, which speak to tensions that can arise when disruptive modes of politics become popularized.

Sarah Banet-Weiser characterizes popular feminisms as having three dimensions. First, she suggests, "feminism manifests in discourses and practices that are circulated in popular and commercial media, such as digital spaces like blogs, Instagram, and Twitter, as well as broadcast media. As such, these discourses have an accessibility that is not confined to academic enclaves or niche groups" (2018: 1). In addition, Banet-Weiser continues, popular feminism holds a more generic meaning, signifying "the condition of being liked or admired by like-minded people and groups, as *popularity*" (1). As well as being characterized by accessibility and popularity "the 'popular' is, as cultural theorist Stuart Hall argued, a terrain of struggle, a space where competing demands for power battle it out. This means that there are many different feminisms that circulate in popular culture at the moment and some of these feminisms are more visible than others" (Banet-Weiser, 2018: 1). Some of the feminisms that are circulating in popular culture might have progressive potential; digital media platforms such as Twitter and Instagram, for instance, have played an important role in circulating Black, intersectional and trans-inclusive feminisms to wider audiences (Jackson, Bailey and Foucault Welles, 2018, 2020). Other iterations of popular feminisms are more dangerous, in centering white, middle-class, cisgender women while erasing other experiences (Phipps, 2020).

Some of the most prominent, individualized expressions of feminism, which have been criticized in academic contexts, for instance, are those grouped together under the label "postfeminism" (see Gill, 2007, 2017). This term is used in reference to media depictions of empowerment that shift the focus away from collective action and structural change, instead treating empowerment as being all about individual women's freedom of choice. Empowerment in this context is commonly articulated through consumption (Butler, 2013: 46), with practices that were formerly seen as perpetuating patriarchal social relations or gender stereotypes—high heels, glamour modeling, pole-dancing, plastic surgery—recast as empowering acts of re-appropriation on the part of individuals. While the politics of these shifts are complex and can hold a messier relationship to social norms than is often assumed (Holliday and Sanchez Taylor, 2006), important questions have been posed about *who* is able to choose to engage in these individualistic expressions of empowerment and indeed whether the valorization of the individual's freedom to choose makes it more difficult to critique structural oppressions.

In recent years, high-profile instances of animal rights campaigns in general and vegan campaigns specifically have been read as postfeminist texts (Fegitz and Pirani, 2018). Perhaps unsurprisingly, in light of the issues discussed in the previous chapters, an archetypal example of postfeminist media culture can be found in some of PETA's activism. Their prominent "lettuce ladies" campaigns, for example, encourage volunteers to wear bikinis made of salad leaves to promote veganism in public spaces. The webpage for these volunteers describes how they "embody empowerment," because: "Lettuce Ladies *choose* to turn heads to protect animals, improve people's health, and help fight climate change." Additionally, they suggest that "in a society that uses scantily clad models to sell everything from cars to cheeseburgers, those who use their bodies as a political or an emotional statement to call for justice and compassion—as our Lettuce Ladies do—are a breath of fresh air" (PETA, 2020b). It is in light of such narratives that Corey Lee Wrenn argues that the ascendancy of postfeminism and "choice feminism" actively makes it difficult to address the ongoing exploitation of women's emotional and affective labor within animal activism (Wrenn, 2015; Wrenn, 2016: 94–5). PETA's description of their lettuce ladies, for instance, evokes a narrative of empowerment through individual choice, to deflect the complex politics of *who* is able to make certain choices (here the choice to use a particular, heteronormative construction of sexuality to promote veganism) without bearing the stigma attached to other women who engage in these practices as work.[1] Or, indeed, without reflecting upon how initiatives such as "lettuce ladies" perpetuate social norms, which mean only those with the "right" body-type could ever hope to be a lettuce lady in the first place (cf Wright, 2015: 137).

As elucidated by the "lettuce ladies" campaign, the individualistic conceptions of empowerment centralized by postfeminism are dangerous for two reasons. First, the notion that empowerment is something that can be enacted on an individual level ignores connections between oppressions. A large body of critical research about postfeminism has pointed out, for instance, that not everyone has the social or economic resources to attain conventional social markers of "success" and this lack of opportunity is invariably entangled with race, class, and sexual inequalities as well as gender (see Littler, 2017). The dynamics of postfeminism, therefore, speak to A. Breeze Harper's (2012) criticism of post-race foodscapes that have a similar emphasis on the individual (see previous chapter); wherein veganism is framed as an ethically empowering personal choice, in a manner that neglects the structural constraints that need to be overcome in order to access such choices.

The second criticism leveled at postfeminism is perhaps more specific to this form of media culture and associated with the way that individualistic empowerment narratives are mediated. Angela McRobbie (2004, 2009) frames the dynamics of postfeminism as a "double entanglement" of feminism and anti-feminism, where the former is consistently undermined by the latter. In postfeminist media culture, feminist values—of equality, liberation, and empowerment—appear repeatedly, only to be undercut by anti-feminist themes (see also Gill, 2007, 2017). Sometimes this undercutting takes the form of overtly anti-feminist content, such as narratives of "independent women" being infused with gender stereotypes, objectification, or ironic sexism. These trends are evident, for example, in some of the "classic" postfeminist texts that were focused on in early scholarship about this brand of media culture such as *Sex and the City* (1998–2004), *Ally McBeal* (1997–2002), or the film series *Bridget Jones's Diary* (2001, 2004, 2016) (see Kim, 2001; McRobbie, 2004, 2009; Tasker and Negra, 2005). PETA's lettuce ladies could, likewise, easily be added to this list.

It is important, however, not to use these campaigns (or PETA in general) as a straw man in support of pro- or anti-vegan narratives. While the campaign is a straightforward instance of postfeminist media culture, other popular vegan texts are not postfeminist in themselves but instead bear structural similarities to what Gill (2007) describes as a "postfeminist sensibility" in more subtle ways. One of the central arguments made about postfeminist media culture is that it reflects a wider shift in media depictions of feminism, where collective change has been displaced by narratives of individual empowerment (Mendes, 2012). The reason why this configuration is so dangerous is that the collective action that is necessary to instigate structural change is not just marginalized but stigmatized; while generalized notions of gender equality might be foregrounded, the tools to actually attain this equality—and indeed the label "feminism" itself—are "feared, hated, and fiercely repudiated" (Gill, 2007: 161). These tensions are because postfeminism's emphasis upon the individual over the collective means that sometimes feminism that focuses on structural change is itself portrayed as repressive for restricting individual freedom. As Jo Littler (2017) argues, however, while emphasizing individual self-determination and agency at the expense of structural change might be beneficial for those who *already* possess particular cultural or monetary resources, this politics consecrates the marginalization of those who lack them by foreclosing scope to contest these social formations. Postfeminism, from this perspective, is a media culture that has the veneer of empowerment, while normalizing the very social relations that are placing the conditions to attain equality out of reach for many.

In the rest of this chapter, I argue that parallels can be drawn between the double entanglements of postfeminism and key developments in the popularization of veganism. While some texts associated with veganism might themselves be postfeminist (such as "lettuce ladies," or the *Skinny Bitch* vegan diet books, described in further depth later) what I am more concerned with here are the *structural* parallels between postfeminism and a strand of popular veganism. While post-veganism is certainly not culturally dominant in the same manner as postfeminism (Gill, 2017), the emphasis on individual choice and the entanglement of competing political tendencies is nonetheless present. The most prominent source of tension relates to vegan food itself. Turning to recent debates about food politics is therefore useful as an initial starting point for sketching out the contours of what I refer to in this chapter as post-veganism.

Just a Diet?

One of the biggest sources of ambivalence associated with contemporary veganism is the shift from it being difficult to live as a vegan, to vegan food becoming readily available. Indeed, when asked about the biggest change they had experienced over the past three years in relation to veganism, the majority of my interviewees responded "food" or, more specifically, the widespread availability of food. Interviewees often jokingly describing how they were delighted at being able to take train journeys without relying on crisps and peanuts (Chris, vegan fourteen years) or being able to go for a meal with friends without packing their own bottle of soya milk and vegan margarine (Ali, vegan twelve years). This line of reflection is perhaps best crystallized by Ginny (vegan fourteen years) who states:

> It's wild in comparison to what it was a few years ago . . . vegan food and the understanding of veganism within food outlets has become so well-known and popular, that I've almost started to become complacent! Because it's like . . . well why isn't there a vegan chocolate éclair for me to eat right now?! [laughs]

These shifts were often articulated not just in terms of food availability, but marketing; Saskia, (vegan twenty-five years) for instance, describes how she was initially able to "block out" a lot of marketing as it just wasn't relevant to her, but now increasingly feels "shouted at" by vegan brands being promoted in the "urban environment."

As these reflections suggest, though product availability was often discussed in positive terms, there was also a creeping sense of ambivalence, with individuals concerned that the flipside of accessibility was a de-politicization of what it means to be vegan. For some interviewees, its commercialization ran the risk of disconnecting veganism not only from other social issues but even from animal ethics itself. The ramifications of a narrow focus on vegan food, as opposed to veganism as something that is more than a way of eating, came to the fore throughout discussions. Interviewees voiced concern that the long-standing emphasis on the importance of making vegan food more accessible—once important for sustaining veganism (see Chapter 3)—has now, paradoxically, become a barrier to realizing more expansive understandings of vegan ethics.

Several interviewees voiced concern that key sites for promoting vegan politics, such as vegan fairs and festivals, have undergone a shift, arguing that what were once radical spaces that drew attention to different forms of animal exploitation and supported community-building have shifted to a more individualistic emphasis on food:

> I mean on the one hand it's really good to see these vegan fairs going on and the really big ones that attract tens of thousands of people, you know, they're alright but it's all about food! There's very little activist groups there, there's very little ethics there, it's all about me—what can I eat! (Sol, vegan forty-three years)

Others voiced wider concerns about the limitations of going to chain restaurants with new vegan options as opposed to "your classic vegan café that has . . . you know posters for your local environmental group or whatever . . . ALF stickers, hunt sab stickers, cultural signifiers of something that goes further than just 'this is about what I spend my money on'" (Graham, vegan twelve years). Ali echoed these concerns, again worrying that in recent years the emphasis had been placed on a liberal-individualist push to expand consumer choices rather than instigating structural change: "it is now more about the accessibility and . . . fashionability of veganism and trying to attract as many people to go vegan as possible rather than focusing on actually like setting up vegan structures," arguing instead that "we do need to take the focus off the individual and put it on the corporations and stuff who are still doing all of this farming, and who are the ones that even if everyone turned vegan tomorrow would just change their style into producing vegan food."

Two things are especially worth dwelling on in relation to these reflections. The first is the way that people were actively drawing connections between the widespread availability of vegan food and the depoliticization of vegan practice, due to this process maximizing individual choice within the constraints of existing systems without fundamentally transforming these systems (a point that was reiterated by almost all of my interviewees). The choice to eat whatever one desires was thus seen as coming at the expense of reflecting on how the systems producing particular foods are entangled with other forms of animal—let alone human—oppression. The second notable point relates to the commodification of veganism. It would be easy to make the argument that the rise of plant-based capitalism is primarily due to the actions of corporations who have seen the potential of new vegan markets. Questions also need to be asked, however, about whether some of these developments have been aided and abetted by certain strands of the vegan advocacy movement itself, which has tended to centralize food politics (as argued by Ko, 2019: 8–9). Perceptions of the inaccessibility and expense of veganism are often perceived as one of the key barriers to entry. Tensions can arise, however, if food—and dietary choice in particular—is centralized in awareness campaigns in ways that become entangled with corporate strategies.

Corporate Veganism(s)

As suggested by interviewees, one of the central facets of "post-veganism" relates to political shifts that have arisen due to the newfound availability of vegan products. Fast-food companies that were formerly targets of protest (see Chapter 4) now stock vegan products: from KFC serving Quorn "chicken" in the UK, to Burger King's Impossible Whopper, and McAloo Tikki burgers (which have long been available in India to tailor for Hindu markets, but have only been made available in other locations from 2018). Indeed, vegan lifestyle website *Live Kindly* contains a list of twelve vegan items that can be obtained by McDonald's globally.[2] These developments, and such lists in particular, crystallize tensions surrounding the rising popularity of veganism. Echoing Harper's critique of the label "cruelty free" (2010a), framing such products as "kinder" options elides other social and political tensions associated with corporations such as McDonald's (related to labor and environmental politics as well as their ongoing implication in animal products). While these products might not contain animal ingredients, they are not vegan in the more expansive sense of the term.

The wave of multinational fast-food restaurants offering vegan products helps to elucidate tensions related to veganism becoming "just a diet" or personal food choice. As George Ritzer (2013) argues in his influential theory of McDonaldization, in order to maximize profits, McDonald's places an emphasis on efficiency, calculability, rationality, and control. Everything, from products to workers' movements to consumer behavior, has to be carefully monitored and regulated, to ensure that resources are used as efficiently as possible, they cost as little money as possible, and, as such, profits can be maximized. This form of efficiency, as Susan Leigh Star (1991) points out, has stark consequences. First, the scale and size of McDonald's means it has the power to affect norms and standards in a range of other industries: from farming (where it often has a high level of influence in setting animal welfare standards, by determining prices and inducing farmers to cut costs), to the catering industry (where its deliberate organization of kitchens to rationalize workflow is used to justify employing minimum wage, unskilled workers). Indeed, during the McLibel trial (see Chapter 4) it was ruled that the corporation had depressed wages in the catering industry as a whole and was culpable for animal cruelty due to its disproportionate influence over farming as the world's largest purchaser of beef (see also Giraud, 2019: 21–45). Second, Star (1991: 40–1) points out that these norms and standards are not only difficult to reverse (because of the vast scale and quantities involved) but often become naturalized as the way things are: echoing the well-worn "there is no alternative" logic of neoliberal capitalism (cf Fisher, 2009).

It is worth dwelling on earlier critiques of McDonaldization due to their significance to contemporary developments in popular veganism(s). When describing factors that could expose infrastructural norms embodied by fast-food corporations, Star describes how exclusionary standards are often only revealed when they clash with the needs of those who do not "fit" with these norms; in her words:

> McDonald's appears to be an ordinary, universal, ubiquitous restaurant chain. *Unless* you are: vegetarian, on a salt free diet, keep kosher, eat organic foods, have diverticulosis (where the sesame seeds on the buns may be dangerous for your digestion), housebound, too poor to eat out at all—or allergic to onions. (1991: 36)

In my previous work (Giraud, 2018, 2019) I have argued that anti-McDonald's activism that emerged from the context of grassroots vegan campaigning work played an important role in unsettling norms associated with McDonald's. What contemporary events illustrate is that such potentials are not guaranteed. One of the (many) reasons why Star's work is so prescient is her argument that practices which pose resistance to existing norms and standards can be co-opted back into the systems they criticize, if they evolve into new marketing niches that are worth catering to.

Again, some of my interviewees reflected on these developments. Dani (vegan thirteen years), for instance, stated: "I remember the first time soya milk was in my local supermarket. You know it was, wow, soya milk—here! You don't need to go and look for it in a special shop!" Since then, he continued, "it's just been bombing with special products that are labelled vegan, marketed at vegans, trying to imitate lots of types of non-vegan products from cheese to milk, and now you go and you have 20 types of milk in the supermarket that is marketed as vegan milk." One of the notable changes accompanying these shifts, he suggested, is that the term "accidentally vegan" has changed its meaning. Initially this label was used by campaigning groups to assist transitions to veganism by listing easily accessible products that happened to be vegan. Now, he points out, the label has still more resonance as "so many products that are vegan are labelled vegan, so if something happens to be vegan and it's not labelled now that's the exception." Such reflections are significant, as they point to dramatic changes over the past decade and a half wherein veganism has shifted from something marginal to a selling point. In 2007, for instance, the large UK supermarket chain Sainsbury's began to drop their vegan labeling, which led to much criticism in online vegan communities and resulted in the eventual reinstatement of this information.[3] It should be noted that this was not a matter of vegans calling for *new* products, but instead asking for packaging on products which already "happened" to be vegan to retain their vegan labeling. The notion that veganism had an insufficient market to make it worthwhile labeling foods as such lies in stark contrast with more recent activities by the supermarket, such as a report it produced in 2019 entitled the *Future of Food*. The document begins with a scenario:

> Julia has just returned home to her parents from university in London where she is studying her degree in eco-health. Tomorrow is her mother's 60th birthday

and she's planning to cook a meal for all the family. She opens up her meal planner app and asks it to update the quantities for seven, taking into account her sister's gluten intolerance, her brother's love of Italian and her grandparents' MIND diet—designed to prevent dementia and loss of brain function as you age. She smiles gleefully at the thought of showing her dad that the entirely vegan meal has surpassed daily recommended nutrition guidelines. Secretly he would prefer to eat steak, but she's determined that the whole family follow a more flexitarian diet. (2019: 5)

This scenario offers a launchpad for the supermarket's headline statement, that "with the rise of an ecologically aware new generation, driven by health concerns and environmental determination, vegetarians (including vegans) look set to make up a quarter of British people in 2025, and flexitarians just under half of all UK consumers" (2019: 6). Preceding these developments, the supermarket had launched new plant-based food ranges to coincide with Veganuary as well as what they described as the UK's first "plant-based butcher" later that year (Mannering, 2019).

There is much in Sainsbury's statements to unpack that parallels narratives about postfeminism: the emphasis on flexibility, the focus on environmentalism and health, and the lack of reference to animal ethics marking a few significant features of the *Future of Food*'s opening scenario. While these discourses are explored in further depth shortly (when I argue they should be understood as core features of post-vegan food cultures), before doing so I wish to dwell a little longer on some of the more complicated affordances of veganism's emergence as a viable market as revealed by this report. What documents such as the *Future of Food* report mark, to draw upon Star's (1991) arguments, is the sense that veganism—bluntly put—is now a big enough market to bother co-opting. From a vegan perspective, while the sharp growth in the practice might be read in positive terms, its co-option is perhaps less positive. However, it remains difficult to ascertain whether the relationship between veganism's growth and its commercialization can be meaningfully disentangled.

The issues surrounding processes of popularization and co-option are difficult to interpret and perhaps mark a departure—or at least complication—from the logic that characterizes postfeminism. While contemporary food cultures and branding are increasingly understood in postfeminist terms, especially narratives of empowerment-through-food that emphasize individual agency through consumption (O'Neill, 2020), the commercial accessibility of vegan food is more complex than a straightforward march toward individualized consumer-oriented practice. On the one hand, the corporatization of veganism marks a transition from a way of eating that was formerly outside of certain social norms—and thus, in line with Star, able to denaturalize them—to instead being incorporated smoothly into existing food infrastructures. On the other hand, these developments cannot be read entirely critically due to their democratizing potentials.

For instance, even activists who had been long-term campaigners against the ethical practices of particular fast-food corporations and supermarkets stated:

It's all very well to say oooh Tescos are not very ethical are they? Well, they might not be but they're selling food half the price. . . . You can get a sausage roll from Greggs, or go to [place name removed] vegan market and buy a sausage roll for £2; you know, if you're a family on a budget you're better going to Greggs and buying sausage rolls for you and your family for £1 a pop rather than trying to go to an ethical vegan wholefoods store, where you'll be paying twice the price. I don't know quite how you deal with that from an ethical consumer perspective, because it is expensive being a small ethical trader. (Scotty, vegan thirty-four years)

Echoing Scotty's reflections, these issues caused huge dilemmas for all of my interviewees. As touched on previously, many people I spoke to were wary about the co-option of veganism by fast-food corporations in particular. Yet, as with Scotty, people also recognized the democratizing potentials of the widespread availability of food, especially from a class perspective. Although Sol, as quoted earlier, was heavily critical of the food-focus of contemporary veganism, he also recognized that his confidence in cooking vegan food from scratch meant that new products and fast-food were less significant for him and he was wary of being critical of what others might need to support vegan practice. Others similarly emphasized that it was not just a matter of accessibility but also time and resources, which could—at least in part—be redressed by the wider availability of vegan food.

What is evident in all of these reflections is something more nuanced than simply praising or condemning fast-food corporations that sell vegan products; there is a recognition that plant-based consumerism offers routes for people to engage with particular forms of food ethics in the constraints of existing food systems riddled with inequalities. At the same time, there remained a sense among my interviewees that uncritically celebrating the newfound accessibility of vegan food is dangerous if it fails to engage with how these actions can perpetuate inequalities associated with food production. These narratives reflect one of the core dilemmas for an activist-vegan politics that is committed to recognizing other forms of inequality (White, 2018). If long-term activists are critical of contemporary veganism then this is framed as elitist and exclusionary, interpreted as purist activist identity politics. If, in contrast, corporate veganism is uncritically celebrated, this can erase other structural problems within food systems. One of the main contexts where these tensions are at their most explicit is when vegan politics intersects with long-standing tensions surrounding green consumerism and greenwashing.

Greenwashing and the Green Premium

While this chapter has focused on postfeminism as a valuable framework for approaching popular veganisms, other useful concepts could be drawn from fields such as the sociology of consumption, particularly research that has focused on the phenomenon of greenwashing. This term "encompasses a range of communications that mislead people into adopting overly positive beliefs about an organization's environmental performance, practices, or products" (Lyon and Montgomery, 2015: 225). Plant-based capitalism, in many ways, is an instance of greenwashing; a number of products straightforwardly use the connotations associated with "plants" to promote food as somehow natural and good for the planet (as well as healthy for those who consume it).

What makes these issues difficult to parse in contemporary foodscapes is that this particular form of "veganwashing" (Alloun, 2020) often gains momentum not just through generalized appeals to being environmentally friendly, but by gesturing toward more radical expressions of veganism as an *activist* practice; as explicit in the framing of plant milks as a dramatic break from the norm (see Clay et al., 2020, discussed in Chapter 1).[4] Nathan Clay et al. frame these developments as an instance of co-option, wherein the aesthetics of more politicized food choices are incorporated into the branding of foods that are far from radical in their labor politics or environmental and animal ethics. In these contexts, the term "plant-based" retains its connotations as something radical even as, in practice, the politics behind vegan ethics are displaced. Yet, although the retention of vegan signifiers and displacement of its ethics is clearly one component of the growth of plant-based markets, again these processes are messier and more ambivalent than they appear on the surface.

The majority of interviewees who I spoke to saw environmental politics as a key driver of veganism's popularization. Saskia (vegan twenty-five years) saw the "new climate movements" as heralding more sustained connection-making between animal ethics and environmentalism, while Len (vegan ten years) suggested that "the thing about climate change and the climate emergency is that things are moving so fast and are getting to such a critical point . . . that actually the climate change message is the one that's really coming through as the most powerful message." Others felt that the connections being made between veganism and environmentalism were drawing attention to concerns that had already been present in early Vegan Society publications, but were often absent from popular conceptions of what veganism means today: "of course the language of climate change didn't exist—but a lot of the other things that we're still talking about like . . . soil erosion, and waste of fresh water, squandering of plant foods for livestock feed, all this kind of thing . . . all that was in the vegan movement right back then" (Chris, vegan fourteen years).

However, although the present moment is one in which expressions of vegan and environmental activism are coming together in more politicized ways, it is also a moment in which both movements are being drawn into attempts to commodify their radical politics, with the significance and implications of these developments still unfolding. This coming together of (often opposing) socioeconomic and political developments has resulted in multiple directions of travel and sites of contestation. Green- or veganwashing itself, for instance, is complicated as it is not just about fast-food corporations adding additional products to their lines in order to (re-)capture new environmentally conscious consumers, but is also bound up with a slightly different trend in which cheap ingredients are turned into products that can be branded as healthy, environmentally friendly alternatives in order to justify higher prices (often described as a "green premium").

The phenomenon of cauliflower steaks perhaps best illustrates this point, offering a lightning rod for debates about the comparative expense of vegan food in mainstream media discourse. Premium supermarket Marks and Spencer, for instance, were mocked on social media for selling a £2.50 plastic tub of cauliflower slices while charging £1 for whole cauliflowers (with this story subsequently picked up by the print media, which resulted in the withdrawal of the product; Cloake, 2018). British pub chain Young's were subject to similar criticism, after charging £14 for their cauliflower steak dish. One commentary on this revelation argues, "Whichever way you slice it, £14 for a dish with a main component that costs less than a pound feels grabby" (Naylor, 2019).

Thus, echoing broader suspicion toward greenwashing on the part of consumers, who often feel such approaches are purely a branding exercise (Lyon and Montgomery, 2015), attempts to charge a premium for vegan products have not gone uncontested in wider media culture. Interviewees likewise reflected critically on these trends: "often vegan products are at a premium so you can see that from their catalytic viewpoint that that's attractive to businesses because they think 'well here's a product that we can charge more for'" (Thomas, vegan fourteen years); "green consumerism is not a new thing and companies have been using very vague green politics to sell things to people for a long time and [vegan consumerism] fits nicely into that sort of realm" (Graham, vegan twelve years). In addition, interviewees articulated further systemic problems shaping vegan consumerism:

> people who have got these environmental and ethical drives are willing to pay more for that, you know, and be loyal to that sort of branding as well. . . . I mean, vegan food—grains and cereals and things—they should be inordinately more affordable than meat and dairy and, as we know, it isn't the case, it's just extraordinary levels of subsidy! (Will, vegan ten years)

As argued by Will, in the context of food the "green premium" is more complex than simply marking an attempt to profit from new markets of ethical consumerism. Alongside this, the "green premium" also relates to, and emerges from, the historical entrenchment of certain aspects of industrial food production that result in the comparative cheapness of animal products.

Talk of a "green premium," moreover, is highly context specific; the pricing of "meat" and "vegan" products is not universal, but bound up with specific cultural values and associations. Indeed, on the other end of the spectrum, many of my interviewees described finding vegan food much cheaper than other ways of eating once they had learned to cook from scratch, particularly when moving beyond convenience foods and branded products or the Anglo-centric conception of meat as some sort of centerpiece that had to be replaced with expensive alternatives (Karima, vegan twenty-two years; see Chapter 6). From this perspective, the concern was that recent developments—and the focus on specialized meat alternatives in particular—were making veganism more expensive and inaccessible for many people than it had been previously. Even if awareness of veganism had increasingly resulted in it being perceived as a viable option for those with higher levels of disposable income, its wider democratization was being undercut by the expense of prominent plant-based products.

Again, therefore, it is important to avoid making generalizations about the meanings that have become attached to veganism in the contemporary moment and instead explore how specific discourses of consumption are embedded and enacted in particular institutional contexts (to again reiterate Cudworth, 2014). A way of approaching these questions in relation to the discourse of popular veganism, for instance, is to ask what meanings become attached to terms such as "plant-based" as they travel between contexts, and how they assume particular meanings while distancing themselves from others.

Ethical Displacement?

It would be easy to see the forms of displacement that have arisen in relation to, say, plant "mylks" and other green- or vegan-washed products as a straightforward jettisoning of more radical modes of vegan politics, even as the aesthetics of vegan practice are retained. One area where this process seems especially apparent is in the context of punk aesthetics. Veganism has historically played an important role in the context of straightedge subcultures (especially in North America) and anarcho-punk in the UK, resulting in the material culture surrounding certain forms of veganism being bound to an anti-consumerist, DIY ethos and aesthetic (Clark, 2004; Haenfler, 2004; Giraud, 2013a). These links have persisted as veganism emerged as a viable consumer market in the late 1990s and early 2000s, with more professionalized recipe books still maintaining subcultural links, such as Tanya Barnard and Sarah Kramer's *How It All Vegan* (1999) and *Garden of Vegan* (2002), or Isa Chandra Moskowitz's *Vegan with a Vengeance* (2005) and her follow-up with Terry Hope Romero, *Veganomicon* (2007), with authors often being heavily tattooed, or wearing retro or punk clothing (see Inness, 2006 and Carey, 2016 for more in-depth analysis of these texts).

More importantly, these books were bound up with vegan community-building. Moskowitz's work, for instance, fed into early vegan social media: including Livejournal community "vegantestkitchn" where people experimented with recipes, and later a large, vibrant website and forum, the Post Punk Kitchen. The forum in particular went beyond food (with sections focused on politics and social issues, which often criticized the emergence of the sort of phenomena discussed in the previous chapter, such as T*** Kitchen). The potential for veganism to have connections with other social justice movements was also explored in Moskowitz's recipe books. *Vegan with a Vengeance*, for instance, contained pages detailing the value of anarcho-feminist potlucks, encouraged people to get involved with anti-poverty food activist group Food Not Bombs (see Chapter 4), and offered tactics for sourcing cheap ingredients or acquiring low-priced kitchen equipment in thrift stores.

It is these, more politicized, forms of connection-making, however, that seem to have waned in recent years, even as the punk aesthetics of this strand of veganism have been retained. For example, during an interview, Ginny (vegan fourteen years) suggested that, at times, the aesthetics associated with vegan counterculture have been adopted in particular settings while veganism itself is displaced. She described how in recent years there has been

> a kind of a hipness around an aesthetic that felt vegan to me! I don't know how I can put my finger on it, but I'd get so frustrated when you'd go into a café that felt and looked like a vegan café [laughs] and you're like, it's not even a fucking vegan café! They've got oat milk you know and the cool cafés, oh I can get oat milk but I can't get soya milk though, cause that's not cool! . . . But it's the same with loads of movements, loads of subcultural movements, where there's an aesthetic that's cool and then it's taken on and diluted and diluted and reproduced in other spaces.

Yet, as Ginny continues, and a number of other interviewees reiterated, seeing these developments in terms of a straightforward displacement of vegan ethics is overly simplistic. Like the multiple iterations of feminism that constitute popular feminisms (Banet-Weiser, 2018), there are different strands of popular veganism. In addition, it is important to recognize that countercultural spaces and animal activism still exist and, in some instances, are gaining increased visibility (see Chapter 4). To draw on the terminology of Ernesto Laclau (2005), perhaps instead of marking a process of ethical displacement and depoliticization it is more productive to see terms like "plant-based" as "floating signifiers," which have competing—and often fundamentally opposing—meanings attached to them by those committed to different political projects. That said, it is also necessary to acknowledge that those involved in contestations over meaning often have unequal levels of resources at their disposal to aid in these struggles. Those who already have media access and financial resources have more opportunities to push for their meanings to become dominant, something that comes to the fore when turning to another term gaining popular purchase in association with veganism: flexitarianism.

Flexible Veganism

The term "flexitarian" has grown in popularity throughout the first two decades of the twenty-first century. Though the term received the accolade of "most useful" word of the year by the American Dialect Society in 2004 (Flail, 2011), it was not added to the *Oxford English Dictionary* until 2014 (BBC, 2020). Since then, the usage of "flexitarian" has grown rapidly and over the past two years it has been repeatedly referred to as a major trend by food industry bodies and marketers. As evoked by Sainsbury's aforementioned *Future of Food* report, these developments are repeatedly associated with veganism (which is, again, often used interchangeably with plant-based).

Echoing the potentials and tensions that have accompanied the newfound accessibility of vegan products, the rise of flexitarianism is sometimes read in positive terms as something democratizing. Pro-vegan initiatives such as Veganuary, which encourages individuals to try out veganism for the month of January, have had a record number of subscribers in recent years, with 400,000 people signing up to the scheme in the UK alone in 2020 (Peat, 2020). Other highly successful, ecologically minded initiatives such as Meat Free Mondays have focused less on veganism explicitly and more on the logic of cutting down animal products for environmental purposes. What these developments seem to share is an emphasis on moving beyond the (alleged) purism of "activist veganism" (White, 2018) to instead emphasize reduction, trying out plant-based products, and making consumer choices based on individual needs and circumstances.

However, again, an ambivalent picture is revealed by attending more closely to the *way* that veganism and flexitarianism are associated with one another in these narratives, with the two modes of food ethics often pitched *against* each other. A BBC article titled "Vegan v Flexitarian," for instance, states: "because a vegan diet can seem so restrictive, eating a varied diet that includes a small amount of animal products could be more realistic and achievable for more people—and the only way for diet changes to have an impact is en masse." Despite the article including the caveat "seems," its framing still slides into long-standing tropes of veganism as an ascetic, restrictive way of living that have been circulated both by social science research and in mainstream media narratives (Cole, 2008; Cole and Morgan, 2011).

The BBC is not alone in framing flexitarianism as a more sensible, moderate alternative to eliminating animal products entirely. Carol Morris's research into media depictions of Meat Free Mondays (MFM) maps how such depictions are part of a wider media discourse that—echoing the tendencies of postfeminist media culture—shifts the focus away from institutional and structural change toward choice narratives. Morris examined representations of MFM in UK print media and found that although positive coverage outweighed negative, the political and ethical framing of these articles was somewhat muted and focused on three key messages: "MFM is good for your health; the message of the campaign is moderate, sensible and achievable; MFM is good for the environment" (Morris, 2018: 439–40). What is notable across these discussions of Meat Free Mondays is what was *missing*; only 1 article out of the 125 pieces that Morris examined mentioned animals, and connections between the movement and structural or institutional change were made infrequently. Echoing Kaitlyn Mendes's (2012) analysis of media depictions of feminist activism, choice-based narratives of empowerment on an individual level came here at the expense of questioning broader institutional arrangements.

Yet, even as reducing animal products is routinely framed by the media as preferable to eschewing them, at other times *conflations* were made between these practices. Again, reports such as the *Future of Food* illustrate these slippages (binding veganism, choice, animal product reduction, health, and flexibility together in the same scenarios), but these relationships are also inscribed in narratives beyond food marketing. The landmark 2019 EAT-Lancet report on food and planetary health, for example, also calls explicitly for a "flexitarian diet, which is largely plant-based but can optionally include modest amounts of fish, meat and dairy foods," in order to feed 10 billion people while securing human and planetary health (EAT-Lancet Commission, 2019: 11). In narratives of flexitarianism, I suggest, it is this simultaneous blurring and distancing between acts of reducing versus eliminating animal products, which serves to situate flexible food practice as part of more radical ethical and environmental lineages of vegan practice without adhering to the (apparent) strictures of these ways of living.

Concerns about emergent discourses connecting veganism and flexitarianism are often interpreted as a form of purity politics or boundary policing, as discussed in Chapters 3 and 4. For instance, allegations of purity politics are often leveled at both vegan individuals and activist groups who maintain clear definitions of what veganism means. While it is important to recognize that these criticisms are not without purchase, with certain forms of lifestyle politics sometimes serving as identity markers to demarcate insiders and outsiders of particular activist communities (as outlined in Chapter 4), tropes such as the "angry vegan," "vegan police," or "preachy vegan" are frequently deployed as rhetorical tactics to dismiss important ethical concerns out of hand (see Stephens Griffin, 2017). Again, therefore, parallels can be drawn with critiques of postfeminist media culture, which have, likewise, elucidated how the figure of the "angry feminist" is routinely leveraged to undermine calls for social change (McRobbie, 2009).

Other critical engagements with postfeminist media culture offer a sense of how flexibility discourse emphasizes individual empowerment at the expense of structural transformation. As noted earlier, neoliberalism is tightly associated with postfeminism. Postfeminist media culture is often seen as a specific, neoliberal articulation of feminism due to its emphasis on individualism and empowerment as manifested through consumer choice. A further trait that understands postfeminism as a neoliberal iteration of feminism is its emphasis on flexibility (Gregg, 2008), wherein contemporary women are portrayed as being capable of "having it all"—work, family, empowerment—so long as they are flexible enough to juggle the often competing requirements associated with these needs (see Littler, 2017: 179–211). The emphasis on modeling oneself as a flexible, resilient subject is central to wider analyses of the gig economy (Bull and Allen, 2018; Gill and Orgad, 2018). Feminist scholarship has examined how this phenomenon manifests in often overlooked contexts ranging from care-work to establishing home-run businesses that can be juggled with childcare (what Littler dubs "Mumpreneurism").

The significance of flexibility in relation to vegan politics and ethics can be drawn out more clearly when turning to a situated example of plant-based capitalism: Burger King's launch of a plant-based burger, the Rebel Whopper, to coincide with Veganuary 2020. The advertisements themselves featured a logo stamped with the slogan "the vegetarian butcher," a further logo stating "100% Whopper 0% Beef," and a background that displayed the word "rebel" repeatedly in large, green type. The advertisement's use of the term "plant-based" seemed designed to carry some of the connotations of "veganism"—those palatable with commodification—while rejecting others. The product's name and branding, for instance, evokes both the alternative, punk aesthetic of veganism and youth rebellion associated with the new climate movements, without the structural critique integral to earlier understandings of veganism and called for by environmentalist activism. Indeed, later that year Burger King were found guilty of misleading advertising (BBC, 2020). The Rebel Whopper was ultimately not only unsuitable for vegans (due to containing egg-based mayonnaise) but many vegetarians, as it was cooked on the same grill as meat. Especially notable was the company's defense of their branding, which deliberately took advantage of cultural slippage between plant-based, flexitarianism and veganism to argue that although the product was unsuitable for *ethical* vegans their branding was not misleading as the product itself contained "no beef" and was intended for a "flexitarian" audience.

Though the Rebel Whopper might be an extreme case, it crystallizes something important about the dynamics of plant-based capitalism. Although it might be straightforward to co-opt plant-based food as a flexible option for omnivorous diets, it is less easy to incorporate the ethical commitments associated with earlier meanings of veganism. In a practical sense, as highlighted by Star (1991), kitchen technologies can only be smooth and efficient if everything is standardized. If the need for radically different forms of preparation (e.g., alternative mayonnaise) or different preparation methods (a separate cooking area for vegetarian food) cannot be accommodated, neither can the ethical commitments of less "flexible" definitions of veganism that require these changes. Despite the "lure of flexibility" (Star, 1991: 37) promised by large-scale fast-food infrastructures that claim to cater to all preferences, it is often not systems themselves but *individuals* who are encouraged to be more flexible, conforming to, rather than rebelling against, corporate needs. Post-vegan notions of flexibility, then, actively enable the co-option of veganism into green capitalism by foreclosing critical reflection on the norms, standards, and ethical questions associated with particular socio-technical arrangements.

Yet, as with all of the cases discussed in this chapter, even flexitarianism carries a seed of a more hopeful, or at least ambivalent, politics. One of my interviewees, for instance, reflected on the way flexitarian narratives have been taken up in other institutional contexts, such as the UK Food, Farming and Countryside Commission's *The Future of the Land* (RSA, 2019), a response to EAT-Lancet's report:

> Their phrasing was really interesting. They went: we need to move toward a global flexitarian plant-based diet, i.e. they know we need to move to a plant-based diet, but they know that people won't like that . . . so it's got to be people's choices—so they put the word flexitarian in front of it. (Len, vegan ten years)

For Len, though not entirely conflated with an animal activist agenda, these developments nonetheless carried hope: "even if we had that over what we've got today, if it reduces animal suffering by 80, 90% it's got to be better than what we've got now!" Perhaps more importantly, he suggested that, even if animal ethics was perhaps lost in mainstream flexitarian discourse, more radical groups nonetheless play an important role in initiating conversations that feed into these shifts. Rather than a straightforward displacement of radical politics, therefore, a more complex picture of post-veganism can be constructed. Despite all of their problems it is perhaps important to remain hopeful about the accessibility offered by flexitarian narratives, while recognizing that at times these hopes can be stretched to their limits as highlighted by the final example I focus on in this chapter: the relationship between veganism and "healthiness."

Health-Food Veganism and "Heganism"

Out of all of the facets of post-veganism, narratives about the relationship between veganism and the body, or, more specifically, the "healthy" body resonate most strongly with concerns articulated by critical analyses of postfeminism. As Gill points out, the body assumes an uneasy role within postfeminist media culture where it is "presented simultaneously as women's source of power and as always unruly, requiring constant monitoring, surveillance, discipline, and re-modelling (and consumer spending) in order to conform to ever-narrower judgements of female attractiveness" (2007: 149). While previous forms of feminist activism criticized the policing of female bodies, postfeminism not only embraces this policing but also reframes it as empowering.

Vegan bodies, as Wright points out, have similarly been a site of scrutiny, often pathologized or stigmatized within popular culture, with veganism sometimes framed as a tactic for masking eating disorders such as anorexia or orthorexia (Wright, 2015: 96–102). Wright's, and others', response to the pathologization of veganism has been to contest its association with disordered eating, drawing on a range of dietary studies to do so. I wish to adopt a slightly different approach here. Rather than debunking these connections, I instead examine how they are reinscribed in popular culture. Postfeminist discourse and practice are key sites where the connections between veganism and norms surrounding the body are articulated, due to health-based discourse about veganism aligning uneasily with wider postfeminist narratives of bodily self-surveillance where a vegan diet is positioned as a means of empowering oneself through taking control of the body. Again, however, empowerment in this context translates to an adherence to a narrow set of cultural norms about the body, primarily related to losing weight, although general appeals to veganism's capacity to improve health and even cure particular ailments are also recurring themes.

Important work has been undertaken on the part of charities and advocacy groups to combat veganism's extreme pathologization, with the UK Vegan Society, for instance, producing detailed guidance to support people in being healthy at any age (Vegan Society, 2020: "Nutrition and Health"). However, problems can arise when veganism is depicted as *intrinsically* healthier than the consumption of animal products. The dangers of health-based empowerment narratives are evident in certain discourses that have circulated *within* the vegan community, such as the infamous *Skinny Bitch* books that rose to prominence in the early

2000s (Freedman and Barnouin, 2005, 2007) which promoted vegan, organic, unprocessed diets in order to attain a desirable body. As with PETA's lettuce ladies, *Skinny Bitch* could straightforwardly be read as a postfeminist text. Media scholar Alison Winch, for instance, classes the books among other archetypal postfeminist "conduct books" that promote notions of a "consumer-oriented self where sexual attractiveness is sold as a source of power over patriarchy" (Winch, 2011: 361). This framing is certainly evident in the original 2005 book, which features a cartoon of a glamorous, narrow-waisted woman, wearing a designer dress and accompanied by the tagline "A no-nonsense, tough-love guide for savvy girls who want to stop eating crap and start looking fabulous!" As Winch elucidates, the book effectively serves as a checklist for the aesthetic and discursive hallmarks of postfeminism; focusing on the body as a site of empowerment, while emphasizing the individual's responsibility in attaining this empowerment through ensuring they eat foods that secure thinness. Indeed, this sentiment was articulated still more forcefully by the follow-up recipe book, *Skinny Bitch in the Kitch* (2007), whose subtitle promised "kick ass recipes for hungry girls who want to stop cooking crap and start looking hot." Texts such the *Skinny Bitch* series are part of a wider use of fat-shaming tactics in vegan campaigns wherein sizeism has played a number of strategic roles (Wrenn, 2017b). A common feature of these campaigns is the reframing of veganism as something extreme to something morally acceptable (by linking it to "good health" rather than animal ethics), in order to incorporate vegan practice into a lucrative diet industry where it is turned into one fad among many promoted by celebrity recipe books.

What is classically postfeminist about *Skinny Bitch*, in particular, is that here bodily surveillance is not simply something that re-models the body, or even the lifestyle, but it is also bound up with *ethical* self-development. Sections entitled "Carbs—the truth" or "Sugar is the devil," for instance, are followed immediately by a chapter called "The dead, rotting, decomposing flesh diet." Not only does following the skinny bitch diet improve the body and mind, then, it also offers a makeover for the soul (cf. Gill, 2007). This promotion of narrow models of "hotness" (coded as thinness and whiteness), however, is couched in irony and humor in a manner that makes it difficult to gain critical purchase upon (much like PETA's defense of their appropriation of #TakeAKnee, as outlined in the previous chapter). As Angela McRobbie argues, this tactic is a well-known trait of postfeminism; evoking objectifying discourses and imagery, which were the target of criticism for prior forms of feminism, only to suggest that such concerns belong to a "puritanical" past; as McRobbie puts it, objecting to such imagery "nowadays would run the risk of ridicule. Objection is pre-empted with irony" (2009: 17).

It should be noted, however, that while texts such as *Skinny Bitch* are archetypally postfeminist, they were published prior to the recent popularization of veganism and various academic texts, as well as interviewees, suggest that discourses surrounding veganism and healthiness are shifting. These shifts were detailed by Saskia (vegan twenty-five years), who became vegan at a relatively young age. She recalled a "vivid" memory of attending a vegetarian meet-up event where she was confronted by a middle-aged man who said she "must be anorexic" due to her diet (despite the fact she was in the middle of eating an ice-cream at the time): "cue conversation with my mum: 'what's anorexia'?!" Encounters such as this had a lasting effect, making Saskia feel that as a young, naturally petite woman, she could feed into stereotypes about veganism, which left her feeling wary about vegan public-speaking engagements for years after this moment. As a result, she described experiencing a sense of relief at the recent proliferation of popular veganisms, stating: "I'd rather have popularization than pathologization!" What Saskia's perspective speaks to is not that postfeminist vegan narratives, which associate health with plant-based living, no longer exist. Indeed, discourses of health-food veganism have proliferated (Fegitz and Pirani, 2018; Braun and Carruthers, 2020; Scott, 2020; O"Neill, 2020). Saskia's point, though, is that now health narratives are one of multiple discourses about veganism. Indeed, even health-based discourses themselves have become more pluralistic, as with shifts in depictions of the relationship between veganism and masculinity.

In contrast with discourses surrounding vegan women where stereotypes about veganism mesh neatly with gendered norms, veganism has conventionally been seen to clash with expectations attached to masculinity. A 2014 article by Megan Dean, for instance, turns to the narratives of vegan women to elucidate how veganism offers resistance to patriarchal norms surrounding food, while much-cited work by Annie Potts and Jovian Parry (2010) provides a persuasive analysis of how veganism poses challenges to hegemonic masculinity. This research has been complicated by more recent scholarship that suggests veganism's relationship with patriarchal norms is becoming less straightforward. In their interviews with male vegans, for instance, Jessica Greenebaum and Brandon Dexter (2018) uncovered a messy picture wherein although veganism as a practice has not conventionally sat easily with hegemonic masculinity, the way practitioners justified their lifestyle re-framed veganism in ways that made it conform to masculine stereotypes more readily:

> by emphasizing strength, control and personal empowerment as masculine, by regarding compassion to be an act of courage and rebellion in a society that socializes men to be stoic and uncaring and by asserting men's crucial role in bringing legitimacy to the vegan movement. (2018: 640)

Wright goes further still, identifying the emergence of a new figure in US media culture—the "hegan"—who is "something other than merely vegan; they are so ultramasculine as to be able to be vegan and to make that dietary choice manly as well" (2015: 126). This cultural figure is most often associated with "elite athletics" and serves as a counterpoint to the long-standing vegan backlash "that has worked to associate [veganism] with femininity, idealism, and disordered consumption," instead portraying plant-based food "as a means to masculine physical strength and prowess" (Wright, 2015: 144). Five years after *The Vegan Studies Project* was originally published, the "hegan" has crossed the Atlantic and become an increasingly prominent media figure.

Perhaps most notably, texts such as documentary *The Game Changers* (2018) have centralized the idea that veganism is not just compatible with hegemonic masculinity but actively enhances the physical qualities necessary to be an elite athlete; notably "improved blood flow, increased muscle efficiency, reduced inflammation, quicker recovery times, and enhanced immune function" (*The Game Changers*, 2019: FAQs). The text is classically "hegan" in Wright's sense, in that it not only emphasizes that veganism can be compatible with athleticism—by focusing on figures such as tennis player Novak Djokovic and racing car driver Lewis Hamilton—but develops this argument by pitching health-oriented vegan practice *against* other stereotypical depictions of veganism as somehow un-masculine. As with other "post-vegan" texts, *The Game Changers'* branding distances itself from "ethical veganism" by instead emphasizing connections between plant-based living, health, and strength while carefully selecting promotional quotes from mainstream media reviews of the documentary that reiterate it is "not haughty or preachy."

This discourse of an accessible, "non-preachy" veganism for men is furthered by other texts such as BBC TV series and recipe book *Dirty Vegan*, both fronted by Mathew Pritchard who is described in promotional materials as an "elite athlete," but perhaps best known for fronting *Dirty Sanchez*, the UK equivalent to the prank/stunt reality series *Jackass*. This genre of television has typically been associated with narratives of "'boys being boys,' ritually acting out an exaggerated hyper-masculine identity" (Lindgren and Lélièvre, 2009: 394), connotations that are integral to *Dirty Vegan*'s framing. Echoing the branding of *T*** Kitchen* (see Chapter 6), the books and series make use of slang, emphasize cheapness and accessibility, and centralize health and nutrition as opposed to animal ethics. Moreover, the punk aesthetic of the books echo concerns that certain stylistic traits, originally associated with subcultural expressions of vegan practice, have been appropriated and perhaps, to use Ginny's turn of phrase, "diluted" as they move between contexts.

Texts such as *Dirty Vegan* thus seem to straightforwardly shift the meaning of veganism to support rather than oppose specific constructions of hegemonic masculinity. Yet even these types of "hegan" texts cannot be read as entirely undermining earlier forms of vegan ethics. As Lindgren and Lélièvre (2009) argue, while stunt reality TV seems to adhere to tropes associated with hegemonic masculinity, in making these tropes so explicit this genre deliberately invites criticism and interrogation of such stereotypes. Similar arguments could be made about *Dirty Vegan*. While adhering to a depoliticized post-vegan reading in many ways, these texts also seem to recognize and work to ameliorate the problems of "heganism" by deliberately going beyond expectations about their audiences to reflect on the nutritional requirements of various different demographics of people. Marketing for the recipe books, for instance, highlights their examination of how veganism could meet the nutritional needs of pensioners, and women's sporting teams, as well as the elite male athlete as embodied by Pritchard. These texts, therefore, somewhat uneasily leverage the hegan as a means of departing from narrow notions of who veganism is stereotypically for (namely health-conscious women, ethical extremists, and hippies) to instead articulate it as being for "everyone," due to this figure of the ultramasculine elite athlete straying so far from stereotypes about the typical vegan. The *success* of this discourse, however, still relies on perpetuating notions of the preachy ethical vegan, by positioning this trope as the version of veganism which it both defines itself against and that needs to be moved beyond.

As heganism illustrates, the relationship between veganism and the body has changed significantly over the past decade. Yet what has been intensified by more recent depictions of health-food veganism is a further departure from veganism as a mode of structural critique, to instead depicting it as a means of individual self-realization and empowerment. Echoing criticisms of postfeminism, discourses of healthism again take the form of an individualistic, neoliberal mode of politics that shifts attention away from structural change driven by commitment to animal ethics, toward individual empowerment through dietary change.[5] Due to these constructions of veganism evolving so rapidly, the question that still needs to be addressed is whether—for all their problems—some sense of political possibility can still be found in these discourses; in other words, is there future potential for accessibility and ethics to be reconciled rather than pitched against one another?

Conclusion: Finding Hope Amid Unmeshed Oppressions?

This chapter has explored several trends and recurring motifs in popular depictions of veganism that, collectively, can be understood as form of "post-veganism," which echoes some of the key characteristics of postfeminism. In particular, these developments reflect a focus on empowerment via individual consumer choice, the emergence of new commercial products tailored to this choice, and an exhortation to move away from the apparent rigidity of earlier forms of vegan praxis toward a more flexible approach (in this context in relation to eating). Though these shifts do carry democratizing potentials, they also pose important questions about the risks that can arise as political practices shift to the mainstream. These risks are underlined in Aph Ko's observation that what makes it so difficult to articulate complex arguments that draw together animal ethics, feminist theory, and critical race studies is that these conversations are taking place against a backdrop of capitalist-led vegan politics that "has equated veganism with kale or processed food products, rather than a critical intervention into race, power, animality, and thought" (2019: 8). Thus, echoing McRobbie's (2009) characterization of postfeminism as "undoing" the work of earlier forms of feminism, questions need to be asked about whether the emergence of post-veganism—as an individualistic, consumerist food politics—undoes the emphasis on enmeshed oppressions that has been engaged with in more expansive vegan theory and activism.

As with popular feminisms (Banet-Weiser, 2018), it is important to note that these developments are just *one* strand of contemporary veganism. Rather than understanding post-veganism as straightforwardly displacing or undermining more politicized expressions of "activist veganism" (White, 2018), it is valuable to recognize the coexistence of different forms of veganism and the potential for traffic between them. Indeed, this scope for traffic is something that many of the people I interviewed drew hope from, suggesting that, for all of its problems, the newfound visibility of veganism for people who had previously perceived it as extreme, marginal, or inaccessible was broadly positive. The acid test, and something that is still emerging, is whether these engagements will materialize as a first step towards more complex forms of vegan ethics, which might start with dietary politics but ultimately go beyond it.

One of the key insights that I have drawn from the field of cultural studies (see Chapter 1) is that scope for realizing these, more complex, political, and ethical connections is a site of struggle. Popular culture, as Stuart Hall argues, is necessarily a site of contestation over meaning, which can lead to certain understandings and definitions becoming dominant while others are subjugated. In the context of postfeminism itself things have taken a worrying turn in this regard, with key thinkers such as Gill arguing that what began as one (apolitical) strand of popular feminism, which jostled with other feminist calls for structural change, has become the culturally dominant way that feminism is represented. Due to the manner that postfeminism not only valorizes individual empowerment but also positions collective change as something retrograde that actively impinges on freedom of choice, these shifts are dangerous in placing the tools to attain more meaningful equality out of reach.

In light of how struggles have evolved in the context of popular feminisms, it is particularly important to be attuned to parallels with contemporary vegan practice; identifying the shifting meanings that surround veganism and perhaps recognizing points at which certain trends need to be contested in order to avoid depoliticization. The material and discursive relationships between plant-based food, green capitalism, and veganism that I have sketched out in this chapter are far from exhaustive in terms of themes that could be associated with the emergence of a post-vegan sensibility and further empirical and conceptual work needs to be undertaken to develop a clearer understanding of these developments. What even a tentative exploration of these issues highlights, nonetheless, is that while multiple veganisms might exist at the same time, as with any instance of popular culture, there is likely to be a struggle over which understanding of veganism gains dominance as the commonly understood meaning. In the context of veganism, the stakes of this struggle are high. Will vegan practice be understood as more than a diet—as something that is concerned with wider human-animal relations beyond food—and as something that responds to different forms of human and nonhuman animal oppression, or will "ethical veganism" be carved off as a marginal concern?

Chapter 8

CONCLUSION

MAINTAINING THE "MORE-THAN"

A few years ago my friend gave me a shopping bag containing the best part of two decade's worth of vegan recipes. The majority had been carefully clipped out of magazines, although some were cut from the cardboard packaging of products and one was even on the lid of a margarine tub. Several DIY recipe books were also included, with hand-drawn covers and typewritten pages, which had been photocopied and distributed at vegan festivals. I added these to my own collection of texts that included a 2002 *Animal Free Shopper*, which offered guidance from the UK Vegan Society on which readily available products were vegan (prior to the advent of widespread labeling), along with short recipe pamphlets from the vegan café in my (then) home town.[1] My later involvement with vegan food activism—such as free food giveaways that were incorporated into anti-fast food protests—contributed a further pile of pamphlets in the box, this time ones I had produced myself, that included recipes that were designed to offer a cheap, easy introduction for making bean burgers using simple ingredients. Similar ad hoc collections of leaflets, grassroots recipe books, and activist literature are likely present in the homes of most "long-term" vegans.

The existence of these recipe collections speaks to some of the tendencies that I have traced throughout this book and, in particular, the question I want to focus in on a little more depth in this brief concluding chapter: What happens when a practice such as veganism shifts from the margins to the mainstream? Or, as evoked by my donated recipe collection, what happens when something that has connotations of a fringe, DIY movement—that requires a lot of work, time, and effort—becomes something catered for by existing socio-technical infrastructures and consumer markets? During the course of my interviews, many people reflected on shifts surrounding veganism that speak to these questions; put simply, the resources to support vegan dietary practice have increased so rapidly that the process of recipe curation and product lists, which used to be so important, no longer seem necessary. As Ali (vegan twelve years) states:

> if you wanted a . . . burger you got to buy your dried TVP, put . . . a stock cube in there because it tastes minging on its own, pour in boiling water! You had to make your own stuff! Sosmix in a box! You couldn't just walk into anywhere and get anything!! And you had to be prepared every time you left the house—

soymilk in your bag, butter in your bag, snacks in your bag, because where you were going wouldn't have vegan options!!

Prior to around 2015, these difficulties automatically marked out vegans as different and indeed difficult; potentially generating frictions with familial and friendship networks, due to vegan food practice being awkward to reconcile with communal activities such as family meals and eating out. As existing sociological research suggests (see Chapter 3), vegans have historically struggled against the (sometimes inadvertent) "normalizing pressures" created by a desire to fit in and share experiences with close friends and family. These pressures were often exacerbated by day-to-day feelings of awkwardness, from going hungry on train journeys to negotiating workplace buffets.

Until recently, in the UK at least, everyday normalizing pressures have worked in tandem with socio-technical systems that make certain ways of eating easier than others: from catering ordering systems that fail to have vegan options, to a lack of supermarket products that can be easily turned into vegan dishes at shared family meals. These mundane issues are, of course, quite aside from structural constraints associated with racialized and classed inequalities that might make certain ethical choices difficult to access (Harper, 2012; see also Chapters 6 and 7). Together, therefore, social pressure and systemic constraints have positioned a vegan diet as not only something that is outside of existing cultural norms but also difficult to accommodate within these norms. Though these difficulties are clearly not the most extreme problem that could be associated with food (or indeed other forms of consumption), they nonetheless speak to the fact that—conventionally— veganism has not been the easiest path from a practical or social perspective. Recently, however, things appear to have changed dramatically.

From the perspective of making the experience of practicing veganism easier, more accessible, and less prone to conflict, it is difficult to interpret the recent popularization of vegan food as anything other than a good thing. Certain barriers in terms of accessibility are being removed: from wider awareness of what veganism is and means, to the accommodation of plant-based products in contexts such as workplaces and chain food outlets where this was unthinkable even three or four years ago. In other words, clear steps are being made to resist the sorts of normalizing pressures discussed in earlier research about vegan practice (e.g., Cole, 2008; Stephens Griffin, 2017) by supporting veganism's own normalization. Yet, as described throughout this book, these developments are also a source of ambivalence. While vegan *food* practice has been rendered more accessible, this is not the case for the more fundamental questioning of human-animal relations that is posed by vegan ethics.

Complicating Vegan Narratives

It might seem like making a vegan diet more socially acceptable and less confrontational is unambiguously positive, but—to bring things full circle to Richard White's (2018) distinction between an "activist" and "lifestyle" veganism—at present these processes entail ceding a degree of agency away from vegan communities themselves toward these needs being fulfilled by markets. As White suggests and as argued throughout this book, though lifestyle veganism has some important potentials, if engaged with uncritically this form of vegan practice can undermine both wider critiques of human-animal relations and attempts to articulate connections with other social justice campaigns.

To again reiterate A. Breeze Harper (2010a), a product that is labeled "cruelty free" does not live up to its name if this label smooths over inequalities associated with food systems themselves, including who is able to access particular choices and who is exploited in the production of resources. In other words (to paraphrase Dominick, 2010 [1997]) although vegan food politics *can* offer a route into a more fundamental interrogation of how particular, privileged humans relate to other beings, if treated as an end in itself dietary veganism can also shut down more expansive conversations. The recent "green rush" (Stewart and Cole, 2020) of plant-based capitalism seems to be enacting precisely the mode of single-issue politics that Dominick and Harper warn against: as with the tensions surrounding specific brands of plant mylk (Clay et al., 2020) or Rebel Whoppers (see Chapter 7). For veganism to serve as a more meaningful route into grasping the "multidimensional" relationships between oppressions, it is thus necessary to be wary of initiatives that frame veganism in narrower, food-focused, consumerist terms (Ko, 2019).

However, it is also not a straightforward case of a "good" activist veganism versus a "bad" commercialized lifestyle or food politics. What makes matters especially difficult is that while, on one hand, the emergence of popular veganisms can continue to center neoliberal market-based solutions, these developments do have certain democratizing potentials. For all of their problems it does seem important to recognize the fraught politics of consumer activism and the complexity of practices that are often written off as "lifestyle activism" (Haenfler, 2004; Littler, 2009; Hanefler et al., 2012). Recent research, for instance, suggests that lifestyle activism might begin as individual acts but can coalesce as more complex, collective modes of politics that hold hope for wider change (Evans, Welch and Swaffield, 2017): something some of my interviewees speculated was happening in the context of plant-based food.

Comparisons with postfeminism (Chapter 7) also point to potentials associated with veganism's popularization, for all the ambiguity accompanying its mainstreaming. As illustrated throughout this book, there has not been a straightforward displacement of activist veganism with lifestyle veganism. While a post-vegan sensibility that emphasizes individual, consumer empowerment—and undermines scope for radical change—certainly exists, so do other more radical iterations of veganism. New connections between environmentalism and veganism are emerging in relation to the new climate movements, for instance, which hold as-yet undetermined potentials (see Chapter 4), while alternative media depictions of multispecies relations offer a platform for expressions of animal subjectivity that interrogate carnism on both an ideological and structural basis (Parkinson, 2019; see Chapter 5).

At the same time as recognizing the complexity of ethical food politics, it is critically important not to idealize individual, consumer-oriented solutions or assume they intrinsically lead to social transformation. The reason why it is important to be wary is not just due to lifestyle activism often segueing with the demands of neoliberal economic policy, but because of the specific mechanisms through which these processes occur in the case of veganism. As detailed in Chapter 7, the primary danger of individualized solutions is if they come at the expense of other possibilities. The increasingly hegemonic status of more depoliticized notions of dietary veganism is something that is happening with "post-vegan" discourse in particular, which (much like postfeminism's relationship to other forms of feminist activism) frames other expressions of vegan ethics as something marginal and restrictive that needs to be moved beyond.

It is in relation to the ascendancy of "post-veganism" or "plant-based capitalism" that things become especially complicated in academic terms. Despite coming from very different political places, post-vegan discourses sometimes mesh in unexpected ways with criticisms of veganism within certain strands of cultural theory (see Chapter 3). So-called posthumanist animal studies in particular have been critical of activist veganism due to framing it as an elitist mode of boundary policing that feeds into the hierarchies of purity politics. It is in the wake of these critiques that a huge amount of theoretical (see Chapter 2) and social scientific (Chapter 3) research within vegan scholarship has dedicated itself to complicating characterizations of veganism as something restrictive that denies the complexity of the world (see also Tyler, 2018; Hamilton, 2019). Instead, this body of work has reasserted some of the longer histories of veganism that have positioned it as a route into understanding the situated and complicated ways that human-animal oppressions manifest themselves in particular cultural contexts, treating vegan practice a way into—rather than rejection of—ethical complexity.

Beyond the Purist/Flexible Dichotomy

Briefly turning to a (final) example can help to illustrate, and hopefully complicate, understandings of the sort of tensions that can arise when veganism is seen not as an ethical practice that goes beyond food—and attempts to draw connections with other social justice movements—but something that neglects the complexities of the world. In 2019, recipe book author and activist Jack Monroe published an accessible collection of vegan recipes for those on a budget entitled *Vegan(ish)*. The book built on Monroe's track record of creating recipes that are easy and accessible to those suffering under economic austerity policy in the UK. Some of Monroe's most popular meals—such as their recipe for "9p carrot, cumin and kidney bean burgers"—happened to be already vegan, hinting at scope for vegan politics to be accessible to more than the stereotypical middle-class consumer with disposable income.[2] *Vegan(ish)* built upon these foundations, with straightforward recipes designed explicitly for those on a budget. Yet, for all this promise, the book engendered consternation by certain members of the vegan community. The "ish," for instance, infers veganism is something flexible that can be opted in or out of. Though in Monroe's case these criticisms were unfounded (all the recipes were technically vegan), debate surrounding the book helps to restage questions about the dangers and potentials of more "flexible" understandings of veganism that have emerged with its popularization.

In the wake of *Vegan(ish)*, Monroe reflects on their blog, *Cooking on a Bootstrap*, about various criticisms received (often via social media) for the flexible approach to veganism hinted at by the book:

> nobody likes to be told that they have a degree of privilege, no matter how small the degree appears to be. "But some of the poorest diets in the world are vegan," I hear some of you drafting your indignant replies. And there, dear reader, does the distinction lie. Poverty diets are not a choice. A diet lacking in meat and dairy products for wont of the finances, resources and availability of them, is not the same, not remotely the same, as having access to these products and choosing not to use them. (Monroe, 2019)

As discussed in previous chapters (see Chapter 6 in particular), the classed inequalities that make veganism difficult to realize in certain contexts can also intersect with other racialized structures of oppression (Harper, 2010b, 2012), and these tensions are invariably exacerbated by media discourses and even vegan campaigns that centralize white middle-class vegans (Doyle, 2016).

Yet it is important to ensure that analysis of structural barriers to a vegan diet do not feed into more reductive stereotypes about what veganism is and means. As Ko foregrounds, critiques of vegan practice that frame it as being at odds with human social justice often hinge on conceiving veganism as a dietary phenomenon. Framing veganism purely as a way of eating means that discussions are reduced to whether a diet that eliminates animal products is accessible (or not) within the constraints of existing food systems. For Ko, this framing of vegan praxis is a missed opportunity, which can obscure the more far-reaching questions that it poses:

> Because veganism has become so corporatized and chained to food items, it has become common for most people to dismiss it because it's framed as a diet that's not affordable. Imagine if you heard someone say, "I can't be a Black Lives Matter activist because it costs too much!" or "Being a feminist is too expensive!" These statements are overtly absurd to those of us who understand that these movements are not about items or consumption but powerful conversations for change. (2019: 8)

One of the challenges of making arguments such as Ko's is that, as she has argued elsewhere, wider media constructions of veganism mean that drawing analogies with other social movements can create a hostile reaction (Ko, 2017b: 11). Histories of insensitive comparison-making between women, people of color, and animals by NGOs promoting veganism (see Chapter 5) has created preconceptions about veganism that, in turn, result in more complex and situated analyses of enmeshed oppressions being misconstrued. In the earlier quotation, for instance, it is important to note that Ko is not directly comparing the suffering of those whose struggles lay at the heart of different social movements, but pointing to these movements' shared concern with instigating "powerful conversations" that challenge specific social arrangements (and the oppressions these arrangements perpetuate). Understanding veganism as a conversation for change, rather than consumerist, eating-focused movement, transforms it from something that is about dietary purity and only available to the few, to a way of thinking about and engaging with the world (echoing arguments made in texts such as Wright's *Vegan Studies Project* and Quinn and Westwood's *Thinking Veganism*, 2018).

As argued throughout the book, moreover, changing wider discourses and classifications associated with nonhuman animals is not enough in itself and these processes need to be combined with careful attention to developing modes of "counter conduct" (Wadiwel, 2015), as well as institution-building and developing infrastructures to support new ways of living alongside nonhuman animals. Although transforming practice is difficult, initiatives such as Food Not Bombs, radical catering collectives in protest camps, certain strands of the animal sanctuary movement, and developments in veganic agriculture offer a heterogeneous range of attempts to build different worlds.

A key danger in relation to veganism's popularization is whether these more radical forms of institution-building are perceived as no longer needed in supporting vegan practice. The surge in plant-based food products might carry potentials, but do not seem to have heralded an inevitable march toward the vision put forward in Simon Amstell's *Carnage* (see Chapter 4), where "carnism" itself (Joy, 2011)—rather than veganism—is framed as a nonnormative ideology. Instead, the ascendancy of market-delivered solutions has centralized flexitarianism: where veganism is framed as one option among others, in food systems that can increasingly cater for everyone's individual choices. As touched on in the previous chapter, this stance is not just dangerous due to treating systems that harm both humans and nonhuman animals as something that can be opted out of depending on individual preference, but actively enables these systems to reproduce themselves. Dairy companies diversifying into plant mylks and fast-food corporations producing "rebellious" beef-burgers mean, in Star's (1991) terms, that practices that were formerly resistant can now be smoothly accommodated back into standardizing food infrastructures.

What I have sought to move beyond in this book, therefore, is any sense of a straightforward distinction between a rigid, ethically purist conception of vegan politics and a flexible approach that recognizes structural barriers to veganism. On one hand, flexible, market-based food ethics can, as Ko (2019) puts it, narrow the frame of reference to such an extent that wider "conversations for change" are foreclosed, while, on the other hand, outright condemnation of lifestyle activism can miss some of the complicated ways this activism can serve as an entry-point to more sustained and organized modes of politics. It is thus important to be reflexive about structural inequalities—and how these inequalities might shape the realization of vegan practice—while recognizing the important work that can be accomplished by firm definitions of veganism as a commitment to re-working particular human-animal relations. Likewise, it is important to be critical of the dangers of food-focused consumer veganism, without dismissing it entirely.

To move beyond polarized debates where, at one end of the spectrum, more radical conceptions of veganism as a mode of ethics are dismissed for being purist, while, on the other, dietary lifestyle veganism is framed as wholly apolitical, it is useful to interrogate *how* notions of flexibility are conceived of in both contexts. There is a difference, for instance, between the "social model of veganism" argued for by Sunaura Taylor (2017: 13), which sees barriers to veganism in terms of structural oppressions that need to be *contested*, and a marketized notion of flexitarianism that instead uses appeals for ethical flexibility on the part of consumers to *avoid* structural change.

Here the emphasis on structure is critically important; as Cole (2014) points out, early Vegan Society definitions used the terminology "wherever practical and possible" in relation to eliminating animal products. This phrase, importantly, is not used in reference to individualized choice (that suggests harms to animals, humans, and the environment can be temporarily bracketed to one side if you want to eat a particular item or engage in a particular practice), but in relation to structural difficulties that undermine scope for making these choices in particular contexts. What makes veganism difficult, in line with this conception of "practical and possible," is due to working in the constraints of agricultural and industrial systems that embed particular ways of relating to animals, so that no way of living in these societies is free from being imbricated in these relations. Reasserting an emphasis on socio-technical systems is important in foregrounding the need to resist exclusionary narratives about veganism—by acknowledging structural barriers that make certain ethical choices difficult—without descending into choice discourse that means veganism ceases to function as a useful way of navigating the world and loses its ethical meaning.

Put slightly differently, while it is important to recognize barriers to consuming a vegan diet, it is also important not to stretch out what "practical and possible" means so that it refers to individual choice, as opposed to operating as an ethical aspiration that acknowledges the structural barriers that might complicate this aspiration. The world *is* complex and ethical practice needs to be sensitive and context-specific, but veganism is still a useful heuristic for signaling, as Donna Haraway puts it, a "loud No! as well as an affirmative politics" (2017: 56). This function breaks down if vegan ethics is treated as an optional extra, without engaging with the questions it poses in relation to the overwhelming harms caused by many preexisting ways of relating to humans and nonhuman animals. The danger at present, in other words, is akin to the mechanisms of postfeminism (see Chapter 7) where earlier expressions of veganism are framed as overly strident and moralistic, due to inhibiting individual consumer choice and flexibility: a framing that denigrates conceptual tools and forms of political practice that are valuable in articulating more sustained forms of collective change.

For all of these dangers, I wish to end on a note of hope. Amid the people I interviewed, although the problems, ambivalence, and ambiguity of veganism's rising popularity were constantly articulated, there was also an enduring sense of hopefulness. As Benny (vegan twenty-four years) puts it: "this is that the dawning of the world that we fought for, for so long, and hoped for, and just because it doesn't look exactly the way that we envisaged it would for all this time, we can't be too proprietorial about it." As vegan scholarship, as well as more specific calls for a Vegan Studies (Wright, 2015, 2018, 2019) and "multidimensional" understandings of shared oppressions (Ko, 2019) take hold, it seems valuable to continue pursuing questions of whether vegan practice can retain its hopeful conceptual and political potential to serve as more than a diet: a potential that is gathering force both despite and because of veganism's popularization.

NOTES

Chapter 1

1 I make a distinction here between "human" and "environment" for illustrative purposes, but understand in practice it is difficult to make such distinctions. For more on the entanglements between humans and other beings, see the discussion of posthumanist thought in Chapter 2.
2 The Vegan Society, for instance, state that in the UK alone the number of vegans quadrupled between 2014 and 2019: https://www.vegansociety.com/news/media/stati stics.
3 For a more in-depth discussion on Donald Watson, with reference to his archives, see Cole, Stewart and Craane's plenary at the inaugural Vegan Sociology conference, available: https://www.youtube.com/watch?v=bAHHifclJH0.
4 As outlined in Chapter 4, these assumptions are not unproblematic with the nature of the relationship between veganism and environmentalism currently being a site of political struggle.
5 More recently Oatly have come under criticism for accepting funding from venture capitalist group Blackstone, for their defense of this decision see: https://www.oatly.co m/int/climate-and-capital.
6 Thanks to Seán McCorry for this reflection about the dangers of the (important) sense of there being no ethical consumption under capitalism sliding into doing nothing.
7 The vegan organic network, for instance, attempts to develop forms of agriculture that does not rely on animal agriculture. See: https://veganorganic.net/.
8 For a more detailed sense of these arguments, see Chapter 2 and for a critical appraisal the conclusion of Chapter 5.

Chapter 2

1 For clarification purposes, STS is a field dedicated to the sociological analysis of science and technology; when I make reference to the field of STS, therefore, I am not referring to particular scientific disciplines but *social scientific* work dedicated to understanding both the inner-workings of these disciplines and the wider sociological implications of technoscientific innovations.
2 It should be noted that although Adams referred to her earlier work as "vegetarian" ecofeminism, the praxis she advocates is vegan.
3 Details about this event and the network it instantiated can be found here: http://www .vegansociology.com/.

Chapter 3

1   Other features of Maddox's webpage include a link to PETA's response to the story and an advertisement for his book *Kill the Whales*.

2   A useful instance of this shift is illustrated by Carol Morris's (2018) work, which is discussed in more depth in Chapter 7.

3   Some of the activists I have interviewed in my own research share these concerns, describing negative encounters with angry or judgmental vegans; Scotty (vegan thirty-four years), for instance, stated: "I've been only vegan for 34 years, because when I was first put in touch with veganism, the first vegans I met were angry vegans who . . . and I thought well if that's what vegans are like, I don't want to go there!" Though it is important to recognize that these attitudes do exist, however, it is also important to take care when generalizing; larger surveys about how vegans conceive of their practice, for example, illustrate resistance to seeing veganism as a single-issue cause, which complicates more critical perceptions of it as purity politics (see Wrenn, 2017a).

4   Although the Post Punk Kitchen forums no longer exist, the meme can be found here: https://vegansaurus.com/post/254784826/defensive-omnivore-bingo.

5   Many thanks to Alex Lockwood for raising this point in a previous draft of this chapter.

Chapter 4

1   The story of af Hageby and Schartau, along with other women involved in the early animal rights movement, can be found on the Archiving Activism website (an initiative dedicated to understanding archival practices surrounding radical activism, led by an editorial collective composed of Rachel Tavernor, Sarah Evans, and Catherine Oliver): https://archivingactivism.com/category/animal/.

2   As noted in Chapter 1, these hidden connections between human and animal oppression find their echo in the contemporary racialized dynamic of meat production in the United States (Pachirat, 2011), which have come to the fore most recently in light of the role of meat-processing plants as coronavirus hotspots (Specht, 2020).

3   De-horning by using heat, or "hot iron disbudding," is a routine procedure that is often advocated as the "least painful" way of de-horning cattle (Laven, 2010). Compassion over Killing's undercover footage was used to argue that this procedure is routinely conducted incorrectly in ways that caused additional pain and distress. From the activists' perspective, however, the point was not just to draw attention to a particularly problematic instance of de-horning, but use this instance of abuse to criticize the practice *in general*, thus this tactic ran the risk of undercutting the group's aims. For the footage itself, see: http://cok.net/inv/martinfarms/.

4   For footage from Mercy for Animals, see: https://www.youtube.com/watch?v=dZQ3sl0xNC4.

5   The work of Veggies Catering Campaign is discussed on their website, see http://veggies.org.uk/. The Anarchist Teapot have published texts such as *Feeding the Masses* (ND) that provide recipes as well as documenting their work.

Chapter 5

1 Two informative examples from places I have lived, for instance, are Brinsley Animal Rescue and Tribe Animal Sanctuary Scotland. See http://brinsleyanimalrescue.org/ and https://tribesanctuary.co.uk/.
2 For a similar argument, from an activist perspective, see Stallwood (2014).
3 As touched on in the previous chapter, these approaches have an ocular bias that has been criticized from a critical disability studies perspective (see Taylor, 2017 for a more productive approach that draws disability studies into dialogue with critical animal studies).
4 A number of websites have compiled lists of especially problematic campaigns; see: https://www.buzzfeed.com/copyranter/the-12-absolute-worst-peta-ads-of-all-time and https://www.businessinsider.com/peta-shocking-controversial-ads-2011-10?r=US &IR=T#and-so-did-ron-jeremy-11.
5 The US version of this video is narrated by No Doubt bassist Tony Kanal.
6 As Cassidy points out, similar stereotypes persist about rural populations but the divides between groups who are portrayed as being in opposition to one another are far messier in practice.
7 This short video, from November 19, 2017, can be found here: https://www.facebook .com/estherthewonderpig/videos/1515717948535424/?v=1515717948535424.
8 I wish to thank Naomi Griffin for making this point during workshop discussions at the Vegan Narratives and Storytelling workshop, facilitated by Julie Doyle, Mike Goodman, and Nathan Farrell, December 7, 2018.

Chapter 6

1 An interview by Bénédicte Boisseron (2019) in *Edge Effects* helps to further unpack some of the dangers of insensitive connection-making in animal studies.
2 Stephens Griffin's interviewee is especially striking in elucidating the dilemmas facing vegan activism that tries to recognize inequalities facing different people and how these inform vegan practice. Due to having a neurological condition the interviewee, Claire, took a drug that made her day-to-day life easier but felt deeply uncomfortable at taking animal-tested medication. What is notable is that she was wary of re-joining activist groups not just due to fearing judgment at making this compromise but the opposite: concern that other vegans would "too readily accept the choices she had made as a product of patronizing, ablist pitying" (2017: 87).
3 Zephaniah, a poet and musician whose writing is part of the national curriculum studied in British schools, was perhaps the most famous vegan in the UK media during the 1990s (indeed, the first time I heard anyone refer to themselves as vegan—in the media or in "real life"—was when he read his poem "Talking Turkeys" on a children's television programme). Zephaniah has written several poems focused on veganism, including the collection *The Little Book of Vegan Poems* (2001) and is ambassador for the UK Vegan Society. In the early 2000s he gained particular prominence after rejecting a national honour—an Order of the British Empire (OBE)—due to his anti-colonial commitments.

4　Priestly et al. (2016: 351) gather together some key criticisms from bloggers including Laur M. Jackson, Maya K. Francis, and Akeya Dickson, as well as Bryant Terry and A. Breeze Harper: whose work is discussed in more depth in the main body of this section.

5　These tensions are noted in the FAQs of Sebastian's website, for instance.

6　The opening pages of Harper's *Sistah Vegan* (2010b: XIV) not only critique PETA's insensitive comparisons between slavery and factory farming but also point to erasures that occurred in the backlash to this campaign, as reflected by activist Alka Chandna's concern that the work of animal activists of color is often marginalized and dismissed in the process of "painting [all] animal activists as white racists."

7　As Catherine Oliver (2020b) points out, similar erasures have arisen in relation to gender: with male activist experiences prioritized at the expense of women who were founding figures in the UK animal liberation movement(s).

8　These concerns are revisited in the conclusion, in relation to narratives that conflate plant-based diets that are the result of poverty with veganism.

9　Chatterjee and Subramaniam's forthcoming edited collection *Meat!* (2021) also contains essays examining shifting meanings and interpretations of animal products within particular cultural contexts, including an essay by Neel Ahuja (2021) exploring the relationship between colonialism and conceptions of animal cruelty in Bengal.

Chapter 7

1　For an in-depth argument in favor of understanding sex work as work, see Smith and Mac (2018).

2　One of these lists for instance, can be found here: https://www.livekindly.co/vegan-mcd onalds/.

3　Though many early 2000s online vegan communities are now defunct, a good example of these discussions can be found on the V Bulletin forums (see: http://www.veganforu m.com/forums/showthread.php?13288-Sainsbury-s-is-dropping-vegan-labelling) and there were also lively discussions in Livejournal vegan communities such as Vegan People (a community I was on the moderation team of between 2004 and 2007!), Veganism, and UK Vegans (see https://ukvegans.livejournal.com/131483.html), for example.

4　It is important to note here that while Alloun uses the term "veganwashing" she critically interrogates this concept rather than deploying it straightforwardly, and shows that vegan activists themselves often resist the way that veganism is deployed to hide other ethical issues.

5　It is important to note that discussions of the relationship between veganism and health do not have to be apolitical; the essays in Harper's *Sistah Vegan* (2010b), for instance, offer a range of instances where this subject matter is used as a route into wider questions about health inequalities related to food access.

Chapter 8

1　The sadly now-defunct Treehouse cooperative café in Norwich, UK.

2　For Monroe's 9p kidney bean burger, see: https://cookingonabootstrap.com/2019/11/ 01/carrot-kidney-bean-burger-recipe/.

REFERENCES

Aavik, K. (2019a), "Institutional Resistance to Veganism: Constructing Vegan Bodies as Deviant in Medical Encounters in Estonia." *Health*: 1363plec459319860571.

Aavik, K. (2019b), "The Rise of Veganism in Post-socialist Europe: Making Sense of Emergent Vegan Practices and Identities in Estonia." In L. Wright (ed.), *Through a Vegan Studies Lens: Textual Ethics and Lived Activism*, 146–64. Reno: University of Nevada Press.

Activist History Review eds. (2020), "Anti-Carceral Veganism Webinar." *Activist History Review*. Available online: https://activisthistory.com/2020/06/29/anti-carceral-veganis m-webinar/.

Adams, C. J. (2018), *Protest Kitchen*. Newburyport: Conari Press.

Adams, C. J. (2006), "An Animal Manifesto Gender, Identity, and Vegan-feminism in the Twenty-first Century," interview by T. Tyler. *Parallax*, 12(1): 120–8.

Adams, C. J. (2000), *The Sexual Politics of Meat: A Feminist Vegetarian Critical Theory*. New York: Continuum.

Adams, C. J. and Calarco, M. (2016), "Derrida and the Sexual Politics of Meat." In A. Potts (ed.), *Meat Culture*, 31–53. Boston: Brill.

Adams, C. J. and Gruen, L., eds. (2014), "Introduction." *Ecofeminism: Feminist Intersections with Other Animals and the Earth*, 1–36. New York: Bloomsbury Publishing USA.

Ahmed, S. (2017), *Living a Feminist Life*. Durham, NC: Duke University Press.

Ahmed, S. (2014), *Cultural Politics of Emotion*, 2nd edn. Edinburgh: Edinburgh University Press.

Ahuja, N. (2021), "Oh Phooka: Beef, Milk, and the Framing of Animal Cruelty in Late Colonial Bengal." In S. Chatterjee and B. Subramaniam (eds.), *Meat! A Transnational Analysis*, 213–40. Durham, NC: Duke University Press.

Alaimo, S. (2016), *Exposed: Environmental Politics and Pleasures in Posthuman Times*. Minneapolis: University of Minnesota Press.

Alloun, E. (2020), "Veganwashing Israel's Dirty Laundry? Animal Politics and Nationalism in Palestine-Israel." *Journal of Intercultural Studies*, 41(1): 24–41.

Alloun, E. (2018), "'That's the Beauty of It, It's Very Simple!' Animal Rights and Settler Colonialism in Palestine–Israel." *Settler Colonial Studies*, 8(4): 559–74.

Almiron, N., Cole, M. and Freeman, C. P. (2018), "Critical Animal and Media Studies: Expanding the Understanding of Oppression in Communication Research." *European Journal of Communication*, 33(4): 367–80.

Almiron, N., Cole, M. and Freeman, C. P. (2016), *Critical Animal and Media Studies: Communication for Nonhuman Animal Advocacy*. Abingdon, Oxon: Routledge.

Ambedkar, B. R. (2020), *Beef, Brahmins, and Broken Men: An Annotated Critical Selection from The Untouchables*. New York: Columbia University Press.

Anarchist Teapot (ND), *Feeding the Masses*. London: Active Distribution.

Animal Equality (ND), "iAnimal," *Animal Equality*. Available online: https://ianimal.uk/.

Animal Equality (2016), [YouTube Video] iAnimal: Pig Farms in 160 Degrees. Available:
   https://www.youtube.com/watch?v=X11LIG7P3ME.
Anon (2004), *Beasts of Burden*. London: Active Distribution.
Appia, V. (2018), "Esther the Wonder Pig is Officially Cancer Free – Which is Good
   Because it Would've Been Illegal to Give Her Chemo." *Toronto Star*, September 12.
   Available: https://www.thestar.com/news/gta/2018/09/12/esther-the-wonder-pig-is
   -officially-cancer-free-which-is-good-because-it-wouldve-been-illegal-to-give-her-
   chemo.html.
Arcari, P. (2020), *Making Sense of Food Animals*. Singapore: Palgrave Macmillan.
Avieli, N. and Markowitz, F. (2018), "Slavery Food, Soul Food, Salvation Food: Veganism
   and Identity in the African Hebrew Israelite Community." *African and Black Diaspora:
   An International Journal*, 11(2): 205–20.
Babe (1995), [Film] Dir. C. Noonan. Los Angeles: Universal Pictures.
Ball, T. (2019), "Animal Rebellion: Traders Welcome Vegan Activists Occupying
   Smithfield Meat Market," *The Times*, October 8. Available online: https://www.thetimes
   .co.uk/article/vegan-activists-occupy-london-meat-market-wxnjkbzls.
Banet-Weiser, S. (2018), *Empowered: Popular Feminism and Popular Misogyny*. Durham,
   NC: Duke University Press.
Bao, H. (2020), *Queer China: Lesbian and Gay Literature and Visual Culture under
   Postsocialism*. London: Routledge.
Batt, E. (1964), "Why Veganism," *Candid Hominid*. Available online: http://www.cand
   idhominid.com/p/why-veganism.html.
Barad, K. (2007), *Meeting the Universe Halfway*. Durham, NC: Duke University Press.
Barnard, T. and Kramer, S. (2002), *Garden of Vegan*. Vancouver: Arsenal Pump Press.
Barnard, T. and Kramer, S. (1999), *How It All Vegan*. Vancouver: Arsenal Pump Press.
Barstow, G. (2017), *Food of Sinful Demons: Meat, Vegetarianism, and the Limits of
   Buddhism in Tibet*. New York: Columbia University Press.
BBC Food (2020), "Vegan v. Flexitarian – Which Will Save the Planet?" *BBC Food*.
   Available online: https://www.bbc.co.uk/food/articles/vegan_vs_flexitarian#:~:text=Th
   e%20rise%20of%20flexitarianism,occasionally%20eats%20meat%20or%20fish%22.&t
   ext=This%20is%20twice%20the%20number,vegan%2C%20vegetarian%20or%20pesc
   etarian%20diet.
BBC News (2006), "Turkey Cruelty Workers Sentenced." *BBC News Online*, September 7.
   Available online: http://news.bbc.co.uk/1/hi/england/norfolk/5323190.stm.
Becerril, M. W. (2018), "Invisibilise This: Ocular Bias and Ablist Metaphors in Anti-
   Oppressive Discourse." *Feminist Review*, 120(1): 130–4.
Bekhechi, M. (2013), "Eating Quinoa May Harm Bolivian Farmers, But Eating Meat
   Harms Us All," *The Guardian*, January 22. Available online: https://www.theguardian.c
   om/commentisfree/2013/jan/22/quinoa-bolivian-farmers-meat-eaters-hunger.
Belcourt, B. R. (2015), "Animal Bodies, Colonial Subjects: (Re)Locating Animality in
   Decolonial Thought." *Societies*, 5(1): 1–11.
Berry, M., Garcia-Blanco, I. and Moore, K. (2016), *Press Coverage of the Refugee and
   Migrant Crisis in the EU: A Content Analysis of Five European Countries*. Project
   Report. Geneva: United Nations High Commissioner for Refugees. Available online:
   http://www.unhcr.org/56bb369c9.html.
Best, S. (2009), "The Rise of Critical Animal Studies: Putting Theory into Action and Animal
   Liberation into Higher Education." *Journal for Critical Animal Studies*, 7(1): 9–52.
Best, S., Nocella, A. J., Kahn, R., Gigliotti, C. and Kemmerer, L. (2007), "Introducing
   Critical Animal Studies." *Journal for Critical Animal Studies*, 5(1): 4–5.

Bhopal, K. (2018), *White Privilege: The Myth of a Post-racial Society*. Bristol: Policy Press.

Black Fish (2013), [Film] Dir. G. Cowperthwaite. New York: Magnolia Pictures.

Blanchette, A. (2020), *Porkopolis: American Animality, Standardized Life, and the Factory Farm*. Durham, NC: Duke University Press.

Blythman, J. (2013), "Can Vegans Stomach the Unpalatable Truth About Quinoa?" *The Guardian*, January 16. Available online: https://www.theguardian.com/commentisfree /2013/jan/16/vegans-stomach-unpalatable-truth-quinoa.

Boisseron, B. (2019), "Why Animal Studies Must Be Antiracist." Interview by B. Fielder, *Edge Effects*, March 26. Available online: https://edgeeffects.net/afro-dog-benedicte-bo isseron/.

Boisseron, B. (2018), *Afro-Dog: Blackness and the Animal Question*. New York: Columbia University Press.

Bourdieu, P. (2008), *Outline of a Theory of Practice*. Cambridge: Cambridge University Press.

Bowker, G. C. and Star, S. L. (2000), *Sorting Things Out: Classification and Its Consequences*. Cambridge, MA: MIT Press.

Braidotti, R. (2016), "Posthuman Critical Theory." In D. Banerji and M. Paranjape (eds.), *Critical Posthumanism and Planetary Futures*, 13–32. New Delhi: Springer.

Braidotti, R. (2013), *The Posthuman*. London: Polity.

Braun, V. and Carruthers, S. (2020), "Working at Wellness: A Critical Analysis of Vegan Vlogs." In D. Lupton and Z. Feldman (eds.), *Digital Food Cultures*, 82–96. London: Routledge.

Brown, G., Feigenbaum, A., Frenzel, F. and McCurdy, P., eds. (2017), *Protest Camps in International Context: Spaces, Infrastructures and Media of Resistance*. Bristol: Policy Press.

Brown, G. and Pickerill, J. (2009), "Space for Emotion in the Spaces of Activism." *Emotion, Space and Society*, 2(1): 24–35.

Brueck, J. F. (2019), *Veganism of Color: Decentring Whiteness in Human and Nonhuman Liberation*. Milton Keynes: Sanctuary Books.

Brueck, J. F. (2017), *Veganism in an Oppressive World*. Milton Keynes: Sanctuary Books.

Brueck, J. F. and McNeill, Z. Z. (2020), *Queer and Trans Voices: Achieving Liberation through Consistent Anti-Oppression*. Minton Keynes: Sanctuary Books.

Bull, A. and Allen, K. (2018), "Introduction: Sociological Interrogations of the Turn to Character." *Sociological Research Online*, 23(2): 392–8.

Butler, J. (2013), "For White Girls Only? Postfeminism and the Politics of Inclusion." *Feminist Formations*, 25(1): 35–58.

Calarco, M. (2014), "Being Toward Meat: Anthropocentrism, Indistinction, and Veganism." *Dialectical Anthropology*, 38(4): 415–29.

Calarco, M. (2008), *Zoographies: The Question of the Animal from Heidegger to Derrida*. New York: Columbia University Press.

Callon, M. (1984), "Some Elements of a Sociology of Translation: Domestication of the Scallops and the Fishermen of St Brieuc Bay." In J. Law (ed.), *Power, Action and Belief? A New Sociology of Knowledge?*, 196–223. London: Routledge.

Carey, J. (2016), "Veganism and the Politics of Nostalgia." In J. Castricano and R. R. Simonsen (eds.), *Critical Perspectives on Veganism*, 245–60. Basingstoke: Palgrave Macmillan.

Carnage (2017), [TV programme] Dir. S. Amstell, BBC iPlayer, March 19. Available online: https://www.bbc.co.uk/programmes/p04sh6zg.

Carolan, M. (2011), *Embodied Food Politics*. London: Routledge.

Carrigan, M. (2017), "Revisiting 'The Myth of the Ethical Consumer': Why Are We Still Not Ethical Shoppers?" *Journal of Consumer Ethics*, 1(1): 11–21.

Carter, B. and Charles, N. (2018), "The Animal Challenge to Sociology." *European Journal of Social Theory*, 21(1): 79–97.

Cassidy, A. (2019), *Vermin, Victims and Disease: British Debates over Bovine Tuberculosis and Badgers*. London: Palgrave Macmillan.

Castricano, J., ed. (2008), *Animal Subjects: An Ethical Reader in a Posthuman World*. Waterloo: Wilfrid Laurier University Press.

Castricano, J. and Simonsen, R. R., eds. (2016), *Critical Perspectives on Veganism*. Basingstoke: Palgrave Macmillan.

Chatterjee, S. and Subramaniam, B. (2021), *Meat! A Transnational Analysis*. Durham, NC: Duke University Press.

Chatterton, P. and Pickerill, J. (2010), "Everyday Activism and the Transitions Towards Post-Capitalist Worlds." *Transactions of the Institute of British Geographers*, 35(4): 475–90.

Cherry, E. (2015), "I Was a Teenage Vegan: Motivation and Maintenance of Lifestyle Movements." *Sociological Inquiry*, 85(1): 55–74.

Cherry, E. (2010), "Shifting Symbolic Boundaries: Cultural Strategies of the Animal Rights Movement." *Sociological Forum*, 25(3): 450–75.

Cherry, E. (2006), "Veganism as a Cultural Movement: A Relational Approach." *Social Movement Studies*, 5(2): 155–70.

Chilvers, D. (2016), "Cowspiracy: Stampeding in the Wrong Direction?" *New Internationalist*, February 10. Available online: https://newint.org/blog/2016/02/10/cowspiracy-stampeding-in-the-wrong-direction.

Clark, A., Bottom, K. and Copus, C. (2008), "More Similar Than They'd Like to Admit? Ideology, Policy and Populism in the Trajectories of the British National Party and Respect." *British Politics*, 3(4): 511–34.

Clark, D. (2004), "The Raw and the Rotten: Punk Cuisine." *Ethnology*, 43(1): 19–31.

Clarke, A. and Haraway, D., eds. (2018), *Making Kin Not Population: Reconceiving Generations*. Chicago: Prickly Paradigm Press.

Clay, N., Sexton, A. E., Garnett, T. and Lorimer, J. (2020), "Palatable Disruption: the Politics of Plant Milk." *Agriculture and Human Values*, 37: 945–962.

Cloake, F. (2018), "Forget M&S's £2.50 'Cauliflower Steak': Here's How to Make Your Own." *The Guardian*, January 10. Available online: https://www.theguardian.com/lifeandstyle/shortcuts/2018/jan/10/forget-mss-250-cauliflower-steak-heres-how-to-make-your-own.

Cole, M. (2014), "'The Greatest Cause on Earth': The Historical Formation of Veganism as an Ethical Practice." In N. Taylor and R. Twine (eds.), *The Rise of Critical Animal Studies, from the Margins to the Center*, 203–24. London and New York: Routledge.

Cole, M. (2008), "Asceticism and Hedonism in Research Discourses of Veg* anism." *British Food Journal*, 110(7): 706–16.

Cole, M. and Morgan, K. (2011), "Vegaphobia: Derogatory Discourses of Veganism and the Reproduction of Speciesism in UK National Newspapers." *The British Journal of Sociology*, 62(1): 134–53.

Cole, M. and Stewart, K. (2016), *Our Children and Other Animals: The Cultural Construction of Human-Animal Relations in Childhood*. London: Routledge.

Collard, R.-C. (2014), "Putting Animals Back Together, Taking Commodities Apart." *Annals of the Association of American Geographers*, 104(1): 151–65.

Collins, P. H. (2019), *Intersectionality as Critical Social Theory*. Durham, NC: Duke University Press.

Collins, P. H. (2015), "Intersectionality's Definitional Dilemmas." *Annual Review of Sociology*, 41: 1–20.

Compassion in World Farming (2015), "Ask this Factory Farmer Anything." Compassion in World Farming UK, February 12. Available online: https://www.ciwf.org.uk/news/2 015/02/ask-this-factory-farmer-anything-f1.

Coulter, K. (2016), *Animals, Work, and the Promise of Interspecies Solidarity*. New York: Palgrave Macmillan.

Cowspiracy: The Sustainability Secret (2014), [Film] Dir. K. Anderson and K. Kuhn. Los Angeles: AUM Films/First Spark Media.

Crane, C., Walter, D. and Jenkins, S. (2018), *Happily Ever Esther: Two Men, a Wonder Pig, and Their Life-Changing Mission to Give Animals a Home*. New York: Grand Central Publishing.

Crenshaw, K. (2017), "Kimberlé Crenshaw on Intersectionality, More than Two Decades Later." Columbia Law School (blog), June 8. Available online: https://www.law.colu mbia.edu/news/archive/kimberle-crenshaw-intersectionality-more-two-decades-later.

Crenshaw, K. (1997), "Color-blind Dreams and Racial Nightmares: Reconfiguring Racism in the Post-civil Rights Era." In T. Morrison and C. Brodsky LaCour (eds.), *Birth of a Nation 'Hood: Gaze, Script and Spectacle in the O.J. Simpson Trial*, 97–168. Pantheon: New York.

Crenshaw, K. (1989), "Demarginalizing the Intersection of Race and Sex: Black Feminist Critique of Antidiscrimination Doctrine, Feminist Theory and Antiracist Politics." *University of Chicago Legal Forum*, 1989: 139–68.

Cudworth, D. E. and Hobden, D. S. (2013), *Posthuman International Relations: Complexity, Ecologism and Global Politics*. London: Zed Books.

Cudworth, E. (2014), "Beyond Speciesism: Intersectionality, Critical Sociology and the Human Domination of Other Animals." In N. Taylor and R. Twine (eds.), *The Rise of Critical Animal Studies, from the Margins to the Center*, 19–35. London and New York: Routledge.

Cudworth, E. (2011), *Social Lives with Other Animals: Tales of Sex, Death and Love*. Basingstoke: Palgrave Macmillan.

Dean, M. (2014), "You Are How You Eat? Femininity, Normalization, and Veganism as an Ethical Practice of Freedom." *Societies*, 4(2): 127–47.

Deckha, M. (2012), "Toward a Postcolonial, Posthumanist Feminist Theory: Centralizing Race and Culture in Feminist Work on Nonhuman Animals." *Hypatia*, 27(3): 527–45.

Deckha, M. (2010), "The Subhuman as a Cultural Agent of Violence." *Journal for Critical Animal Studies*, 8(3): 28–51.

Deckha, M. (2008a), "Intersectionality and Posthumanist Visions of Equality." *Wisconsin Journal of Law Gender & Society*, 23: 249–68.

Deckha, M. (2008b), "Disturbing Images: PETA and the Feminist Ethics of Animal Advocacy." *Ethics and the Environment*, 13(2): 35–76.

Dell'Aversano, C. (2010), "The Love Whose Name Cannot be Spoken: Queering the Human-Animal Bond." *Journal for Critical Animal Studies* VIII(1/2): 73–125.

DeLuca, K. (1999), *Image Politics: The New Rhetoric of Environmental Activism*. London: Routledge.

DeMello, M. (2018), "Online Animal (Auto-)Biographies: What Does it Mean When We 'Give Animals a Voice?'" In A. Krebber and M. Roscher (eds.), *Animal Biography*, 243–60. Basingstoke: Palgrave Macmillan.

DeMello, M. (2012), *Animals and Society: An Introduction to Human-Animal Studies*. New York: Columbia University Press.

Derrida, J. (2008), *The Animal That Therefore I Am*, trans. D. Wills. New York: Fordham.

Despret, V. (2016), *What Would Animals Say If We Asked the Right Questions?* Minneapolis: University of Minnesota Press.

Despret, V. (2013), "Responding Bodies and Partial Affinities in Human–Animal Worlds." *Theory, Culture & Society*, 30(7–8): 51–76.

Despret, V. (2006), "Sheep Do Have Opinions." In B. Latour and P. Weibel (eds.), *Making Things Public: Atmospheres of Democracy*, 360–70. Cambridge, MA: MIT Press.

Despret, V. (2004), "The Body We Care For: Figures of Anthropo-Zoo-Genesis." *Body & Society*, 10(2–3): 111–34.

Despret, V. and Meuret, M. (2016), "Cosmoecological Sheep and the Arts of Living on a Damaged Planet." *Environmental Humanities*, 8(1): 24–36.

Dickstein, J., Dutkiewicz, J., Guha-Majumdar, J. and Winter, D. R. (2020), "Veganism as Left Praxis." *Capitalism Nature Socialism*, https://doi.org/10.1080/10455752.2020.18 37895.

Doherty, B., de Moor, J. and Hayes, G. (2018), "The 'New' Climate Politics of Extinction Rebellion," *Open Democracy*, November 27. Available online: https://www.opendemo cracy.net/en/new-climate-politics-of-extinction-rebellion/.

Dominick, B. (2010 [1997]), *Veganism and Social Revolution*. Republished *Anarchist Library*. Available online: https://theanarchistlibrary.org/library/brian-a-dominick-ani mal-liberation-and-social-revolution.

Donaldson, S. and Kymlicka, W. (2015), "Farmed Animal Sanctuaries: The Heart of the Movement." *Politics and Animals*, 1(1): 50–74.

Donaldson, S. and Kymlicka, W. (2011), *Zoopolis: A Political Theory of Animal Rights*. Oxford: Oxford University Press.

Donovan, J. and Adams, C. J., eds. (2007), *The Feminist Care Tradition in Animal Ethics: A Reader*. New York: Columbia University Press.

Downey, J. and Fenton, N. (2003), "New Media, Counter Publicity and the Public Sphere." *New Media & Society*, 5(2): 185–202.

Doyle, J. (2016), "Celebrity Vegans and the Lifestyling of Ethical Consumption." *Environmental Communication*, 10(6): 777–90.

Dutkiewicz, J. and Dickstein, J. (2021) "The Ism in Veganism: The Case for a Minimal, Practice-based Definition." *Food Ethics*, 6(2): 1–19.

Earthlings (1995), [Film] Dir. S. Monson. Burbank: Nation Earth Films.

EAT-Lancet Commission (2019), *Summary Report of the Eat-Lancet Commission*. Available online: https://eatforum.org/content/uploads/2019/07/EAT-Lancet_Comm ission_Summary_Report.pdf.

Eating Animals (2017), [Film] dir. C.D. Quinn. Los Angeles: Big Star Pictures.

Eisenman, S. F. (2016), "The Real 'Swinish Multitude'." *Critical Inquiry*, 42(2): 339–73.

Elston, M. A. (1987), "Women and Anti-vivisection in Victorian England, 1870–1900." In N. A. Rupke (ed.), *Vivisection in Historical Perspective*, 259–87. New York: Routledge.

Esther the Wonder Pig (2019), "About." *Esther the Wonder Pig*. Available online: https://www.estherthewonderpig.com/about.

Evans, D., Welch, D. and Swaffield, J. (2017), "Constructing and Mobilizing 'The Consumer': Responsibility, Consumption and the Politics of Sustainability." *Environment and Planning A*, 49(6): 1396–412.

FAO (2018), "World Livestock: Transforming the Livestock Sector through the Sustainable Development Goals," Rome. Licence: CC BY-NC-SA 3.0 IGO. Available online: http://www.fao.org/3/CA1201EN/ca1201en.pdf.

Fegitz, E. and Pirani, D. (2018), "The Sexual Politics of Veggies: Beyoncé's 'Commodity Veg* ism'." *Feminist Media Studies*, 18(2): 294–308.

Feigenbaum, A., Frenzel, F. and McCurdy, P. (2013), *Protest Camps*. London: Zed Books.

Festinger, L. (1957), *A Theory of Cognitive Dissonance*. Evanston: Row, Peterson.

Fisher, M. (2009), *Capitalist Realism*. Ropley, Hants: O Books.

Fiske, J. (2010), *Introduction to Communication Studies*. London: Routledge.

Fitzgerald, A. J. (2010), "A Social History of the Slaughterhouse: From Inception to Contemporary Implications." *Human Ecology Review*, 17(1): 58–69.

Fitzgerald, A. J. and Taylor, N. (2014), "The Cultural Hegemony of Meat and the Animal Industrial Complex." In N. Taylor and R. Twine (eds.), *The Rise of Critical Animal Studies, from the Margins to the Center*, 165–82. London and New York: Routledge.

Fitzgerald, D. and Callard, F. (2015), "Social Science and Neuroscience Beyond Interdisciplinarity: Experimental Entanglements." *Theory, Culture & Society*, 32(1): 3–32.

Flail, G. J. (2011), "Why 'Flexitarian' Was a Word of the Year." *International Journal of Humanities and Social Science*, 1(12): 83–92.

Flynn, M. and Hall, M. (2017), "The Case for a Victimology of Nonhuman Animal Harms." *Contemporary Justice Review*, 20(3): 299–318.

Fox, N. J. and Alldred, P. (2016), *Sociology and the New Materialism: Theory, Research, Action*. London: Sage.

Fraiman, S. (2012), "Pussy Panic versus Liking Animals: Tracking Gender in Animal Studies." *Critical Inquiry*, 39(1): 89–115.

Francis, S. (2019), "Animal Rebellion Blockade Smithfield Market," *BBC News*, October 8. Available online: https://www.bbc.co.uk/news/uk-england-london-49976197.

Freedman, R. and Barnouin, K. (2010 [2005]), *Skinny Bitch*. Philadelphia: Running Press.

Freedman, R. and Barnouin, K. (2007), *Skinny Bitch in the Kitch*. Philadelphia: Running Press.

Freeman, J. (1984), "The Tyranny of Structurelessness." In J. Freeman and C. Levine (eds.), *Untying the Knot: Feminism, Anarchism and Organisation*, 5–16. Whitechapel: Dark Star and Rebel Press.

French, R. (1975), *Antivivisection and Medical Science in Victorian Society*. Princeton, NJ: Princeton University Press.

Gaard, G. (2011), "Ecofeminism Revisited: Rejecting Essentialism and Re-placing Species in a Material Feminist Environmentalism." *Feminist Formations*, 23(2): 26–53.

Gaard, G. (2002), "Vegetarian Ecofeminism: A Review Essay." *Frontiers: A Journal of Women Studies*, 23(3): 117–46.

Gambert, I. (2019), "Got Mylk? The Disruptive Possibilities of Plant Milk." *Brooklyn Law Review*, 84 (3): 801–71.

Gambert, I. and Linné, T. (2018a), "How the Alt-right Uses Milk to Promote White Supremacy." *The Conversation*, April 26. Available online: https://theconversation.com/how-the-alt-rightuses-milk-to-promote-white-supremacy-94854.

Gambert, I. and Linné, T. (2018b), "From Rice Eaters to Soy Boys: Race, Gender, and Tropes of 'Plant Food Masculinity.'" *Animal Studies Journal*, 7(2): 129–79.

Game Changers (2019), "The Game Changers" Website. Available online: https://gamechangersmovie.com/team/.

Game Changers, The (2018), [Film] Dir. L. Psihoyos. US: ReFuel Productions.

Ganesan, R. (2017), "Vegan Misappropriations of Hinduism." In J. F. Brueck (ed.), *Veganism in an Oppressive World*, 61–8. Milton Keynes: Sanctuary Books.

Garlick, B. (2015), "Not All Dogs Go to Heaven, Some Go to Battersea: Sharing Suffering and the 'Brown Dog Affair.'" *Social and Cultural Geography*, 16(7): 798–820.

Geier, T. (2017), *Meat Markets: The Cultural History of Bloody London*. Edinburgh: Edinburgh University Press.

George, K. P. (2000), *Animal, Vegetable, or Woman?: A Feminist Critique of Ethical Vegetarianism*. New York: SUNY Press.

George, K. P. (1994), "Should Feminists be Vegetarians?" *Signs: Journal of Women in Culture and Society*, 19(2): 405–34.

Giles, D. B. (2018), "Abject Economies, Illiberal Embodiment, and the Politics of Waste." In V. Lawson and S. Elwood (eds.), *Relational Poverty Politics:(Un) Thinkable Forms, Struggles, Possibilities*, 113–30. Athens: University of Georgia Press.

Gill, R. (2017), "The Affective, Cultural and Psychic Life of Postfeminism: A Postfeminist Sensibility 10 Years On." *European Journal of Cultural Studies*, 20(6): 606–26.

Gill, R. (2007), "Postfeminist Media Culture: Elements of a Sensibility." *European Journal of Cultural Studies*, 10(2): 147–66.

Gill, R. and Orgad, S. (2018), "The Amazing Bounce-backable Woman: Resilience and the Psychological Turn in Neoliberalism.." *Sociological Research Online*, 23(2): 477–95.

Gillespie, K. (2018), *The Cow with Ear Tag# 1389*. Chicago: University of Chicago Press.

Gillespie, K. (2017), "Feminist Food Politics." In J. S. Parreñas (ed.), *Gender: Animals, Macmillan Interdisciplinary Handbooks*, 149–63. Farmington Hills, MI: Palgrave Macmillan.

Gillespie, K. (2011), "How Happy is your Meat? Confronting (Dis)connectedness in the 'Alternative' Meat Industry." *The Brock Review*, 12(1): 100–28.

Gillespie, K. and Collard R-C. (2015), *Critical Animal Geographies: Politics, Intersections and Hierarchies in a Multispecies World*. New York: Routledge.

Gillespie, K. and Narayanan, Y. (2020), "Animal Nationalisms: Multispecies Cultural Politics, Race, and the (Un) Making of the Settler Nation-State." *Journal of Intercultural Studies*, 40(1): 1–7.

Gilroy, P. (1991), *"There Ain't No Black in the Union Jack": The Cultural Politics of Race and Nation*. Chicago: University of Chicago Press.

Ginn, F. (2014), "Sticky Lives: Slugs, Detachment and More-than-human Ethics in the Garden." *Transactions of the Institute of British Geographers*, 39(4): 532–44.

Giraud, E. (2019), *What Comes After Entanglement? Activism, Anthropocentrism and an Ethics of Exclusion*. Durham, NC: Duke University Press.

Giraud, E. (2018), "Displacement, 'Failure' and Friction: Tactical Interventions in the Communication Ecologies of Anti-capitalist Food Activism." In T. Schneider, K. Eli, C. Dolan and S. Ulijaszek (eds.), *Digital Food Activism*, 130–50. London: Routledge.

Giraud, E. (2015), "Practice as Theory: Learning from Food Activism and Performative Protest." In K. Gillespie and R.-C. Collard (eds.), *Critical Animal Geographies: Politics, Intersections and Hierarchies in a Multispecies World*, 36–53. New York: Routledge.

Giraud, E. (2013a), "'Beasts of Burden': Productive Tensions Between Haraway and Radical Animal Rights Activism." *Culture, Theory and Critique*, 54(1): 102–20.

Giraud, E. (2013b), "Veganism as Affirmative Biopolitics." *PhaenEx*, 8(2): 47–79.

Giraud, E. and Hollin, G. (2016), "Care, Laboratory Beagles and Affective Utopia." *Theory, Culture & Society*, 33(4): 27–49.

Giraud, E., Hollin, G., Potts, T. and Forsyth, I. (2018), "A Feminist Menagerie." *Feminist Review*, 118(1): 61–79.

Glabau, D. (2017), "Feminists Write the Anthropocene: Three Tales of Possibility in Late Capitalism." *Journal of Cultural Economy*, 10(6): 541–8.

Glasser, C. L. (2011), "Tied Oppressions: An Analysis of How Sexist Imagery Reinforces Speciesist Sentiment." *The Brock Review*, 12(1): 51–68.

Glasser, C. S. (2014), "The Radical Debate: A Straw Man in the Movement?" In N. Taylor and R. Twine (eds.), *The Rise of Critical Animal Studies: From the Margins to the Centre*. London: Routledge.

Goldberg, D. T. (2015), *Are We All Postracial Yet?* Maldon: John Wiley & Sons.

Goldberg, D. T. (2009), *The Threat of Race: Reflections on Racial Neoliberalism*. Malden: Wiley-Blackwell.

Goodman, M. K., Maye, D. and Holloway, L. (2010), "Ethical Foodscapes?: Premises, Promises, and Possibilities." *Environment and Planning A: Economy and Society*, 42(8): 1782–96.

Greenebaum, J. (2012a), "Veganism, Identity and the Quest for Authenticity." *Food, Culture & Society*, 15(1): 129–44.

Greenebaum, J. (2012b), "Managing Impressions: 'Face-Saving' Strategies of Vegetarians and Vegans." *Humanity & Society*, 36(4): 309–25.

Greenebaum, J. and Dexter, B. (2018), "Vegan Men and Hybrid Masculinity." *Journal of Gender Studies*, 27(6): 637–48.

Greenebaum, J. B. (2018), "Vegans of Color: Managing Visible and Invisible Stigmas." *Food, Culture & Society*, 21(5): 680–97.

Greenebaum, J. B. (2017), "Questioning the Concept of Vegan Privilege: A Commentary." *Humanity & Society*, 41(3): 355–72.

Greenhough, B. and Roe, E. (2011), "Ethics, Space, and Somatic Sensibilities: Comparing Relationships between Scientific Researchers and their Human and Animal Experimental Subjects." *Environment and Planning D: Society and Space*, 29(1): 47–66.

Gregg, M. (2008), "The Normalisation of Flexible Female Labour in the Information Economy." *Feminist Media Studies*, 8(3): 285–99.

Gruen, L. (2020), "What Motivates Us to Change What We Eat?" *The Philosopher*, 108(1): 39–43.

Gruen, L. (2015), *Entangled Empathy*. New York: Lantern Books.

Gruen, L. and Weil, K., eds. (2012), "Animal Others," special edition. *Hypatia: A Journal of Feminist Philosophy*, 27(3).

Guthman, J. (2008), "Bringing Good Food to Others: Investigating the Subjects of Alternative Food Practice." *Cultural Geographies*, 15(4): 431–47.

Guthman, J. (2004), *Agrarian Dreams? The Paradox of Organic Farming in California*. Berkeley: University of California Press.

Guthman, J. (2003), "Fast Food/Organic Food: Reflexive Tastes and the Making of 'Yuppie Chow.'" *Social and Cultural Geography*, 4(1): 45–58.

Haenfler, R. (2004), "Rethinking Subcultural Resistance: Core Values of the Straight Edge Movement." *Journal of Contemporary Ethnography*, 33(4): 406–36.

Haenfler, R., Johnson, B. and Jones, E. (2012), "Lifestyle Movements: Exploring the Intersection of Lifestyle and Social Movements." *Social Movement Studies*, 11(1): 1–20.

Halkier, B. (2019), "Political Food Consumerism between Mundane Routines and Organizational Alliance-Building." In M. Boström, M. Micheletti and P. Oosterveer (eds.), *The Oxford Handbook of Political Consumerism*. Oxford: Oxford University Press, 275.

Hall, S. (2010 [1981]). "Notes on Deconstructing 'the Popular.'" In I. Szeman and T. Kaposy (eds.), *Cultural Theory: An Anthology*, 72–80. Chichester: Wiley Blackwell.

Hall, S. (1980), "Encoding/Decoding." In S. Hall (ed.), *Culture, Media, Language: Working Papers in Cultural Studies*, 128–38. London: Hutchinson in association with the Contemporary Cultural Studies, University of Birmingham.

Hamilton, C. (2016), "Sex, Work, Meat: The Feminist Politics of Veganism." *Feminist Review*, 114(1): 112–29.

Hamilton, C. L. (2019), *Veganism, Sex and Politics: Tales of Danger and Pleasure*. Bristol: HammerOn Press.

Hamilton, L. and Taylor, N. (2013), *Animals at Work: Identity, Politics and Culture in Work with Animals*. Leiden: Brill.

Haraway, D. (2017), "Staying with the Manifesto: An Interview with Donna Haraway," interview by Sarah Franklin. *Theory, Culture & Society*, 34(4): 49–63.

Haraway, D. (2016), *Staying with the Trouble*. Durham, NC: Duke University Press.

Haraway, D. (2011), "Species Matters, Humane Advocacy: In the Promising Grip of Earthly Oxymorons." In M. DeKoven and M. Lundblad (eds.), *Species Matters: Humane Advocacy and Cultural Theory*, 17–26. New York: Columbia University Press.

Haraway, D. (2008), *When Species Meet*. Minneapolis: University of Minnesota Press.

Haraway, D. (2003), *The Companion Species Manifesto: Dogs, People, and Significant Otherness*. Chicago: Prickly Paradigm Press.

Haraway, D. (1997), *Modest_Witness@Second_Millennium. FemaleMan@_Meets_ OncoMouse™: Feminism and Technoscience*. New York: Routledge.

Haraway, D. (1988), "Situated Knowledges: The Science Question in Feminism and the Privilege of Partial Perspective." *Feminist Studies*, 14(3): 575–99.

Harper, A. B. (2018), "RIP Intersectionality (Or Is It Too Soon to Quit)." *The Sistah Vegan Project*, January 30. Available online: http://sistahvegan.com/2018/01/30/rip-interse ctionality-or-is-it-too-soon-to-quit/.

Harper, A. B. (2014), "On Ferguson, Thug Kitchen, and Trayvon Martin." *The Sistah Vegan Project*, October 9. Available online: http://sistahvegan.com/2014/10/09/on-ferguson -thug-kitchen-and-trayvon-martin-intersections-of-postrace-consciousness-food-ju stice-and-hip-hop-vegan-ethics/.

Harper, A. B. (2012), "Going Beyond the Normative White 'Post-Racial' Vegan Epistemology." In P. Williams-Forson and C. Counihan (eds.), *Taking Food Public: Redefining Foodways in a Changing World*, 155–74. New York: Routledge.

Harper, A. B. (2010a), "Race as a 'Feeble Matter' in Veganism: Interrogating Whiteness, Geopolitical Privilege, and Consumption Philosophy of 'Cruelty-Free' Products." *Journal for Critical Animal Studies*, 8(3): 5–27.

Harper, A. B. (2010b), *Sistah Vegan: Black Female Vegans Speak on Food, Identity, Health, and Society*. New York: Lantern Books.

Harvie, D., Milburn, K., Trott, B. and Watts, D., eds. (2005), *Shut Them Down! The G8, Gleneagles 2005 and the Movement of Movements*. Leeds: Dissent!; Brooklyn: Autonomedia.

Hayes, G. and Doherty, B. (2019), "What Next for Extinction Rebellion?" *The Political Quarterly*, April 29. Available online: https://politicalquarterly.blog/2019/04/29/what -now-for-extinction-rebellion/.

Hebdige, D. (2005 [1997]), *Subculture: The Meaning of Style*. London: Routledge.

Helmreich, S. (2009), *Alien Ocean: Anthropological Voyages in Microbial Seas*. Berkeley: University of California Press.

Hemmings, C. (2005), "Telling Feminist Stories." *Feminist Theory*, 6(2): 115–39.

Hetherington, K. (2020), *The Government of Beans: Regulating Life in the Age of Monocrops*. Durham, NC: Duke University Press.

Heynen, N. (2010), "Cooking Up Non-violent Civil-Disobedient Direct Action for the Hungry." *Urban Studies*, 47(6): 1225–40.

Hilson, C. J. (2016), "Environmental SLAPPs in the UK: Threat or Opportunity?" *Environmental Politics*, 25(2): 248–67.

Hodge, P., McGregor, A., Springer, S., Véron O. and White, R. J. (2021), *Vegan Geographies: Spaces Beyond Violence, Ethics Beyond Speciesism*. New York: Lantern.

Holliday, R. and Sanchez Taylor, J. J. (2006), "Aesthetic Surgery as False Beauty." *Feminist Theory*, 7(2): 179–95.

Hollin, G. (2017), "Failing, Hacking, Passing: Autism, Entanglement, and the Ethics of Transformation." *BioSocieties*, 12(4): 611–33.

Huddart Kennedy, E., Parkins, J. R. and Johnston, J. (2018), "Food Activists, Consumer Strategies, and the Democratic Imagination: Insights from Eat-local Movements." *Journal of Consumer Culture*, 18(1): 49–168.

Inness, S. (2006), *Secret Ingredients: Race, Gender, and Class at the Dinner Table*. Basingstoke: Palgrave Macmillan.

Jackson, S. J., Bailey, M. and Foucault Welles, B. (2020), *#HashtagActivism: Networks of Race and Gender Justice*. Cambridge, MA: MIT Press.

Jackson, S. J., Bailey, M. and Foucault Welles, B. (2018), "#GirlsLikeUs: Trans Advocacy and Community Building Online." *New Media & Society*, 20(5): 1868–88.

Jackson, Z. I. (2020), *Becoming Human: Matter and Meaning in an Antiblack World*. New York: New York University Press.

Jackson, Z. I. (2016), "Losing Manhood: Animality and Plasticity in the (Neo) Slave Narrative." *QuiParle: Critical Humanities and Social Sciences*, 25(1–2): 95–136.

Jackson, Z. I. (2015), "Outer Worlds: The Persistence of Race in Movement 'Beyond the Human.'" *Gay and Lesbian Quarterly (GLQ)*, 21(2–3): 215–18.

Jackson, Z. I. (2013), "Animal: New Directions in the Theorization of Race and Posthumanism." *Feminist Studies*, 39(3): 669–85.

Jenkins, S. (2017), "Experience: I Accidentally Bought a Giant Pig." *The Guardian*, February 10. Available online: https://www.theguardian.com/lifeandstyle/2017/feb/10/experience-i-accidentally-bought-a-giant-pig.

Jenkins, S., Walter, D. and Crane, C. (2018), *The True Adventures of Esther the Wonder Pig*. New York: Hachette.

Jenkins, S., Walter, D. and Crane, C. (2017), *Esther the Wonder Pig: Changing the World One Heart at a Time*. New York: Grand Central Publishing.

Jevsejevas, P. (2018), "Their Faces. Building the Semiotic Case of Animal Selfies." *Punctum*, 4(2): 10–32.

Johnson, E. R. (2015), "Of Lobsters, Laboratories, and War: Animal Studies and the Temporality of More-than-human Encounters." *Environment and Planning D: Society and Space*, 33(2): 296–313.

jones, p. (2014), *The Oxen at the Intersection*. New York: Lantern Books.

Joy, M. (2011), *Why We Love Dogs, Eat Pigs, and Wear Cows: An Introduction to Carnism*. San Francisco: Conari Press.

Juna, S. (2017), "Reflections: A Journey Toward Veganism in a Muslim Upbringing." In J. F. Brueck (ed.), *Veganism in an Oppressive World*, 57–60. Milton Keynes: Sanctuary Books.

Juris, J. (2007), *Networking Futures: The Movements Against Corporate Globalization*. Durham, NC: Duke University Press.

Kassam, A. (2017), "Judge Dismisses Case of Woman Who Gave Water to Pigs Headed to Slaughter." *The Guardian*, May 4. Available online: https://www.theguardian.com/world/2017/may/04/canada-anita-krajnc-pigs-water-case-dismissed.

Kay, L. (2020), "League Against Cruel Sports Settles 'Ethical Veganism' Case." *Third Sector*, March 3. Available online: https://www.thirdsector.co.uk/league-against-cruel-sports-settles-ethical-veganism-case/management/article/1675692#:~:text=The%20League%20Against%20Cruel%20Sports,with%20his%20support%20for%20veganism.

Kean, H. (1998), *Animal Rights: Political and Social Change in Britain Since 1800*. London: Reaktion Books.

Keith, L. (2009), *The Vegetarian Myth: Food, Justice, and Sustainability*. Crescent City: PM Press.

Khandker, W. (2020), *Process Metaphysics and Mutative Life: Sketches of Lived Time*. Basingstoke: Palgrave Macmillan.

Khandker, W. (2014), *Philosophy, Animality and the Life Sciences*. Edinburgh: Edinburgh University Press.

Kheel, M. (2004), "Vegetarianism and Ecofeminism: Toppling Patriarchy with a Fork." In S. F. Sapontzis (ed.), *Food for Thought: The Debate Over Eating Meat*, 327–41. Amherst: Prometheus Books.

Kim, C. J. (2015), *Dangerous Crossings: Race, Species and Nature in a Multicultural Age*. Cambridge: Cambridge University Press.

Kim, C. J. (2011), "Moral Extensionism or Racist Exploitation? The Use of Holocaust and Slavery Analogies in the Animal Liberation Movement." *New Political Science*, 33(3): 311–33.

Kim, L. S. (2001), "'Sex and the Single Girl' in Postfeminism: The F Word on Television." *Television & New Media*, 2(4): 319–34.

Ko, A. (2019), *Racism as Zoological Witchcraft: A Guide to Getting Out*. New York: Lantern Books.

Ko, A. (2017a), "#AllVegansRock: The All Lives Matter Hashtag of Veganism." In A. Ko and S. Ko (eds.), *Aphro-Ism: Essays on Pop Culture, Feminism, and Black Veganism from Two Sisters*, 13–19. New York: Lantern.

Ko, A. (2017b), "Bringing our Digital Mops Home." In A. Ko and S. Ko (eds.), *Aphro-Ism: Essays on Pop Culture, Feminism, and Black Veganism from Two Sisters*, 7–12. New York: Lantern.

Ko, S. (2017), "We Can Avoid the Debate about Comparing Human and Animal Oppressions If We Simply Make the Right Connections." In A. Ko and S. Ko (eds.), *Aphro-Ism: Essays on Pop Culture, Feminism, and Black Veganism from Two Sisters*, 82–7. New York: Lantern.

Ko, A. and Ko, S. (2017), *Aphro-Ism: Essays on Pop Culture, Feminism, and Black Veganism from Two Sisters*. New York: Lantern.

Krajnc, A. (2016), "Bearing Witness: Is Giving Thirsty Pigs Water Criminal Mischief or a Duty." *Animal Law*, 23: 479–98.

Kristof, N. (2014), "Opinion: Abusing the Chickens we Eat." *New York Times*, December 3. Available online: https://www.nytimes.com/2014/12/04/opinion/nicholas-kristof-abusing-chickens-we-eat.html.

Kurp, J. (2016), "These Vegans Cooking and Eating E.T. the Extra Terrestrial Will Ruin BBQ for You," *Uproxx*, April 20. Available online: https://uproxx.com/viral/et-the-extra-terrestrial-bbq/.

Kusz, K. (2017), "The Road to Charlottesville: The Role of Popular Culture in Priming Young White Men for the White Right." *Activist History Review*, October 20. Available online: https://activisthistory.com/2017/10/20/the-road-to-charlottesville-the-role-of-popular-culture-in-priming-young-white-men-for-the-white-right/.

Kwan, S. and Roth, L. M. (2011), "The Everyday Resistance of Vegetarianism." In C. Bobel and S. Kwan (eds.), *Embodied Resistance: Breaking the Rules in Public Places*, 186–96. Nashville: Vanderbilt University Press.

Laclau, E. (2005), *On Populist Reason*. London: Verso.

Latimer, J. (2013), "Being Alongside: Rethinking Relations Amongst Different Kinds." *Theory, Culture & Society*, 30(7–8): 77–104.

Latour, B. (1993), *We Have Never Been Modern*. Cambridge, MA: Harvard University Press.

Latour, B. (1992), "Where are the Missing Masses? The Sociology of a Few Mundane Artefacts." In W. Bijker (ed.), *Shaping Technology/Building Society*, 225–58. London: MIT Press.

Laven, R. (2010), "Disbudding Calves." *National Association for Disease*. Available online: https://www.nadis.org.uk/disease-a-z/cattle/disbudding-calves/.

LeDuff, C. (2003), "At the Slaughterhouse Some Things Never Die." In C. Wolfe (ed.), *Zootologies: The Question of the Animal*, 183–98. Minneapolis: University of Minnesota Press.

Lewis, S. (2019), *Full Surrogacy Now*. New York: Verso.

Lewis, S. (2018), "Cyborg Uterine Geography: Complicating 'Care' and Social Reproduction." *Dialogues in Human Geography*, 8(3): 300–16.

Lewis, S. (2017), "Cthulu Plays No Role for Me." *Viewpoint Magazine*. Available online: https://www.viewpointmag.com/2017/05/08/cthulhu-plays-no-role-for-me/.

Leys, R. (2017), *The Ascent of Affect: Genealogy and Critique*. Chicago: University of Chicago Press.

Lindgren, S. and Lélièvre, M. (2009), "In the Laboratory of Masculinity: Renegotiating Gender subjectivities in MTV's Jackass." *Critical Studies in Media Communication*, 26(5): 393–410.

Linné, T. (2016), "Cows on Facebook and Instagram: Interspecies Intimacy in the Social Media Spaces of the Swedish Dairy Industry." *Television & New Media*, 17(8): 719–33.

Littler, J. (2017), *Against Meritocracy*. Abingdon, Oxon: Routledge.

Littler, J. (2009), *Radical Consumption: Shopping for Change in Contemporary Culture*. New York: Open University Press.

Lockwood, A. (2021), "A Useful Uselessness: Vegan Geographies of Bearing Witness at the Slaughterhouse Gates." In P. Hodge, A. McGregor, S. Springer, O. Véron and R. J. White (eds.), *Vegan Geographies: Spaces Beyond Violence, Ethics Beyond Speciesism*. New York: Lantern.

Lockwood, A. (2019a), "Dr Alex Lockwood on Public Vigils for Nonhuman Animals," Australasian Animal Studies Association [blog], March 5. Available online: http://animalstudies.org.au/archives/6576.

Lockwood, A. (2019b), "'Are You a Plant?'" *The New Veganism*, Oxford University, November 13–14.

Lockwood, A. (2019c), "How We Sent Mixed Messages in Excluding Other Calls for Veganism." *Animal Rebellion*, August 30. Available online: https://medium.com/animal-rebellion/how-we-sent-mixed-messages-in-excluding-other-calls-for-veganism-ae0bdcc617c3.

Lockwood, A. (2018), "Bodily Encounter, Bearing Witness and the Engaged Activism of the Global Save Movement." *Animal Studies Journal*, 7(1): 104–26.

Lockwood, A. (2016a), "Graphs of Grief and Other Green Feelings: The Uses of Affect in the Study of Environmental Communication." *Environmental Communication*, 10(6): 734–48.

Lockwood, A. (2016b), *The Pig in Thin Air: An Identification*. Brooklyn: Lantern Books.

Lorimer, J. (2013), "Multinatural Geographies for the Anthropocene." *Progress in Human Geography*, 36(5): 593–692.

Lorimer, J. (2015), *Wildlife in the Anthropocene*. Minneapolis: University of Minnesota Press.

Lorimer, J. (2007), "Nonhuman Charisma." *Environment and Planning D: Society and Space*, 25(5): 911–32.

Loughnan, S., Bastian, B. and Haslam, N. (2014), "The Psychology of Eating Animals." *Current Directions in Psychological Science*, 23: 104–8.

Loughnan, S., Haslam, N. and Bastian, B. (2010), "The Role of Meat Consumption in the Denial of Moral Status and Mind to Meat Animals." *Appetite*, 55: 156–9.

Lyon, T. P. and Montgomery, A. W. (2015). "The Means and End of Greenwash." *Organization & Environment*, 28(2): 223–49.

MacCormack, P. (2016), *Posthuman Ethics: Embodiment and Cultural Theory*. London: Routledge.

Maeckelbergh, M. (2011), "Doing is Believing: Prefiguration as Strategic Practice in the Alterglobalization Movement." *Social Movement Studies*, 10(1): 1–20.

Mannering, R. (2019), "Sainsbury's Reacts to Consumer Trends with 'UK's First' Meat-Free Butchers." *Convenience Store*, June 24. Available online: https://www.convenie ncestore.co.uk/news/sainsburys-reacts-to-customer-trends-with-uks-first-meat-free -butchers/594732.article.

Maron, D. F. (2020), "Did a Mink Just Give Coronavirus to a Human?" *National Geographic*, May 23. Available online: https://www.nationalgeographic.co.uk/animals/ 2020/05/did-a-mink-just-give-the-coronavirus-to-a-human-heres-what-we-know.

Martindill, M. (2015), "Lessons in White Fragility: When Vegan Abolitionists Appropriate Intersectionality." *Vegan Feminist Network*, May 6. Available online: http://veganfem inistnetwork.com/lessons-in-white-fragility/.

Mason, P. (1997), *The Brown Dog Affair: The Story of a Monument that Divided the Nation*. London: Two Sevens.

McCausland, C., O'Sullivan, S. and Brenton, S. (2013), "Trespass, Animals and Democratic Engagement." *Res Publica*, 19(3): 205–21.

McCorry, S. and Miller, J. (2019), *Literature and Meat Since 1900*. Basingstoke: Palgrave Mcmillan.

McKay, R. (2018), "A Vegan Form of Life." In E. Quinn and B. Westwood (eds.), *Thinking Veganism in Literature and Culture: Towards a Vegan Theory*, 249–72. Basingstoke: Palgrave Macmillan.

McKenna, M. (2017), *Plucked! The Truth about Chicken*. London: Little Brown.

McKenna, M. (2015), "The Poultry Industry Responds to an Activist Farmer." *Wired*, February 23. Available online: https://www.wired.com/2015/02/watts-response/.

McLibel: Two People Who Wouldn't Say Sorry (2005), [Film] Dirs F. Armstrong and K. Loach. London: Spanner Films.

McMahon, J. (2019), "Inside the UK Protests against Bloodied Abattoir Animal Deaths." *Vice*, February 12. Available online: https://www.vice.com/en_uk/article/yw833m/save -movement-pig-chicken-protests-essex-london-feature.

McRobbie, A. (2009), *The Aftermath of Feminism: Gender, Culture and Social Change*. London: Sage.

McRobbie, A. (2004), "Notes on Postfeminism and Popular Culture: Bridget Jones and the New Gender Regime." In A. Harris (ed.), *All About the Girl: Culture, Power and Identity*, 3–14. London: Routledge.

McRobbie, A. (1990), *Feminism and Youth Culture: From "Jackie" to "Just Seventeen."* Basingstoke: Palgrave Macmillan.

Mendes, K. (2012), "'Feminism Rules! Now, Where's my Swimsuit?' Re-evaluating Feminist Discourse in Print Media 1968–2008." *Media, Culture & Society*, 34(5): 554–70.

Michael, M. and Birke, L. (1994), "Enrolling the Core Set: The Case of the Animal Experimentation Controversy." *Social Studies of Science*, 24(1): 81–95.

Milburn, J. (forthcoming), "The Analytic Philosophers: Peter Singer and Tom Regan." In L. Wright (ed.), *Routledge Handbook of Vegan Studies*. New York: Routledge.

Mitchell, D. and Heynen, N. (2009), "The Geography of Survival and the Right to the City." *Urban Geography*, 30(6): 611–32.

Mizelle, B. (2011), *Pig*. London: Reaktion.

Monroe, J. (2019), *Vegan(ish): 100 Simple, Budget Recipes that Don't Cost the Earth*. Stuttgart: Pan Macmillan.

Moore, J. W. (2017), "The Capitalocene, Part I." *The Journal of Peasant Studies*, 44(3): 594–630.

Morgenmuffel, I. (2005), "The Feeding of the Five-thousand." In D. Harvie, K. Milburn, B. Trott and D. Watts (eds.), *Shut Them Down!* Brooklyn: Dissent!/Autonomedia.

Morris, C. (2018), "'Taking the Politics out of Broccoli': Debating (de) Meatification in UK National and Regional Newspaper Coverage of the Meat Free Mondays Campaign." *Sociologia Ruralis*, 58(2): 433–52.

Moskowitz, I. C. (2005), *Vegan with a Vengeance*. New York: Marlowe & Company.

Moskowitz, I. C. and Romero, T. H. (2007), *Veganomicon*. New York: Marlowe & Company.

Mukherjee, R. (2016), "Antiracism Limited: A Pre-history of Post-race." *Cultural Studies*, 30(1): 47–77.

Mummery, J. and Rodan, D. (2017), "Mediation for Affect: Coming to Care about Factory-Farmed Animals." *Media International Australia*, 165(1): 37–50.

Munro, L. (2005), "Strategies, Action Repertoires and DIY Activism in the Animal Rights Movement." *Social Movement Studies*, 4(1): 75–94.

Narayanan, Y. (2018), "Cow Protection as 'Casteised Speciesism': Sacralisation, Commercialisation and Politicisation." *South Asia: Journal of South Asian Studies*, 41(2): 331–51.

Narayanan, Y. (2017), "Street Dogs at the Intersection of Colonialism and Informality: 'Subaltern Animism' as a Posthuman Critique of Indian Cities." *Environment and Planning D: Society and Space*, 35(3): 475–94.

Narayanan, Y. and Gillespie, K. (2020), "Radical Intimacies: A Multispecies Politics of Care and Kinship." *Call for Papers*. Available online: https://www.dcasn.com/new-page-4.

Nash, J. C. (2018), *Black Feminism Reimagined: After Intersectionality*. Durham, NC: Duke University Press.

Naylor, T. (2019), "The £14 Cauliflower Steak: Is this the Cost of Vegan Cooking Being Taken Seriously?" *The Guardian*, June 16. Available online: https://www.theguardian.com/food/shortcuts/2019/jan/16/the-14-cauliflower-steak-is-this-the-cost-of-vegan-cooking-being-taken-seriously.

Neubert, C. (2020), "The Anthropocene Stinks! Odor, Affect, and the Entangled Politics of Livestock Waste in a Rural Iowa Watershed." *Environment and Planning D: Society and Space*, 0263775820919768.

Nibert, D. (2002), *Animal Rights/Human Rights: Entanglements of Oppression and Liberation*. Lanham: Rowman and Littlefield.

Nicholson, M. A. (2000), "McLibel: A Case Study in English Defamation Law." *Wisconsin International Law Journal*, 18: 1–144.

Nocella, A. J. II and George, A. (2019), *Intersectionality of Critical Animal Studies*. New York: Peter Lang.

Noske, B. (1997), *Beyond Boundaries: Humans and Animals*. New York: Black Rose Books.

Nunes, R. (2005), "Nothing Is What Democracy Looks Like." In D. Harvie, K. Milburn, B. Trott and D. Watts (eds.), *Shut Them Down! The G8, Gleneagles 2005 and the Movement of Movements*, 299–320. Leeds: Dissent!; Brooklyn: Autonomedia.

Oliver, C. (2020a), "Beyond-Human Research: Negotiating Silence, Anger and Failure in Multispecies Worlds." *Emotion, Space and Society*, 35. https://doi.org/10.1016/j.emospa.2020.100686.

Oliver, C. (2020b), "Towards a Beyond Human Geography." PhD thesis, University of Birmingham, UK.

O'Neill, R. (2020), "Glow from the Inside Out: Deliciously Ella and the Politics of 'Healthy Eating'." *European Journal of Cultural Studies*. doi: 10.1177/1367549420921868.

O'Sullivan, S. (2011), *Animals, Equality and Democracy*. Basingstoke: Palgrave Macmillan.

Ouzounian, G. (ND), "Guiltless Grill? Is There Another Kind?." *Best Page in the Universe*. Available online: http://www.thebestpageintheuniverse.net/c.cgi?u=grill (accessed March 19, 2019).

Pachirat, T. (2011), *Every Twelve Seconds: Industrialized Slaughter and the Politics of Sight*. New Haven, London: Yale.

Papoulias, C. and Callard, F. (2010), "Biology's Gift: Interrogating the Turn to Affect." *Body & Society*, 16(1): 29–56.

Parkinson, C. (2019), *Animals, Anthropomorphism and Mediated Encounters*. London: Routledge.

Paxson, H. (2008), "Post-Pasteurian Cultures: The Microbiopolitics of Raw-milk Cheese in the United States." *Cultural Anthropology*, 23(1): 15–47.

Peaceable Kingdom (2004), [Film] Dir. J. Stein. New York: Tribe of Heart.

Peaceable Kingdom: The Journey Home (2009), [Film] Dir. J. Stein. New York: Tribe of Heart.

Peat, J. (2020), "Record Numbers Complete Veganuary as Vegan Products Flood the High Streets." *The London Economic*, February 3. Available online: https://www.thelondoneconomic.com/food-drink/record-numbers-complete-veganuary-2020-as-new-vegan-products-flood-britains-high-streets/03/02/.

Pedersen, H. and Stanescu, V. (2014), "Future Directions of Critical Animal Studies." In N. Taylor and R. Twine (eds.), *The Rise of Critical Animal Studies, from the Margins to the Center*, 262–75. London and New York: Routledge.

Peggs, K. (2013), "The 'Animal-advocacy Agenda': Exploring Sociology for Non-human Animals." *The Sociological Review*, 61(3): 591–606.

Pendergrast, N. P. (2018), "PETA, Patriarchy and Intersectionality." *Animal Studies Journal*, 7(1): 59–79.

PETA (2020a), "Too Hot for the Big Game: PETA's Banned Super Bowl Ads," *PETA*. Available online: https://www.peta.org/features/peta-banned-super-bowl-commercials-ads-nsfw/.

PETA (2020b), "The Naked Truth About Sex Appeal." *PETA*. Available online: https://headlines.peta.org/lettuce-ladies-banana-boys-why-does-peta-use-nudity/.

Philo, C. (1995), "Animals, Geography, and the City: Notes on Inclusions and Exclusions." *Environment and Planning D: Society and Space*, 13(6): 655–81.

Philo, C. and MacLachlan, I. (2018), "The Strange Case of the Missing Slaughterhouse Geographies." In S. Wilcox and S. Rutherford (eds.), *Historical Animal Geographies*, 100–20. London: Routledge.

Phipps, A (2020), *Me Not You: The Trouble with Mainstream Feminism*. Manchester: Manchester University Press.

Pick, A. (2018), "Vegan Cinema." In E. Quinn and B. Westwood (eds.), *Thinking Veganism in Literature and Culture: Towards a Vegan Theory*, 125–46. Basingstoke: Palgrave Mcmillan.

Pick, A. (2012), "Turning to Animals between Love and Law." *New Formations*, 76: 68–85.

Pickerill, J. (2003), *Cyberprotest: Environmental Activism On-Line*. Manchester: Manchester University Press.

Pickerill, J. and Chatterton, P. (2006), "Notes Towards Autonomous Geographies: Creation, Resistance and Self-management as Survival Tactics." *Progress in Human Geography*, 30(6): 730–46.

Plumwood, V. (2003), "Animals and Ecology: Towards a Better Integration." Available online: https://openresearch-repository.anu.edu.au/bitstream/1885/41767/3/Vegpap6.pdf.

Polish, J. (2016), "Decolonizing Veganism: On Resisting Vegan Whiteness and Racism." In J. Castricano and R. R. Simonsen (eds.), *Critical Perspectives on Veganism*, 373–91. Basingstoke: Palgrave Macmillan.

Potts, A., ed. (2016), *Meat Culture*. Boston: Brill.

Potts, A., ed. (2010), "Women, Psychology and Nonhuman Animals," special edition *Feminism & Psychology*, 20(3).

Potts, A. and Haraway, D. (2010), "Kiwi Chicken Advocate Talks with Californian Dog Companion." *Feminism & Psychology*, 20(3): 318–36.

Potts, A. and Parry, J. (2010), "Vegan Sexuality: Challenging Heteronormative Masculinity Through Meat-Free Sex." *Feminism & Psychology*, 20(1): 53–72.

Priestley, A., Lingo, S. K. and Royal, P. (2016), "The Worst Offense Here is the Misrepresentation: Thug Kitchen and Contemporary Vegan Discourse." In J. Castricano and R. R. Simonsen (eds.), *Critical Perspectives on Veganism*, 349–72. Basingstoke: Palgrave Macmillan.

Probyn, E. (2016), *Eating the Ocean*. Durham, NC: Duke University Press.

Probyn, E. (2000), *Carnal Appetites: FoodSexIdentities*. London: Routledge.

Probyn-Rapsey, F., O'Sullivan, S. and Watt, Y. (2019), "'Pussy Panic' and Glass Elevators: How Gender Is Shaping the Field of Animal Studies." *Australian Feminist Studies*, 34(100): 198–215.

Puig de la Bellacasa, M. (2017), *Matters of Care: Speculative Ethics in More than Human Worlds*. Minneapolis: University of Minnesota Press.

Puig de la Bellacasa, M. (2012), "'Nothing Comes without its World': Thinking with Care." *The Sociological Review*, 60(2): 197–216.

Puig de la Bellacasa, M. (2011), "Matters of Care in Technoscience: Assembling Neglected Things." *Social Studies of Science*, 41(1): 85–106.

Quinn, E. (2020), "Notes on Vegan Camp." *PMLA*, 135(5): 914–30.

Quinn, E. and Westwood, B. (2018), *Thinking Veganism in Literature and Culture: Towards a Vegan Theory*. Basingstoke: Palgrave Macmillan.

Ramsden, E. (2011), "From Rodent Utopia to Urban Hell: Population, Pathology, and the Crowded Rats of NIMH." *Isis*, 102(4): 659–88.

Ramsden, E. and Wilson, D. (2014), "The Suicidal Animal: Science and the Nature of Self-Destruction." *Past & Present*, 224(1): 201–42.

Rasmussen, C. (2015), "Pleasure, Pain and Place." In K. Gillespie and R.-C. Collard (eds.), *Critical Animal Geographies: Politics, Intersections and Hierarchies in a Multispecies World*, 54–70. New York: Routledge.

Ritzer, G. (2013), *The McDonaldization of Society*. London: Sage.

Robinson, M. (2013), "Veganism and Mi'kmaq Legends." *The Canadian Journal of Native Studies*, 33(1): 189–96.

Robinson, M. (2014), "Animal Personhood in Mi'kmaq Perspective." *Societies*, 4(4): 672–88.

Robinson, M. (2017), "Intersectionality in Mi'kmaw and Settler Vegan Values." In J. F. Brueck (ed.), *Veganism in an Oppressive World*, 71–88. Milton Keynes: Sanctuary Books.

Royal Society for the Encouragement of Arts, Manufacturers and Commerce (RSA), Food, Farming and Countryside Commission (2019), *Our Future in the Land*. Report.

Available online: https://www.thersa.org/globalassets/reports/rsa-ffcc-our-future-in
-the-land.pdf.

Safran Foer, J. (2010), *Eating Animals*. London: Penguin.

Sainsbury's (2019), *Future of Food Report*. Report. Available online: https://www.about.sa
insburys.co.uk/~/media/Files/S/Sainsburys/pdf-downloads/future-of-food-08.pdf.

Salih, S. (2014), "Vegans on the Verge of a Nervous Breakdown." In N. Taylor and R.
Twine (eds.), *The Rise of Critical Animal Studies, from the Margins to the Center*, 52–68.
London and New York: Routledge.

Sandelin, E. and Unsworn Industries (2015), "Eating E.T." In E. Andersson Cederholm,
A. Björck, K. Jennbert and A.-S. Lönngren (eds.), *Exploring the Animal Turn: Human-
Animal Relations in Science, Society and Culture*, 47–56. Lund: Pufendorf Institute for
Advanced Studies.

Saunders, C. (2008), "Double-Edged Swords? Collective Identity and Solidarity in the
Environment Movement." *The British Journal of Sociology*, 59(2): 227–53.

Sbicca, J. (2013), "The Need to Feed: Urban Metabolic Struggles of Actually Existing
Radical Projects." *Critical Sociology*, 40(6): 817–34.

Scott, E. (2020), "Healthism and Veganism." In D. Lupton and Z. Feldman (eds.), *Digital
Food Cultures*, 68–81. London: Routledge.

Seager, J. (2003), "'Pepperoni or Broccoli?' On the Cutting Wedge of Feminist
Environmentalism." *Gender, Place and Culture: A Journal of Feminist Geography*, 10(2):
167–74.

Sebastian, C. (2020), "In Response to Harriet Hall: The White Saviour is You, Not Joaquin
Phoenix." *Christopher Sebastian*, February 13. Available online: https://www.christop
hersebastian.info/post/in-response-to-harriet-hall-the-white-savior-is-you-not-joaqui
n-phoenix.

Sebastian, C. (2018), "If Veganism is Racist and Classist, Bad News for Nonveganism."
Christopher Sebastian, October 20. Available online: https://www.christophersebastian
.info/post/2018/10/20/if-veganism-is-racist-and-classist-bad-news-for-nonveganism.

Serpell, J. (2003), "Anthropomorphism and Anthropomorphic Selection—Beyond the
'Cute Response.'" *Society & Animals*, 11(1): 83–100.

Sexton, A. (2016), "Alternative Proteins and the (Non)Stuff of 'Meat.'" *Gastronomica: The
Journal of Critical Food Studies*, 16(3): 66–78.

Sexton, A. E., Garnett, T. and Lorimer, J. (2019), "Framing the Future of Food: The
Contested Promises of Alternative Proteins." *Environment and Planning E: Nature and
Space*, 2514848619827009.

Shah, K. (2018), "The Vegan Race Wars: How the Mainstream Ignores Vegans of Color."
Thrillist, January 26. Available online: https://www.thrillist.com/eat/nation/vegan-race
-wars-white-veganism.

Shapiro, R. (2016), "Outrageous New PETA Ad Compares Cows with Rape Victims."
Huffington Post, April 11. Available online: https://www.huffingtonpost.co.uk/entry/p
eta-ad-rape_n_581befcfe4b0aac624836a29.

Shotwell, A. (2017), "The Folly of Purity Politics," Interview by Julie Beck, *The Atlantic*,
January 20. Available online: https://www.theatlantic.com/health/archive/2017/01/puri
ty-politics/513704/.

Shotwell, A. (2016), *Against Purity: Living Ethically in Compromised Times*. Minneapolis:
University of Minnesota Press.

Shukin, N. (2009), *Animal Capital: Rendering Life in Biopolitical Times*. Minneapolis:
University of Minnesota Press.

Singer, P. (2015 [1975]), *Animal Liberation*. London: The Bodley Head.

Slaven, M. and Heydon, J. (2020), "Crisis, Deliberation, and Extinction Rebellion." *Critical Studies on Security*, 8(1): 59–62.

Slocum, R. (2007), "Whiteness, Space and Alternative Food Practice." *Geoforum*, 38(3): 520–33.

Smith, M. and Mac, J. (2018), *Revolting Prostitutes: The Fight for Sex Workers' Rights*. London: Verso.

Spataro, D. (2016), "Against a De-politicized DIY Urbanism: Food Not Bombs and the Struggle over Public Space." *Journal of Urbanism: International Research on Placemaking and Urban Sustainability*, 9(2): 185–201.

Specht, J. (2020), "Cash Cows: Meatpacking and the Specter of Coronavirus." *The Baffler*, May 4. Available online: https://thebaffler.com/latest/cash-cows-specht.

Stallwood, K. (2014), *Growl*. New York: Lantern Books.

Stanescu, J. (2013), "Beyond Biopolitics: Animal Studies, Factory Farms, and the Advent of Deading Life." *PhaenEx*, 8(2): 135–60.

Stănescu, V. (2018), "'White Power Milk': Milk, Dietary Racism, and the 'Alt-Right'". *Animal Studies Journal*, 7(2): 103–28.

Stanescu, V. (2014), "Crocodile Tears, Compassionate Carnivores and the Marketing of 'Happy Meat'." In J. Sorenson (ed.), *Thinking the Unthinkable: New Readings in Critical Animal Studies*, 216–33. Toronto: Canadian Scholars Press.

Star, S. L. (1991), "Power, Technology and the Phenomenology of Conventions: On Being Allergic to Onions." In J. Law (ed.), *A Sociology of Monsters: Essays on Power, Technology and Domination*, 26–56. London: Routledge.

Starhawk (2005), "Diary of a Compost Toilet Queen." In D. Harvie, K. Milburn, B. Trott and D. Watts (eds.), *Shut Them Down! The G8, Gleneagles 2005 and the Movement of Movements*, 185–202. Leeds: Dissent!; Brooklyn: Autonomedia.

Stephens, N. (2013), "Growing Meat in Laboratories: The Promise, Ontology, and Ethical Boundary-work of Using Muscle Cells to Make Food." *Configurations*, 21(2): 159–81.

Stephens, N., Di Silvio, L., Dunsford, I., Ellis, M., Glencross, A. and Sexton, A. (2018), "Bringing Cultured Meat to Market: Technical, Socio-Political, and Regulatory Challenges in Cellular Agriculture." *Trends in Food Science & Technology*, 78: 155–66.

Stephens Griffin, N. (2020), "'Everyone was Questioning Everything': Understanding the Derailing Impact of Undercover Policing on the Lives of UK Environmentalists." *Social Movement Studies*, 1–19. doi: 10.1080/14742837.2020.1770073.

Stephens Griffin, N. (2017), *Understanding Veganism: Biography and Identity*. London: Routledge.

Stephens Griffin, N. (2014), "Doing Critical Animal Studies Differently: Reflexivity and Intersectionality in Practice." In N. Taylor and R. Twine (eds.), *The Rise of Critical Animal Studies, from the Margins to the Center*, 111–36. London and New York: Routledge.

Stewart, K. and Cole, M. (2020), "Veganism Has Always Been More About Living an Ethical Life than Just Avoiding Meat and Dairy." *The Conversation*, January 7. Available online: https://theconversation.com/veganism-has-always-been-more-about-living-an -ethical-life-than-just-avoiding-meat-and-dairy-129307.

Stewart, K. and Cole, M. (2009), "The Conceptual Separation of Food and Animals in Childhood," *Food, Culture & Society*, 12(4): 457–76.

Sturgeon, N. (2009), "Considering Animals: Kheel's Nature Ethics and Animal Debates in Ecofeminism." *Ethics & the Environment*, 14(2):153–62.

Sundberg, J. (2014), "Decolonizing Posthumanist Geographies." *Cultural Geographies*, 21(1): 33–47.

TallBear, K. (2017), "Beyond the Life/Not Life Binary: A Feminist-Indigenous Reading of Cryopreservation, Interspecies Thinking and the New Materialisms." In J. Radin and E. Kowal (eds.), *Cryopolitics: Frozen Life in a Melting World*, 179–200. Cambridge, MA: MIT Press.

Tasker, Y. and Negra, D. (2005), "In Focus: Postfeminism and Contemporary Media Studies." *Cinema Journal*, 44(2): 107–10.

Taylor, N. (2016), "Suffering Is Not Enough: Media Depictions of Violence to Other Animals and Social Change." In N. Almiron, M. Cole and C. P. Freeman (eds.), *Critical Animal and Media Studies: Communication for Nonhuman Animal Advocacy*, 42–55. New York: Routledge.

Taylor, S. (2017), *Beasts of Burden: Animal and Disability Liberation*. New York: The New Press.

Terry, B. (2014), "The Problem with 'Thug' Cuisine." *CNN*, October 10. Available online: https://edition.cnn.com/2014/10/10/living/thug-kitchen-controversy-eatocracy/index .html.

Terry, B. (2009), *Vegan Soul Kitchen*. Cambridge, MA: Da Capo Press.

Todd, Z. (2016), "An Indigenous Feminist's Take on the Ontological Turn: 'Ontology' Is Just Another Word for Colonialism." *Journal of Historical Sociology*, 29(1): 4–22.

Trachsel, M. (2019), "Befriending Your Food: Pigs and People Coming of Age in the Anthropocene." *Social Sciences*, 8(4). Available online: https://www.mdpi.com/2076 -0760/8/4/106/htm.

Tronto, J. C. (1993), *Moral Boundaries: A Political Argument for an Ethic of Care*. London: Routledge.

Tsing, A. L. (2015), *The Mushroom at the End of the World: On the Possibility of Life in Capitalist Ruins*. Princeton: Princeton University Press.

Tsing, A. L. (2011), *Friction: An Ethnography of Global Connection*. Princeton: Princeton University Press.

Turnbull, J., Searle, A. and Adams, W. M. (2020), "Quarantine Encounters with Digital Animals." *Journal of Environmental Media*, 1. doi.org/10.1386/jem_00027_1.

Twine, R. (2017), "Materially Constituting a Sustainable Food Transition: The Case of Vegan Eating Practice." *Sociology*, 52(1): 166–81.

Twine, R. (2014), "Vegan Killjoys at the Table—Contesting Happiness and Negotiating Relationships with Food Practices." *Societies*, 4(4): 623–39.

Twine, R. (2010), *Animals as Biotechnology: Ethics, Sustainability and Critical Animal Studies*. London: Earthscan/Routledge.

Taylor, N. and Twine, R. (2014), *The Rise of Critical Animal Studies: From the Margins to the Centre*. London: Routledge.

Tyler, T. (2018), "Trojan Horses." In E. Quinn and B. Westwood (eds.), *Thinking Veganism in Literature and Culture: Towards a Vegan Theory*, 107–24. Basingstoke: Palgrave MacMillan.

Tyler, T. (2012), *CIFERAE: A Bestiary in Five Fingers*. Minneapolis: University of Minnesota Press.

Tyler, T. (2006), "Four Hands Good, Two Hands Bad." *Parallax*, 12(1): 69–80.

Tyler, T. (2003), "If Horses Had Hands…." *Society & Animals*, 11(3): 267–81.

Urbanik, J. (2012), *Placing Animals: An Introduction to the Geography of Human-animal Relations*. London: Rowman & Littlefield.

United Nations (2015), "UN Human Rights Chief Urges U.K. to Tackle Hate Speech, after Migrants called 'Cockroaches.'" United Nations Human Rights, April 24. Available online: https://www.ohchr.org/en/NewsEvents/Pages/DisplayNews.aspx?NewsID=1588 5&LangID=E.

Valpey, K. R. (2020), *Cow Care in Hindu Ethics*. Basingstoke: Palgrave Macmillan.

Vegan Society (2020a), "Key Facts." *Vegan Society*. Available online: https://www.vegansoc iety.com/about-us/further-information/key-facts.

Vegan Society (2020b), "Nutrition and Health." *Vegan Society*. Available online: https://ww w.vegansociety.com/resources/nutrition-and-health.

Véron, O. (2016), "(Extra)Ordinary Activism: Veganism and the Shaping of Hemeratopias." *International Journal of Sociology and Social Policy*, 36(11/12): 756–73.

Véron, O. (2016b), "From Seitan Bourguignon to Tofu Blanquette: Popularizing Veganism in France with Food Blogs." In J. Castricano and R. R. Simonsen (eds.), *Critical Perspectives on Veganism*, 287–306. Basingstoke: Palgrave Macmillan.

Vidal, J. (1997), *McLibel: Burger Culture on Trial*. Chatham: Pan Books.

Wadiwel, D. (2015), *The War Against Animals*. Leiden: Brill.

Webster, F. (2004), "Cultural Studies and Sociology at, and after, the Closure of the Birmingham School." *Cultural Studies*, 18(6): 847–62.

Weil, K. (2012), *Thinking Animals: Why Animal Studies Now?* New York: Columbia University Press.

Weisberg, Z. (2009), "The Broken Promises of Monsters: Haraway, Animals and the Humanist Legacy." *Journal for Critical Animal Studies*, 7(2): 22–62.

Whatmore, S. (2006), "Materialist Returns: Practising Cultural Geography in and for a More-than-Human World." *Cultural Geographies*, 13(4): 600–9.

Whistleblower Lawyer Team (2016), "2015's Whistleblower of the Year Award Goes to… Perdue Chicken Farmer Craig Watts." *Whistleblower Group*, February 9. Available online: https://constantinecannon.com/2016/02/09/years-whistleblower-year-award -goes-perdue-chicken-farmer-craig-watts/.

White, R. (2018), "Looking Backward, Moving Forward: Articulating a 'Yes, BUT…!' Response to Lifestyle Veganism." *Europe Now*, September 5. Available online: https:// www.europenowjournal.org/2018/09/04/looking-backward-moving-forward-articulat ing-a-yes-but-response-to-lifestyle-veganism/.

White, R. (2015), "Animal Geographies, Anarchist Praxis and Critical Animal Studies." In K. Gillespie and R.-C. Collard (eds.), *Critical Animal Geographies: Politics, Intersections, and Hierarchies in a Multispecies World*, 19–35. London: Routledge.

White, R. and Cudworth, E. (2014), "Challenging Systems of Domination from Below." In A. J. Nocella II, J. Sorenson, K. Socha and A. Matsuoka (eds.), *Defining Critical Animal Studies: An Intersectional Social Justice Approach for Liberation*, 202–20. New York: Peter Lang.

White, R. and Springer, S. (2018), "For Spatial Emancipation in Critical Animal Studies." In A. Matsuoka and J. Sorenson (eds.), *Critical Animal Studies: Towards Trans-species Social Justice*, 160–83. London: Rowman and Littlefield.

Wiegman, R. (2012), *Object Lessons*. Durham, NC: Duke University Press.

Wilkie, R. (2015), "Multispecies Scholarship and Encounters: Changing Assumptions at the Human-animal Nexus." *Sociology*, 49(2): 323–39.

Winch, A. (2011), "'Your New Smart-mouthed Girlfriends': Postfeminist Conduct Books." *Journal of Gender Studies*, 20(4): 359–70.

Winter, D. R. (2015), "Doing Liberation: The Story and Strategy of Food Not Bombs." In A. J. Nocella II, R. J. White and E. Cudworth (eds.), *Anarchism and Animal Liberation: Essays on Complementary Elements of Total Liberation*, 59–70. Jefferson: McFarland.

Wolfe, C. (2012), *Before the Law: Humans and Animals in a Biopolitical Frame*. Chicago: University of Chicago Press.

Wolfe, C. (2010), *What Is Posthumanism?* Minneapolis: University of Minnesota Press.

Wolfe, C. (2003), *Animal Rites: American Culture, the Discourse of Species, and Posthumanist Theory*. Chicago: University of Chicago Press.

Wolfson, D. (1999), *The McLibel Case and Animal Rights*. London: Active Distribution.

Womack, C. S. (2013), "There Is No Respectful Way to Kill an Animal." *Studies in American Indian Literatures*, 25(4): 11–27.

Wrenn, C. L. (2020), *Piecemeal Protest: Animal Rights in the Age of Nonprofits*. Ann Arbor: University of Michigan Press.

Wrenn, C. L. (2019), "The Vegan Society and Social Movement Professionalization, 1944–2017." *Food and Foodways*, 27(3): 190–210.

Wrenn, C. L. (2017a), "Trump Veganism: A Political Survey of American Vegans in the Era of Identity Politics." *Societies*, 7(4): 32.

Wrenn, C. L. (2017b), "Fat Vegan Politics: A Survey of Fat Vegan Activists' Online Experiences with Social Movement Sizeism." *Fat Studies*, 6(1): 90–102.

Wrenn, C. L. (2016), *A Rational Approach to Animal Rights*. New York: Palgrave Macmillan.

Wrenn, C. L. (2015), "The Role of Professionalization Regarding Female Exploitation in the Nonhuman Animal Rights Movement." *Journal of Gender Studies*, 24(2): 131–46.

Wrenn, C. L. (2014), "The Thug Kitchen Cookbook and the Problem of Vegan Blackface." *Corey Lee Wrenn*, February 27. Available online: http://www.coreyleewrenn.com/the -thug-kitchen-cookbook-and-the-problem-of-vegan-blackface/.

Wrenn, C. L. (2013), "Resonance of Moral Shocks in Abolitionist Animal Rights Advocacy: Overcoming Contextual Constraints." *Society & Animals*, 21(4): 379–94.

Wrenn, C. L. (2011), "Resisting the Globalization of Speciesism: Vegan Abolitionism as a Site for Consumer-Based Social Change." *Journal for Critical Animal Studies*, 9(3): 8–27.

Wright, L., ed. (2019), *Through a Vegan Studies Lens: Textual Ethics and Lived Activism*. Reno and Las Vegas: University of Nevada Press.

Wright, L., ed. (2018), "Vegan Studies and Ecocriticism." Special cluster *ISLE: Interdisciplinary Studies in Literature and Environment*, 24(4): 737–802.

Wright, L. (2015), *The Vegan Studies Project: Food, Animals, and Gender in the Age of Terror*. Athens: University of Georgia Press.

Yarborough, A. and Thomas, S., eds. (2010), "Women of Color in Critical Animal Studies." Special edition, *Journal for Critical Animal Studies*, 8(3).

Zephaniah, B. (2001), *The Little Book of Vegan Poems*. Edinburgh, London: AK Press.

INDEX